Building Software with Vibe Coding

From idea to production with AI

Ambuj Agrawal

www.bpbonline.com

First Edition 2026

ISBN: 978-93-78544-323

LIMITS OF LIABILITY AND DISCLAIMER OF WARRANTY

The information contained in this book is true and correct to the best of author's and publisher's knowledge. The author has made every effort to ensure the accuracy of these publications, but the publisher cannot be held responsible for any loss or damage arising from any information in this book.

All trademarks referred to in the book are acknowledged as properties of their respective owners but BPB Publications cannot guarantee the accuracy of this information.

Distributors:

BPB PUBLICATIONS
20, Ansari Road, Darya Ganj
New Delhi-110002
Ph: 23254990/23254991

DECCAN AGENCIES
4-3-329, Bank Street,
Hyderabad-500195
Ph: 24756967/24756400

MICRO MEDIA
Shop No. 5, Mahendra Chambers,
150 DN Rd. Next to Capital Cinema,
V.T. (C.S.T.) Station, MUMBAI-400 001
Ph: 22078296/22078297

To View Complete BPB Publications Catalogue Scan the QR Code:

Published by Manish Jain for BPB Publications, 20 Ansari Road, Darya Ganj, New Delhi-110002 and Printed by him at Repro India Ltd., Rewari.

www.bpbonline.com

Dedicated to

My beloved wife:

Samaira Agrawal

and

My beloved parents:

Anil Agrawal

Saroj Agrawal

About the Author

Ambuj Agrawal is a distinguished technology leader and founder of GenMB. He has established himself as a prominent expert in machine learning and advanced technological solutions. His professional expertise spans critical domains including machine learning, compiler design, vibe coding and enterprise level AI transformation strategies.

Recognized for his exceptional contributions, Ambuj has garnered multiple prestigious innovation awards from renowned institutions such as Imperial College London, Ministry of Justice UK, Citibank and University of Bristol. He is also one of the youngest recipients of exceptional talent visa in digital technology from the UK government for his groundbreaking work in compiler design and machine learning.

Beyond his corporate and technological achievements, Ambuj has established himself as a thought leader and influential speaker. He has delivered presentations at prominent international conferences including Money20/20 Europe, Fin.Techsummit Europe, Future of Work Summit in London and the Automation Summit in Paris. His speaking engagements primarily focus on exploring the critical themes of AI, automation and the evolving landscape of work in the digital era.

As an accomplished author, Ambuj has further contributed significantly to technical literature having written comprehensive books on generative AI, enterprise automation using Python and no-code AI. These publications highlight his commitment to making advanced technological concepts accessible and practical for professionals and organizations seeking digital transformation.

About the Reviewers

- **Gaurav Singh** is a staff machine learning engineer focused on building the next generation of agentic AI systems that can reason, remember, and continuously improve over time. With over seven years of experience in machine learning and natural language processing, they have developed and deployed large-scale production systems at leading technology companies, including Amazon (Alexa), Yahoo, and Binance.

  Gaurav holds a PhD in natural language processing from University College London, and his research work has been published at top-tier conferences such as EMNLP, NAACL, and AAAI. He is currently working at the forefront of agentic AI, which designs reliable and safe AI agent workflows using frameworks like LangChain and LangGraph.

  Gaurav is also the co-founder of Versanova, a platform aimed at enabling AI agents to learn from experience and adapt over time with minimal engineering overhead. Through his work, Gaurav aims to bridge cutting-edge research with practical, scalable AI systems, and is interested in connecting with engineers and researchers working on AI agents, LLMs, and autonomous systems—anyone curious about the future of AI.

- **Shubhankar Shilpi** is a senior technology executive with over 16 years of experience in enterprise payments, banking platforms, and large-scale technology modernization. As SVP, software engineering director II at Truist, he leads engineering and operational initiatives across mission-critical payment ecosystems, including ACH, wire transfer, treasury, and merchant services platforms, with a strong focus on resilience, observability, production stability, and transformation at scale.

  His technical expertise includes platform engineering, legacy modernization, distributed systems reliability, mainframe-to-modern architecture evolution, cloud adoption strategy, DevOps, AIOps, and intelligent automation. Across leadership roles at Truist, Infosys, NTT DATA, and IBM, he has contributed to high-impact programs involving payment processing, enterprise integration, incident reduction, performance optimization, and support model maturity for highly regulated financial environments.

  Shubhankar is also an inventor, researcher, reviewer, and speaker with growing contributions in AI-enabled operations, secure financial technology, and next-generation software engineering practices. His work reflects a strong interest in applying automation and engineering intelligence to improve system scalability, reliability, and delivery efficiency.

Acknowledgement

I would first like to thank my wife whose extraordinary support transcended mere encouragement. Throughout the book's development she was not just a supportive partner but a critical intellectual collaborator. Her meticulous manuscript review went far beyond proofreading and she provided incisive feedback that fundamentally improved the book's structure, clarity and analytical depth. Her commitment to my professional growth and intellectual pursuits made this book possible.

My parents were instrumental for nurturing my creative and intellectual spirit since childhood. Their consistent encouragement to express ideas freely, to think critically and to pursue ambitious projects created the foundational confidence that ultimately enabled this book's completion. They instilled confidence in me that ideas are worth pursuing regardless of initial complexity or potential challenges. Their belief in my potential was the silent yet powerful force driving this book's creation.

The BPB Publication team provided professional guidance, constructive feedback and unwavering support which helped me immensely in refining the book and bringing it to publication. Each team member from BPB Publication from editors to technical reviewers contributed unique perspectives that refined the book's quality.

My mentors, colleagues, family and friends provided crucial support during the process. My mentors challenged my thinking, colleagues provided domain specific insights, family offered emotional sustenance and friends maintained a crucial perspective of genuine enthusiasm and encouragement. To everyone who contributed directly or indirectly, I would like to thank you for making this book possible.

Preface

Vibe coding is transforming the software development landscape and offers unprecedented capabilities to build, iterate and ship functional applications without writing a single line of traditional code. From conversational prompting techniques to AI powered development platforms, vibe coding is rapidly evolving to become a critical methodology that promises to revolutionize how we create software, prototype ideas and bring digital products to life.

This book explores the cutting edge developments in the field of AI-powered software development from its foundational principles to the most advanced vibe coding techniques available today. We will delve into the paradigm shift from code-first to prompt-first development, examine how vibe coding is disrupting industries from healthcare to finance and investigate the tools, platforms and practices that make this methodology so powerful. Our journey will take us through the conversational development model, architectural considerations of AI assisted applications and ambitious real world projects that demonstrate what is truly possible when you simply describe what you want and let AI figure out the rest.

This book is intended for startup founders, creators, CTOs, business leaders and anyone who believes that moving fast and shipping products matters more than getting bogged down in legacy software engineering concepts. This book provides a comprehensive guide to the current state of vibe coding, its practical applications across industries and its potential to redefine the future of software development entirely. By exploring both the technical workflows and the broader creative possibilities, we aim to provide you with a holistic and hands-on understanding of this transformative methodology that is reshaping how the world builds software.

This book is divided into 9 chapters. These chapters will cover the foundations of vibe coding, its applications across industries, the types of software best suited for this approach, the leading AI tools and platforms, hands-on web and mobile application development, workflow automation and the future trends shaping this exciting field. The details of the chapters are listed below.

Chapter 1: Introduction to Vibe Coding—In this chapter we will understand the fundamentals of vibe coding and learn how it differs from traditional programming. We will explore the paradigm shift from code-first to prompt-first development, the human-AI collaboration model and the key principles of conversational software development. We will also master the anatomy of an effective software development prompt and understand iterative prompt refinement strategies.

Chapter 2: Vibe Coding Applications Across Industries — This chapter showcases how vibe coding is revolutionizing software development across sectors from healthcare to entertainment. We will examine industry specific use cases and demonstrate how different sectors leverage this approach to solve unique challenges supported by real-world case studies.

Chapter 3: Types of Software Suitable for Vibe Coding — This chapter categorizes different types of software applications and analyzes applications that are best suited for vibe coding development. We will explore systems and applications such as web applications, mobile applications, data visualization tools, automation systems and machine learning powered applications that can be developed using vibe coding tools.

Chapter 4: AI Models, Tools and Practices for Vibe Coding — In this chapter we will explore the essential AI models, platforms and tools that power vibe coding development. We will also provide practical guidance on selecting the right tools for your projects while addressing version control and UI/UX design considerations in vibe-coded applications.

Chapter 5: Building Your First Web Application with Vibe Coding — This hands-on chapter guides readers through creating a complete web application using only prompts and AI assistance. We will build a task management system from conception to deployment demonstrating the entire vibe coding workflow including responsive interfaces, backend functionality, authentication and performance optimization.

Chapter 6: Building Mobile Applications with Vibe Coding — This practical chapter focuses on creating mobile applications using vibe coding techniques. We will develop a fitness tracking app from concept to deployment demonstrating cross platform mobile development through natural language prompts including device features, data persistence, push notifications and app store preparation.

Chapter 7: Automating Tasks and Workflows with Vibe Coding — This chapter explores how vibe coding can streamline business processes and automate repetitive tasks. We will build a comprehensive automation suite handling email processing, data synchronization and report generation showing how vibe coding excels at workflow automation and integration with existing business tools.

Chapter 8: Advanced Vibe Coding Projects and Limitations — This chapter tackles sophisticated software projects while honestly addressing the current limitations of vibe coding. We will examine the fundamental limitations and constraints that vibe coding platforms face when applied to production software development.

Chapter 9: Future Trends in Vibe Coding — In this final chapter we will look ahead at the emerging technologies, evolving platforms and shifting paradigms that will define the next generation of vibe coding. We will examine how advances in AI models, agentic development and natural language programming will continue to lower the barriers to software creation for everyone.

Coloured Images

Please follow the link to download the *Coloured Images* of the book:

https://rebrand.ly/90e081

We have code bundles from our rich catalogue of books and videos available at https://github.com/bpbpublications. Check them out!

Errata

We take immense pride in our work at BPB Publications and follow best practices to ensure the accuracy of our content to provide an indulging reading experience to our subscribers. Our readers are our mirrors, and we use their inputs to reflect and improve upon human errors, if any, that may have occurred during the publishing processes involved. To let us maintain the quality and help us reach out to any readers who might be having difficulties due to any unforeseen errors, please write to us at:

errata@bpbonline.com

Your support, suggestions and feedback are highly appreciated by the BPB Publications' Family.

Piracy

If you come across any illegal copies of our works in any form on the internet, we would be grateful if you would provide us with the location address or website name. Please contact us at **business@bpbonline.com** with a link to the material.

If you are interested in becoming an author

If there is a topic that you have expertise in, and you are interested in either writing or contributing to a book, please visit **www.bpbonline.com**. We have worked with thousands of developers and tech professionals, just like you, to help them share their insights with the global tech community. You can make a general application, apply for a specific hot topic that we are recruiting an author for, or submit your own idea.

Reviews

Please leave a review. Once you have read and used this book, why not leave a review on the site that you purchased it from? Potential readers can then see and use your unbiased opinion to make purchase decisions. We at BPB can understand what you think about our products, and our authors can see your feedback on their book. Thank you!

For more information about BPB, please visit **www.bpbonline.com**.

Join our Discord space

Join our Discord workspace for latest updates, offers, tech happenings around the world, new releases, and sessions with the authors:

https://discord.bpbonline.com

Table of Contents

Chapter 1
Introduction to Vibe Coding

Introduction

The emergence of **vibe coding** represents a fundamental shift in software development, transitioning from traditional code-centric approaches to conversational approaches that use the power of **artificial intelligence** (**AI**) collaboration. Vibe coding is the practice of building software through natural language prompts and conversational iteration with AI systems and is emerging as a transformative development paradigm. This chapter explores prompt-first development, where developers describe their requirements in plain language rather than writing code directly. We trace this methodology from early natural language processing experiments to modern **large language model** (**LLM**) implementations, examining how the shift from traditional coding has democratized software creation while introducing new patterns of human-AI collaboration. Through strategies for iterative prompt refinement, we demonstrate how developers can progressively enhance their requests to achieve precise and robust software outcomes.

Structure

In this chapter, we will cover the following topics:

- Origins of vibe coding
- Vibe coding versus traditional programming
- Code first to prompt first development
- Understanding the human-AI collaboration model
- Key principles of conversational software development
- Structure of an effective software development prompt
- Techniques for describing functionality and user requirements
- Iterative prompt refinement strategies
- Context management in vibe coding
- Common vibe coding pitfalls

Objectives

This chapter will provide a comprehensive introduction to the fundamental concepts of vibe coding methodology and conversational software development. It will equip you with the essential knowledge and practical skills needed to transition from traditional programming approaches to AI collaborative development environments. By the end of this chapter, you will understand the historical evolution and core principles that distinguish vibe coding from conventional programming practices. Additionally, you will master iterative refinement techniques that allow you to progressively enhance your prompts for more precise and robust software outcomes. Furthermore, you will develop proficiency in context management strategies that maintain coherence and continuity across extended vibe coding sessions. Finally, you will acquire knowledge of common vibe coding pitfalls and proven mitigation strategies, enabling you to navigate challenges effectively while maximizing the collaborative potential between human creativity and AI capability in your software development projects.

Origins of vibe coding

Vibe coding is a programming paradigm where humans develop software with an artificial intelligence system, especially an LLM. Vibe coding practice places emphasis on creative flow, rapid iteration, and organic problem solving rather than strict adherence to syntax or traditional code review. The modern use of the term *vibe coding* in the context of AI was coined by computer scientist *Andrej Karpathy* in February 2025. Karpathy described a new approach to programming that relies on letting LLMs handle the coding based on conversational and natural language instructions rather than manual line-by-line coding. Karpathy's original use of the term in this context was meant to characterize an improvisational and flow-based way of coding with AI assistants, where the human provides high-level goals and feedback and accepts AI-generated code without deep inspection.

The origins of vibe coding can be traced to decades of incremental technological progress. In the early 2000s, development tools introduced features like code autocomplete and snippets, which are early forms of assistance that streamlined the writing process but did not fundamentally change the programmer's core role. These tools paved the way for smarter code completion systems in the following years. A significant shift emerged in the early 2020s when products such as *GitHub Copilot* and *OpenAI's Codex* began generating entire functions from simple comments or high-level descriptions. While powerful, these systems still required the developer to review, debug, and integrate AI-generated code, thus limiting automation's full potential.

A key moment in the evolution of vibe coding occurred when Andrej Karpathy famously stated *the hottest new programming language is English* in 2023. This sentiment highlighted the reliance on natural language as the new interface for programming, which is a foundation upon which vibe coding now thrives. The capability of modern LLMs to comprehend and execute English instructions enables the shift away from traditional programming languages.

Although the term is attributed to Andrej Karpathy, the spirit of vibe coding was alive in developer communities well before its formal naming. Independent creators, social media influencers, and tech streamers began promoting a more intuitive and expressive style of coding. The *vibes* of coding with energy, mood, and improvisation tapped into a broader cultural trend seeking to reduce burnout and lower the barriers to software creation.

What sets vibe coding apart is its embrace of imperfection, conversational and iterative workflow. Bugs are fixed by further prompting and not by manual troubleshooting. The priority becomes getting working software through high-level direction. The rise of vibe coding has not been without controversy. Advocates celebrate its democratization of software creation and potential to boost productivity, but critics voice concerns over code quality, security, and maintainability. Accepting code without full comprehension introduces risks, especially for production or security-sensitive systems.

By 2025, vibe coding gained recognition in mainstream dictionaries as a trending term, with companies like *Google* and *Apple* starting to integrate vibe coding modes into their development platforms. The practice made its way from niche online circles to professional toolsets, marking a notable shift in human-AI collaboration. As AI systems grow more capable, the programmer's job increasingly centers on creativity, intent, and vision while the heavy lifting is handled by the machine. In the next section, we will look at the differences and similarities between vibe coding and traditional programming.

Vibe coding versus traditional programming

The landscape of software development is experiencing a profound shift with the emergence of vibe coding, which is a fundamentally different approach to programming that prioritizes intuitive exploration over rigid planning. This methodology signals a departure from decades of established software engineering practices. Vibe coding embraces uncertainty, rapid iteration, and trusting one's instincts about what feels right in the moment. Traditional programming emphasizes careful specification, detailed documentation, and methodical implementation.

LLMs have evolved from autocomplete into real-time programmers that can scaffold entire applications from natural language prompts. The following *Figure 1.1* shows an AI-generated image comparing vibe coders to traditional programmers:

***Figure 1.1**: AI-generated image comparing vibe coders to traditional programmers*

Traditional programming has long been anchored in structured methodologies that mirror engineering disciplines. The waterfall model, agile frameworks, and test-driven development all share a common thread where they attempt to bring predictability and control to the inherently chaotic process of creating software. Developers following traditional approaches begin with requirements gathering, proceed through design phases, implement according to specifications, and validate against predetermined criteria. This approach has led us to build the software infrastructure that powers our modern world, from banking systems to space exploration programs, where reliability and predictability are paramount.

Traditional programming started when memory was scarce and compilers unforgiving, and every instruction was explicit, deterministic, and authored by humans who had complete accountability for failures. Core practices such as structured control flow, static typing, modular design, and exhaustive unit tests were codified in programming languages such as C, *Pascal,* and later *Java*. This led to highly maintainable and performant systems that power banking, aviation, and operating systems, where downtime or undefined behavior is intolerable. The trade-off is a steep learning curve, lengthy delivery cycles, and repetitive boilerplate, which can prove difficult for newcomers and slow teams seeking rapid iteration. However, the predictability, auditability, and longevity of traditional code remain unmatched for mission-critical workloads.

Vibe coding, on the other hand, delegates the development process to the AI model, and the human's role changes to ideation, prompt crafting, and high-level steering while accepting that the underlying implementation may grow too large or opaque to grasp line by line. Early adopters report prototypes delivered up to 70% faster with vibe coding than manual efforts, especially for green field web apps, data pipelines, and one-off scripts. One of vibe coding's greatest promises is broadening participation by all users. Teachers experimenting with AI-driven simulators report that non-programmers can build interactive medical training tools at a fraction of the previous cost and time. Researchers find that non-technical users and even screen reader users close gaps in productivity when an AI assistant handles boilerplate, letting them focus on conceptual intent. Start-ups can prototype revenue-generating MVPs without hiring full engineering teams.

Where vibe coding has advantages, but this may create an illusion of competence where surface-level success masks fragile underpinnings. This is especially true when scaling applications in the real world with real traffic and malicious users. Security researchers have demonstrated that AI-suggested code may include SQL injection paths, unsafe memory handling, and misconfigured authentication. A CodeSignal benchmark found that vibe coding excels at trivial algorithms but struggles with holistic system design, error handling, and edge cases where nuanced reasoning is imperative. This may change as the AI technology advances with more intelligent models trained for handling real traffic and malicious users when building software applications.

The following *Figure 1.2* illustrates two different approaches to software development and highlights key characteristics for these approaches. Vibe coding represents a more intuitive flow-based approach to programming where developers prioritize creative expression and rapid iteration over rigid structure. This methodology emphasizes getting into a productive flow state where solutions emerge organically through experimentation and intuitive problem-solving. In contrast, traditional programming follows a structured and process-driven methodology that prioritizes systematic planning, detailed documentation, and quality assurance protocols. The choice between these approaches often depends on project requirements, team dynamics, timeline constraints, and the specific domain in which these software systems will operate.

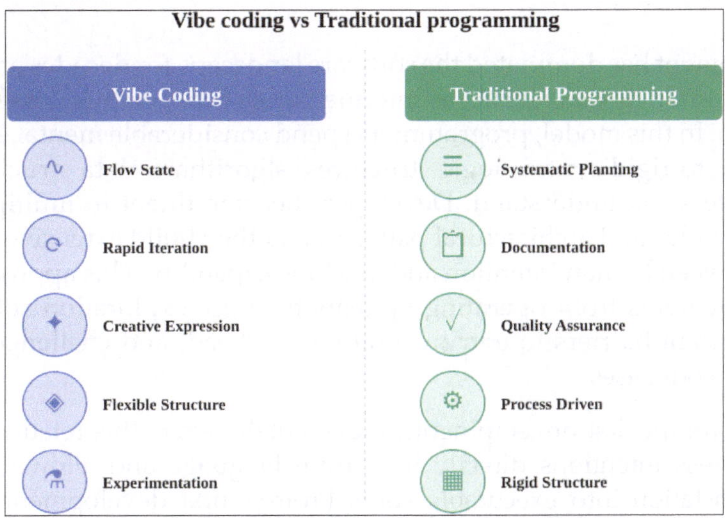

Figure 1.2: *Vibe coding versus traditional programming*

The future is not a battle for supremacy of one programming methodology but a natural evolution of software development practices. Research on agentic AI proposes systems that oscillate between intuitive prompt-driven (vibe) and autonomous test-driven refinement loops, producing production-grade applications with human-in-the-loop oversight. Companies like *IBM* and *Google* advocate governance layers such as policy enforcement, dependency scanning, and explainability dashboards to channel vibe coding's creative speed into secure and maintainable deliverables. Seasoned engineers who embrace LLM copilots while retaining foundational principles stand to amplify their output as well. In the long run, vibe coding can become an extension to professional software development that reassigns keyboard time to conceptual design and invites a broader, diverse community to invent the software of the future. In the next section, we will look at the evolution from code-first to prompt-first development.

Code first to prompt first development

The software development industry is going through one of its most significant paradigm shifts since the advent of high-level programming languages, and it is evolving from code-based instructions to AI-driven natural language interactions. The emergence of prompt-first development, also known as prompt-driven development (part of vibe coding), represents a fundamental reimagining of how software is conceived, designed, and implemented. The traditional code-first approach required developers to translate human intentions into precise syntactic instructions. On the other hand, prompt-first development enables direct communication of intent through natural language prompts to LLMs. This transformation is not merely about new tools, but it represents a philosophical shift toward treating AI as a collaborative partner rather than a passive executor of pre-written instructions. This is often described as the progression to Software 3.0, where prompts serve as the new form of programming.

Code-first development has dominated the software landscape for decades and has established a practice where human developers act as intermediaries between business requirements and machine execution. In this model, programmers spend considerable mental energy translating conceptual ideas into rigid syntax, logic structures, algorithms, data structures, and control flows that computers can understand. Developers become fluent in multiple programming languages, frameworks, and architectural patterns, and they build extensive mental models to bridge the gap between human intention and machine capability. This approach has produced remarkable achievements from operating systems to space exploration software, but it has also created significant barriers to entry, cognitive overhead, and challenges in maintaining consistency across codebases.

The transition to prompt-first development fundamentally alters this relationship by enabling developers to express intentions directly in natural language and allowing the AI systems to handle the translation into executable code. Prompt first development starts with clear articulation of desired outcomes, constraints, and context through structured prompts instead of beginning with decisions about programming languages, frameworks, and implementation details. Humans describe what they want to achieve rather than how to achieve it, and shift their role from implementation specialists to intention architects who collaborate with AI agents. This approach leverages the pattern recognition and code generation capabilities of LLMs to bridge the gap between human communication and machine execution directly. This leads to lower barriers to entry and enables non-traditional programmers to create sophisticated applications.

The cognitive implications of this shift are profound and far-reaching. Code-first development requires developers to maintain complex mental models of system architecture, language syntax, and implementation details simultaneously while solving business problems, often leading to high cognitive load that reduces productivity and increases frustration. This burden can become so substantial that developers spend more time managing technical complexity than focusing on user needs or creative problem-solving. Prompt first development dramatically reduces this cognitive load by abstracting away many implementation details, allowing developers to focus primarily on problem definition, solution design, and outcome validation. This mental bandwidth liberation enables deeper focus on user experience, business logic, and creative innovation, with research showing it can improve comprehension and reduce burnout in early-stage engineering.

Prompt engineering emerges as a critical skill in this new paradigm, requiring developers to master the art of communicating effectively with AI systems through precise and context-rich prompts. Unlike traditional programming, where precision means exact syntax and explicit logic, prompt engineering demands expertise in intent communication, context setting, constraint specification, and iterative refinement to guide LLMs toward accurate outputs. Humans must learn to provide sufficient context for AI systems to generate appropriate solutions and avoid over-specification that might limit creative possibilities. The most effective prompt engineers develop an intuitive sense for how to *think alongside* AI systems rather than simply directing them, and they blend analytical rigor with creative problem-solving.

Industry adoption of prompt-first development varies dramatically across different domains and organizational contexts. Rapidly evolving sectors like web development, content management, and prototyping have enthusiastically embraced prompt-first approaches and have often achieved significant productivity gains through AI-powered tools that auto-generate code and optimize workflows. However, industries with stringent reliability requirements, such as aerospace, medical devices, and financial systems, approach this transition more cautiously due to concerns about predictability, auditability, and regulatory compliance. The most successful implementations often employ hybrid approaches that leverage prompt-first development for appropriate use cases like rapid prototyping, while maintaining code-first practices where precision and control remain paramount.

The following *Figure 1.3* illustrates the evolution from code-first to prompt-first development. In the traditional code-first era, developers needed to master complex programming languages, intricate syntax rules, and multiple frameworks to build applications. The barriers to entry were extremely high, and it required years of study to become proficient in languages, along with deep knowledge of debugging, architecture design, and framework-specific conventions. The AI revolution fundamentally transformed this landscape, ushering in the first development era. Instead of writing lines of code, humans can now describe their intentions in natural language and have AI systems generate functional applications within minutes or hours. This shift democratizes software development by lowering the technical barriers and allowing people to focus on problem-solving and creative thinking rather than syntax mastery. This transformation represents a fundamental change in how we approach building software. The shift from *writing code* to *describing intent* means that the core skill of programming is evolving from technical syntax fluency to effective communication and problem decomposition.

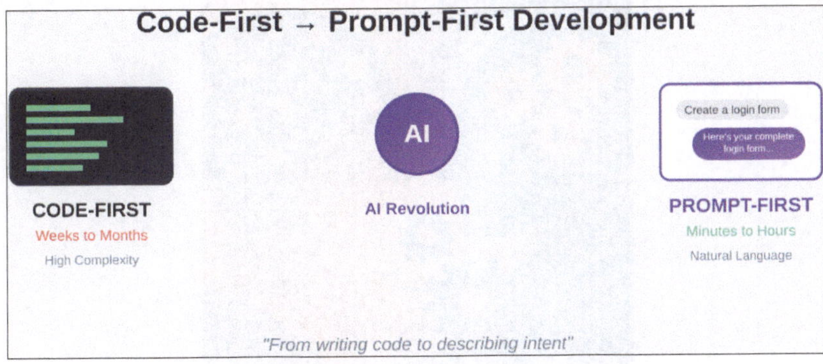

***Figure 1.3**: Code first to prompt first development*

The future trajectory of software development likely involves the continued evolution and refinement of prompt-first development. We can expect prompt first approaches to handle increasingly complex development tasks as AI systems become more sophisticated and reliable. The most successful organizations will be those that master the art of seamless collaboration between human creativity and AI by utilizing the strengths of both to create software solutions that exceed what either could achieve independently. In the next section, we will look at the human-AI collaboration model and how this impacts the development of software systems.

Understanding the human-AI collaboration model

The emergence of human-AI collaboration in software development represents a fundamental reimagining of how intelligence, creativity, and problem solving intersect in the AI age. This collaboration model goes beyond the traditional tool user relationship where humans operate software as passive machines and evolves into a dynamic partnership where both human and AI contribute complementary capabilities to achieve outcomes that neither could accomplish by themselves.

The human-AI collaboration model involves key elements like tasks, goals, interactions, and task allocation. Tasks can range from simple data analysis to complex decision-making, where AI processes vast information quickly, and humans interpret results with real-world understanding. Shared goals drive this partnership, whether improving efficiency in a business or enhancing patient care in healthcare. Effective interaction relies on clear communication, such as AI providing explainable outputs that humans can easily understand and refine. Task allocation involves dynamically assigning roles based on strengths, where AI is used for speed and pattern recognition and humans for ethical oversight and creativity to create a balanced system.

The major advantage of the human-AI collaboration model is boosted productivity and enhanced decision-making by combining AI's data insights with human judgment. The following *Figure 1.4* shows an AI-generated visualization of human-AI collaboration:

***Figure 1.4**: AI-generated visualization of human-AI collaboration*

The future evolution of the human-AI collaboration model points toward increasingly sophisticated partnerships that blur the boundaries between human and artificial contributions while maintaining clear accountability and oversight. This is especially true in the field of software development with vibe coding. As AI systems become more intelligent, the context-aware collaboration interfaces will likely become more intuitive and reduce the cognitive overhead required for effective AI interaction. The fundamental principles of complementary capabilities, calibrated trust, and iterative refinement will likely remain central to successful collaboration. The most transformative potential lies not in AI systems becoming more human-like or humans becoming more machine-like but in developing new forms of hybrid intelligence that leverage the unique strengths of both biological and artificial cognition to solve problems and create solutions that transcend the capabilities of either partner alone. In the next section, we will look at the key principles of conversational software development.

Key principles of conversational software development

Conversational software development emerges as a new field that treats the creation of software as an ongoing dialogue between human intent and artificial intelligence. This approach recognizes that software development is inherently a communication-intensive process traditionally mediated through formal programming languages, which is now increasingly conducted through natural language exchanges that more closely mirror human thought patterns and problem-solving approaches. The conversational model acknowledges that the most effective software solutions often emerge from iterative exchanges of ideas, requirements clarification, and collaborative refinement rather than from linear execution of predetermined specifications.

The following *Figure 1.5* illustrates the key principles of conversational software development. The foundation of this approach lies in clear communication, where humans must articulate their intentions precisely and unambiguously. The iterative refinement principle acknowledges that conversational development is inherently experimental and encourages humans to build in small increments, test frequently, and continuously refine their requests based on the results they receive. Context awareness becomes crucial as humans must provide relevant background information, technical constraints, and environmental details to ensure the AI generates appropriate solutions. The collaborative mindset principle positions AI as an intelligent pair programming partner capable of suggesting alternatives, identifying potential issues, and contributing creative solutions. Problem decomposition is essential for managing complexity as humans learn to break down ambitious features into manageable components that can be addressed systematically through focused conversations. Finally, the quality focus principle ensures that conversational development does not sacrifice code quality for speed.

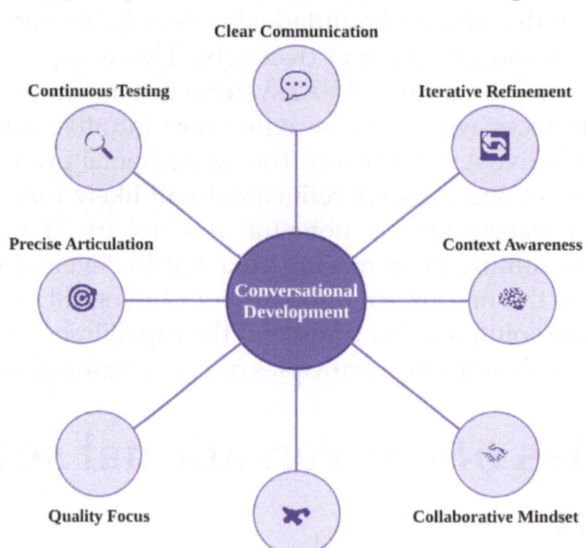

***Figure 1.5**: Key principles of conversational software development*

The key principles of conversational software development highlight the transformative potential of conversational software development, where human ingenuity and AI capabilities converge to foster high-quality outcomes. By prioritizing clear communication, iterative refinement, context awareness, a collaborative mindset, problem decomposition, and focus on quality, developers can harness AI as a dynamic partner in navigating complex projects. This approach not only mitigates common pitfalls of traditional methods but also promotes innovation through experimentation and adaptability, leading to more robust and scalable software solutions that evolve seamlessly with user needs and technological advancements. In the next section, we will look at the structure of an effective software development prompt.

Structure of an effective software development prompt

The structure of effective software development prompts represents a critical skill that determines the quality, relevance, and usability of AI-generated software. Unlike casual conversational prompts, software development prompts must balance technical precision with communicative clarity while providing sufficient context for AI systems to generate appropriate, functional, and maintainable code. Understanding the anatomy of these prompts involves recognizing that they serve as bridges between human conceptual thinking and AI pattern recognition. They require careful consideration of how information is presented, organized, and prioritized to maximize the likelihood of successful outcomes.

The following *Figure 1.6* illustrates the anatomy of an effective software development prompt with a structured framework that transforms vague requests into actionable instructions that AI can execute successfully. The foundation begins with establishing a clear context where humans set the technical scene by specifying their technology stack, project type, and current development state. The second critical component involves defining a specific goal that articulates exactly what functionality or outcome the human wants to achieve. This goes beyond generic requests like *create a component* to provide detailed specifications, such as *create a shopping cart component that displays items, quantities, and total price.* The third critical component involves specifying constraints and requirements that guide the implementation approach, including technical requirements like responsiveness, specific user interactions, edge case handling, and any limitations or standards that must be followed. The final component focuses on output format guidance, where humans specify how they want the AI to structure and present the response. This might include requests for complete code with inline comments, step-by-step explanations, multiple implementation options, or specific documentation formats.

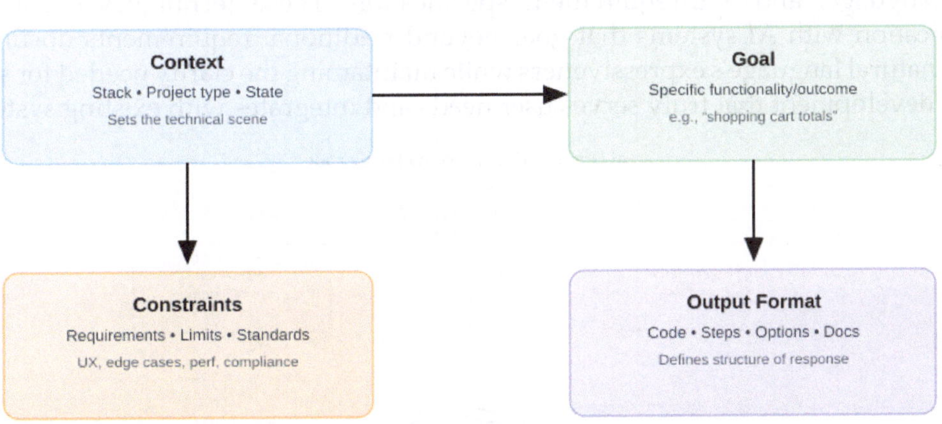

***Figure 1.6**: Anatomy of an effective software development prompt*

When these four components work together in a well-structured prompt, they create a comprehensive brief that enables AI to generate highly relevant and contextually appropriate software solutions. The future evolution of the structure of an effective software development prompt is poised to shift from manually crafted structures and output formats toward more dynamic and self-evolving systems driven by advanced AI capabilities. In the next section, we will look at the techniques for describing functionality and user requirements for AI-driven software development.

Techniques for describing functionality and user requirements

The art of describing functionality and user requirements for AI-driven software development requires mastering communication techniques that translate human needs and behaviors into actionable technical specifications while preserving the nuance and context that make software truly useful. Unlike traditional requirements documentation, descriptions for AI systems must balance precision with flexibility and provide enough detail to guide implementation while remaining open to beneficial variations and optimizations. This communication demands new approaches that leverage natural language's expressiveness while maintaining the clarity and completeness necessary for successful software development.

The following *Figure 1.7* illustrates a comprehensive framework for communicating software requirements to AI systems centered around the challenge of balancing precision with flexibility while preserving essential context. The framework encompasses five key techniques that work together to create effective AI-oriented requirements. The five key techniques are user story transformation, behavioral specification, process flow documentation, domain-specific language, and anti-requirement specification. These techniques enable efficient communication with AI systems that goes beyond traditional requirements documentation and uses natural language's expressiveness while maintaining the clarity needed for successful software development that truly serves user needs and integrates with existing systems.

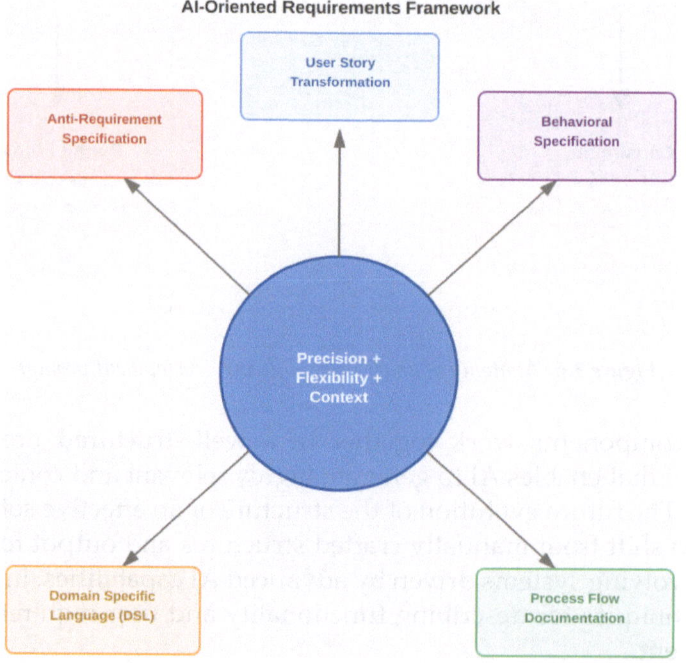

Figure 1.7: *Techniques for describing functionality and user requirements*

User story transformation represents one of the most effective techniques for describing functionality, and it adapts the familiar *As a [user] I want [functionality] so that [benefit]* framework to provide AI systems with rich context about user motivations and expected outcomes. However, effective AI-oriented user stories often require expansion beyond traditional formats to include environmental context, emotional considerations, and workflow integration details. Enhanced user stories might describe not just what users want to accomplish but how they currently approach similar tasks, what frustrations they experience, and what would constitute a delightful solution rather than merely a functional one.

Behavioral specification techniques focus on describing how software should behave in various scenarios, enabling AI systems to leverage their pattern recognition capabilities to identify optimal implementation approaches. This involves describing system responses to user actions, data transformations, error conditions, and edge cases in terms of observable behaviors and outcomes. Effective behavioral specifications often use scenario-based descriptions that walk through complete user journeys, including normal usage patterns, exception handling, and recovery scenarios. These descriptions help AI systems understand the full context of functionality requirements while remaining implementation-agnostic.

Process flow documentation provides AI systems with an understanding of how functionality fits into broader user workflows and business processes, enabling the generation of solutions that integrate smoothly with existing systems and user habits. Effective process descriptions trace the journey of data, decisions, and actions through complete workflows, highlighting decision points, dependencies, and handoffs that influence software design. These descriptions often benefit from visual thinking translated into narrative form, describing how information flows, transforms, and accumulates throughout processes while identifying opportunities for automation, optimization, or user experience enhancement.

Domain-specific language utilization involves incorporating the terminology, concepts, and mental models native to the problem domain being addressed. This helps AI systems generate solutions that align naturally with user expectations and industry standards. This technique requires identifying and consistently using the specific vocabulary that domain experts employ when discussing problems and solutions, including technical terms, process names, role definitions, and conceptual frameworks that shape thinking within the domain. Effective domain language usage helps AI systems tap into learned patterns from similar contexts while ensuring generated solutions feel familiar and appropriate to domain experts.

Anti-requirement specification involves explicitly describing what functionality should not do, what user experiences to avoid, and what implementation approaches to reject based on known problems or user preferences. This negative space definition helps AI systems avoid common pitfalls, inappropriate solutions, or approaches that might seem technically sound but create poor user experiences. Anti-requirements might include performance bottlenecks to avoid, user interface patterns that create confusion, security vulnerabilities to prevent, or integration approaches that create maintenance problems. This technique helps bound the solution space by eliminating known problematic approaches. In the next section, we will look at iterative prompt refinement strategies that can help systematically improve the AI interactions through structured feedback cycles.

Iterative prompt refinement strategies

Iterative prompt refinement is a practice of systematically improving AI interactions through structured feedback cycles and transforming rough communications into precise requirements for generating high-quality software solutions. This approach recognizes that the first prompt rarely captures the full complexity of a development challenge and that the most effective AI collaborations emerge through deliberate iteration rather than hoping for perfect initial results. Successful refinement strategies treat each AI response as valuable data about both the problem space and the AI system's interpretation capabilities. This information can be used to progressively sharpen the focus and improve the alignment between human intent and AI output.

The following *Figure 1.8* illustrates the iterative prompt refinement process as a systematic cycle for improving AI interactions to generate high-quality software solutions. The process flows through four key stages, starting with an initial prompt, receiving an AI response, evaluating the output, and refining the prompt based on findings. This central cycle is supported by four strategic approaches positioned around it, which are an evaluation framework that assesses functional correctness, code quality, and architectural alignment, gap analysis that identifies discrepancies between desired and actual outputs across multiple dimensions, incremental specificity that gradually increases prompt precision while preserving AI creativity and meta prompt strategies that engage AI as an active collaborator in the refinement process.

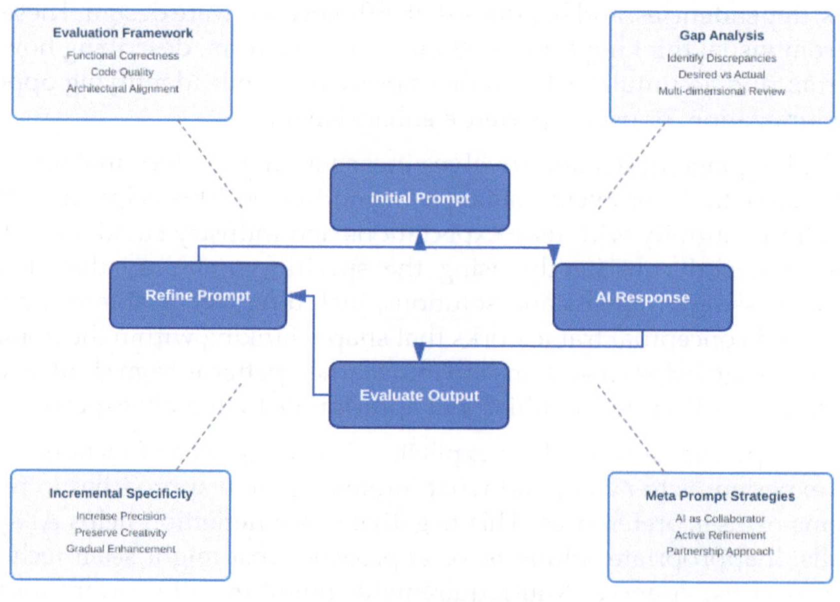

Figure 1.8: Iterative prompt refinement process

The foundation of effective prompt refinement lies in establishing clear evaluation frameworks that enable systematic assessment of AI outputs against intended outcomes.

This involves developing criteria for judging not just functional correctness but also code quality, architectural appropriateness, maintainability, and alignment with project constraints. Effective evaluators look beyond whether code runs successfully to consider factors like readability, performance implications, security considerations, and integration compatibility. The most sophisticated refinement strategies include both immediate functional assessment and long-term considerations about how generated solutions will impact project evolution and maintenance requirements.

Gap analysis forms a critical component of the refinement strategy, involving systematic identification of discrepancies between desired outcomes and actual AI outputs. This analysis examines multiple dimensions simultaneously, such as functional gaps where the code does not perform required operations, architectural gaps where the solution does not align with preferred design patterns, contextual gaps where the AI misunderstood the project requirements, and quality gaps where the output does not meet expected standards. Effective gap analysis avoids simply rejecting unsatisfactory outputs and instead seeks to understand the root causes of misalignment, whether they stem from incomplete problem description, ambiguous requirements, insufficient context, or AI system limitations.

Incremental specificity represents a refinement strategy that gradually increases prompt precision based on observed AI responses, and this approach avoids the trap of either over-specifying initially or under-guiding throughout the process. This approach begins with broader problem descriptions that allow AI systems to demonstrate their understanding and then systematically adds constraints, preferences, and requirements based on how initial responses align with intentions. The strategy recognizes that premature specificity can constrain beneficial AI creativity while insufficient guidance can lead to solutions that miss important requirements or preferences.

Meta prompt strategies involve developing prompts that explicitly guide AI systems to participate in the refinement process by asking clarifying questions, identifying potential ambiguities, or suggesting alternative interpretations of requirements. These strategies treat AI systems as active collaborators in prompt refinement rather than passive recipients of instructions. Meta prompts might ask AI systems to identify assumptions they are making, describe trade-offs they see in different solution approaches, or request additional context required to generate better solutions. This collaborative refinement approach often uncovers misunderstandings or requirements gaps that might not be apparent through traditional prompt response cycles.

Successful application of iterative prompt refinement strategies can lead to better outcomes in software development with vibe coding. With the increase in model intelligence, these can be applied for building more complex software systems. In the next section, we will look at context management in vibe coding, which is critical for effective vibe coding development.

Context management in vibe coding

The effectiveness of vibe coding relies on robust context management. Context management ensures that the AI maintains a coherent understanding of the project's goals, constraints, and evolving requirements. Without proper context management, AI outputs can become inconsistent and lead to inefficient iterations and flawed implementations. Context management in vibe coding involves curating and supplying relevant information, such as project rules, documentation, examples, and prior decisions, to the AI at every step. This process transforms vague *vibes* into structured guidance, preventing the AI from hallucinating or deviating from the intended path. For instance, programmers might maintain a persistent plan file that tracks conversation state, completed tasks, and phase transitions, acting as a shared memory between human and AI. By intentionally engineering this context, programmers can orchestrate complex tasks like feature implementation and ensure that the AI has all the necessary facts without relying solely on its general knowledge.

The shift from casual vibe coding to formalized context engineering addresses the limitations of early AI-assisted development, where intuition often failed at scale. Early vibe coding was like chopping wood with a dull axe, which is quick starts but rapid burnout on real projects. Context engineering emphasizes upfront planning, such as creating **product requirements prompts** (**PRPs**) that outline detailed instructions, rules, and examples before diving into code. This evolution recognizes that AI thrives on structured inputs, turning chaotic conversations into reliable workflows. Effective techniques for context management include breaking down projects into phases like requirements gathering, design, implementation, and testing, with the AI calling functions to determine the next steps based on the current context.

Vibe coding with strong context management allows for vertical slicing of features, implementing end-to-end functionality in incremental steps while continuously updating shared artifacts like plans or rules files. For example, starting with a solid framework and explicit guidelines in a dedicated rules directory can constrain the AI's problem space, making it more predictable and efficient. This approach not only speeds up development but also maintains project coherence across sessions, even when dealing with interruptions or multiple collaborators.

Managing context in vibe coding presents challenges such as the risk of overwhelming the AI's context window with excessive details, which can lead to degraded performance. Vibe coders must balance comprehensiveness with conciseness, often by starting fresh chats for bloated conversations or using summaries to refresh key points. While context engineering enhances reliability, it requires discipline to avoid over-reliance on AI, ensuring human oversight for critical decisions like security or architecture.

The following *Figure 1.9* illustrates the evolution of vibe coding from an intuitive but unreliable approach to a structured methodology centered on robust context management. The left side shows early vibe coding as chaotic and inconsistent, like *chopping wood with a dull axe,* and the right side demonstrates how context engineering transforms AI-assisted development into a predictable process through structured inputs, upfront planning, and PRPs. The diagram maps out a systematic development flow through four key phases, such as *requirements, design, implementation,* and *testing*. It also highlights essential context components like project rules, documentation, and persistent plan files, and addresses practical challenges such as context window overflow and information overload while offering solutions such as fresh chat sessions and balanced detail management. The diagram also states the future of vibe coding, where real-time state tracking and automated refinements will make AI a true collaborative partner in software development.

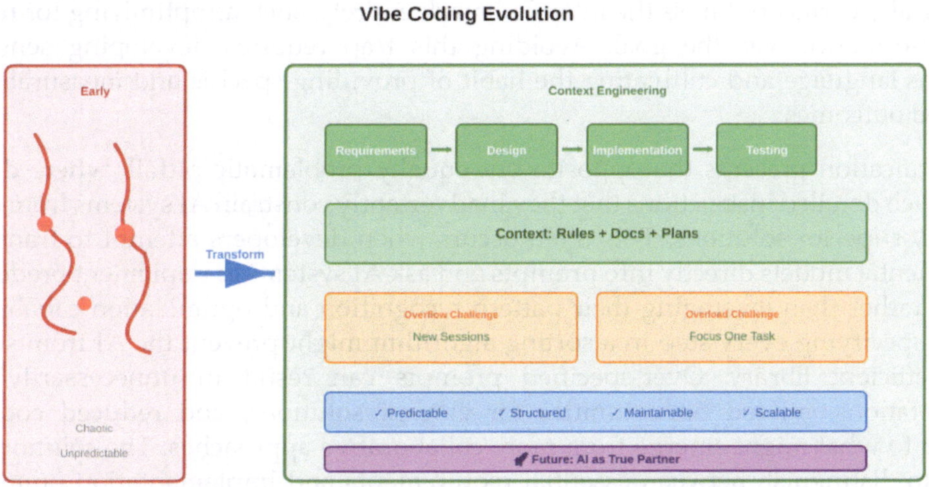

Figure 1.9: Vibe coding and context management evolution

As AI models advance, context management will likely become even more integral to vibe coding. Context management potentially is already being integrated into tools for real-time state tracking and automated refinements. This paradigm will democratize coding further and enable non-experts to build sophisticated apps through guided conversations. Mastering context in vibe coding is not only about better prompts but also about architecting knowledge flows that make AI a true collaborator in creative problem solving. In the next section, we will look at the most common mistakes in vibe coding that can derail even the most well-intentioned efforts.

Common vibe coding pitfalls

The journey toward mastering prompt-driven software development is littered with common mistakes that can derail even the most well-intentioned efforts. Understanding common vibe coding pitfalls and their underlying causes is essential for developers seeking to harness the full potential of AI-assisted coding. These errors often stem from applying traditional programming mindsets to conversational development contexts, underestimating the importance of communication precision or misunderstanding how AI systems interpret and respond to natural language instructions. Recognition of these patterns enables developers to avoid predictable failures while developing more sophisticated prompt crafting skills that lead to consistently better outcomes.

The ambiguity trap represents one of the most common pitfalls in prompt-driven software development, where well-meaning developers provide instructions that seem clear to humans but contain multiple valid interpretations for AI systems. This often manifests when developers use vague language such as *make it better, optimize this* or *add proper error handling* without specifying what *better* means, which optimizations are priorities, or what constitutes *proper* error handling in their specific context. AI systems may then implement solutions that are technically correct but miss the intended mark entirely, such as optimizing for readability when performance was the goal. Avoiding this trap requires developing sensitivity to ambiguous language and cultivating the habit of providing specific and measurable criteria for desired outcomes.

Over-specification presents the opposite but equally problematic pitfall, where developers provide such detailed instructions that they inadvertently constrain AI systems from exploring potentially superior solutions. This often occurs when developers attempt to translate their existing mental models directly into prompts and ask AI systems to implement predetermined solutions rather than leveraging their pattern recognition and optimization capabilities. For example, specifying every step in a sorting algorithm might prevent the AI from suggesting a more efficient library. Over-specified prompts can result in unnecessarily complex implementations, missed opportunities for elegant solutions, and reduced code quality compared to what might emerge from more collaborative approaches. The solution involves learning to distinguish between essential requirements and implementation preferences by providing enough specificity to guide AI systems while maintaining openness to beneficial variations.

Another pitfall is context neglect, which creates significant problems when developers fail to provide sufficient background information for AI systems to make appropriate decisions about implementation details, architectural choices, and integration requirements. This pitfall often occurs as generated code that works in isolation but fails when integrated into existing systems or solutions. These solutions may ignore important constraints like performance requirements, security considerations, or compatibility needs. For example, an AI might generate a database query without knowing it is for a high-traffic e-commerce site, leading to inefficient SQL that causes bottlenecks. AI systems cannot infer missing context, leading them to make default assumptions that may be inappropriate for specific situations. Preventing context neglect requires systematically considering what background information AI systems need to generate contextually appropriate solutions and developing templates or checklists that ensure critical context is consistently provided.

Unrealistic expectation setting leads to frustration and suboptimal outcomes when developers expect AI systems to read their minds, understand implicit requirements, or generate perfect solutions on the first attempt. This pitfall often involves assuming that AI systems have human-like intuition about problem domains, user needs, or preferences without explicitly communicating these considerations. Unrealistic expectations can also manifest as expecting AI systems to handle tasks outside their current capabilities, like generating provably secure cryptography without specialized fine-tuning or maintaining perfect consistency across complex multi-faceted problems. Addressing this pitfall requires developing a calibrated understanding of AI system capabilities and limitations while embracing iterative refinement as a natural part of the collaborative process.

The single-shot fallacy represents a common misconception that effective AI-assisted development should produce perfect solutions in a single prompt exchange. This mindset often leads developers to craft overly comprehensive prompts that attempt to address every possible consideration simultaneously, resulting in unwieldy instructions that are difficult for AI systems to parse effectively. The single-shot approach also prevents the natural refinement and optimization that occurs through iterative dialogue. Overcoming this fallacy involves recognizing that conversational development is inherently iterative and that initial prompts should focus on establishing foundation solutions that can be refined and enhanced through follow-up exchanges, like starting with a basic prototype and iterating based on feedback.

Insufficient validation creates significant risks when developers accept AI-generated solutions without adequate testing, particularly for complex or critical functionality. This pitfall often stems from overconfidence in AI capabilities or time pressure that encourages shortcuts in validation processes. AI systems can generate syntactically correct code that may contain logical errors, security vulnerabilities, or performance issues that only become apparent through careful testing. Avoiding this trap requires establishing systematic validation practices that include code review, functional testing, and integration testing for AI-generated solutions and treating them with the same rigor applied to human-written code.

The following *Figure 1.10* illustrates the major pitfalls that developers encounter when working with AI-assisted coding. The pitfalls are highlighted in the illustration are the *Ambiguity Trap* where vague instructions like *make it better* confuse AI systems, *Over-specification* where excessive detail constrains AI creativity, *Context Neglect* where missing background information leads to poor integration, *Unrealistic Expectations* where developers expect mind reading abilities, *Single-shot Fallacy* where perfect solutions are expected from one prompt and *Insufficient Validation* where generated code is not properly tested.

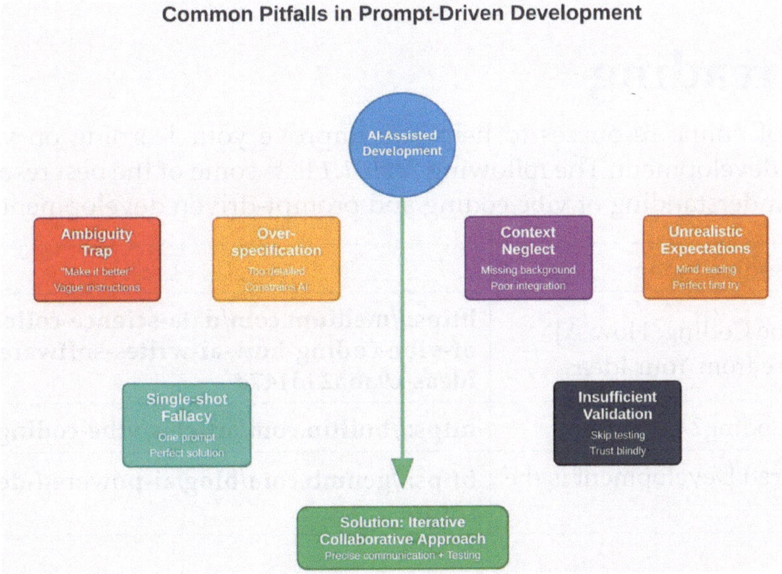

Common Pitfalls in Prompt-Driven Development

***Figure 1.10**: The major pitfalls that developers encounter when working with AI-assisted coding*

Hence, mastering prompt-driven software development requires avoiding these common pitfalls, from ambiguity and over-specification to context neglect and insufficient validation. By drawing on research-backed best practices such as iterative prompting and precise communication, developers can transform AI into a powerful collaborator for software development. As AI technologies evolve, proactively addressing these challenges will enable more efficient, innovative, and reliable coding workflows. The future of software development is vibe coding, and a methodological approach to this can lead to building production-ready software.

Conclusion

In this chapter, we learned about the origins, evolution, and future of vibe coding. We have navigated the evolution from code-first to prompt-first development and identified the similarities between traditional programming and vibe coding. The key principles of conversational software development can help developers utilize AI tools in the most efficient manner. We have looked at the evolution of AI with its improved intelligence and capabilities, paving the way for vibe coding as the new way for software development. We have also addressed critical aspects of vibe coding, such as iterative prompt refinement strategies, and demonstrated how developers can progressively enhance their requests to achieve more precise and robust software outcomes.

In the next chapter, we will look at how vibe coding is revolutionizing software development across various sectors, from healthcare to finance to entertainment. We will examine industry-specific use cases and demonstrate how different sectors leverage vibe coding to solve unique challenges. We will also look at some of the specific case studies for real-world applications for vibe coding.

Further reading

There are lots of online resources to help you improve your learning on vibe coding and prompt-driven development. The following *Table 1.1* lists some of the best resources to further improve your understanding of vibe coding and prompt-driven development.

Resource name	Link
The Rise of Vibe Coding: How AI Writes Software from Your Ideas	**https://medium.com/data-science-collective/the-rise-of-vibe-coding-how-ai-writes-software-from-your-ideas-c9aba25d147d**
What Is Vibe Coding?	**https://builtin.com/articles/vibe-coding**
Why AI-Powered Development is the Future?	**https://genmb.com/blog/ai-powered-development-future**

Resource name	Link
The Rise of Vibe Coding How It's Changing the Future of Software Development	**https://mimo.org/blog/the-rise-of-vibe-coding**
What Is Vibe Coding? How It Works and 5 Quick Tips to Get You Started	**https://www.pcmag.com/explainers/what-is-vibe-coding-how-it-works-and-5-quick-tips-to-get-you-started**
Vibe coding vs traditional coding: Key differences	**https://www.hostinger.com/in/tutorials/vibe-coding-vs-traditional-coding**
Vibe Coding vs. Traditional Coding: 5 Key Differences	**https://zencoder.ai/blog/vibe-vs-traditional-coding**
What is vibe coding?	**https://cloud.google.com/discover/what-is-vibe-coding**
Vibe coding vs traditional programming	**https://graphite.dev/guides/vibe-coding-vs-traditional-programming**
How Does Vibe Coding Differ from Traditional Coding Methods	**https://www.dhiwise.com/post/how-does-vibe-coding-differ-from-traditional-coding-methods**
Vibe Coding vs Traditional Coding: How Do They Compare?	**https://www.index.dev/blog/vibe-coding-vs-traditional-coding**
The Evolution of Prompt-Based Software Development	**https://hackernoon.com/the-evolution-of-prompt-based-software-development**
The Evolution of Coding in the AI Era	**https://thebootstrappedfounder.com/the-evolution-of-coding-in-the-ai-era/**
Prompting in the Wild: An Empirical Study of Prompt Evolution in Software Repositories	**https://arxiv.org/html/2412.17298v2**
Human-AI Collaboration	**https://clanx.ai/glossary/human-ai-colaboration**
Human-AI Collaboration: How to Work Together	**https://www.salesforce.com/agentforce/human-ai-collaboration/**
Evaluating Human-AI Collaboration: A Review and Methodological Framework	**https://arxiv.org/html/2407.19098v1**
Anatomy of an Effective Prompt	**https://www.designgurus.io/course-play/grokking-prompt-engineering-for-software-engineers/doc/anatomy-of-an-effective-prompt**

Resource name	Link
Basic Prompt Structure and Key Parts	**https://learnprompting.org/docs/basics/prompt_structure**
Crafting the Perfect AI Prompts: The Anatomy of an Effective AI Prompt & Common Pitfalls	**https://www.launchconsulting.com/posts/crafting-the-perfect-ai-prompts-the-anatomy-of-an-effective-ai-prompt-common-pitfalls**
Mastering Amazon Q Developer Part 1: Crafting Effective Prompts	**https://aws.amazon.com/blogs/devops/mastering-amazon-q-developer-part-1-crafting-effective-prompts/**
Efficient prompting with Replit AI	**https://docs.replit.com/tutorials/effective-prompting**
Prompt engineering: overview and guide	**https://cloud.google.com/discover/what-is-prompt-engineering**
The Definitive Guide to Prompt Engineering: From Principles to Production	**https://www.sundeepteki.org/advice/the-definitive-guide-to-prompt-engineering-from-principles-to-production**
The 2025 Guide to Prompt Engineering	**https://www.ibm.com/think/prompt-engineering**
Context Engineering is the New Vibe Coding	**https://analyticsindiamag.com/ai-features/context-engineering-is-the-new-vibe-coding/**
Vibe Coding Needs Context Engineering	**https://inferencebysequoia.substack.com/p/vibe-coding-needs-context-engineering**
Vibe coding: programming through conversation with artificial intelligence	**https://arxiv.org/abs/2506.23253**
Context Engineering vs Vibe Coding: Why Systematic Beats Spontaneous	**https://www.thakurcoder.com/blog/2025-07-03-context-engineering-vs-vibe-coding-why-systematic-beats-spontaneous**
A Structured Workflow for "Vibe Coding" Full-Stack Apps	**https://dev.to/wasp/a-structured-workflow-for-vibe-coding-full-stack-apps-352l**
Vibe coding: programming through conversation with artificial intelligence	**https://arxiv.org/html/2506.23253v1**

Table 1.1: *Online resources on vibe coding and prompt driven development*

Questions

1. Who coined the term vibe coding?
2. How did vibe coding emerge?
3. What are the advantages of vibe coding?
4. How does vibe coding compare to traditional programming?
5. What are the disadvantages of traditional programming?
6. What is code first development?
7. How does prompt first development help making software development accessible to all?
8. What are the limitations of prompt first development?
9. How did the AI revolution enable prompt first development?
10. Why is understanding the human-AI collaboration model important?
11. What is the future evolution of the human-AI collaboration model?
12. What are the key principles of conversational software development?
13. Why is clear communication important for vibe coding?
14. What are the advantages of iterative refinement?
15. What is problem decomposition?
16. What are the steps required for composition of effective software development prompts?
17. Why are project constraints important?
18. What are the techniques for describing functionality and user requirements?
19. How do meta-prompt strategies work?
20. What is gap analysis for iterative prompt refinement?
21. How does context management help with vibe coding?
22. What is context engineering?
23. What are the common vibe coding pitfalls?
24. How can you master prompt-driven software development?

CHAPTER 2
Vibe Coding Applications Across Industries

Introduction

Vibe coding is on the path to revolutionize software development by transforming how applications are conceptualized, designed, and deployed across industries. In healthcare, it enables adaptive patient monitoring and personalized treatment interfaces, while finance leverages it for intelligent trading platforms and risk assessment tools that respond to market sentiment. E-commerce applications create hyper-personalized shopping experiences through context-sensitive recommendations, and educational technology produces learning platforms that adapt to individual student needs in real-time. Entertainment industry implementations include innovative content creation tools and immersive experiences that respond to audience engagement patterns. Manufacturing uses vibe coding for predictive maintenance systems and adaptive production workflows that optimize based on operational conditions. The startup ecosystem particularly benefits from accelerated innovation cycles, enabling rapid prototyping and market-responsive development. This evolution spans from experimental tools to industry-specific solutions that fundamentally reshape operational workflows and user experiences.

Structure

In this chapter, we will cover the following topics:

- Rise of vibe coding applications
- Vibe coding applications in healthcare
- Vibe coding applications in finance
- Vibe coding applications in e-commerce
- Vibe coding applications in education
- Vibe coding applications in entertainment
- Vibe coding applications in manufacturing
- Vibe coding applications in start-up ecosystems

Objectives

This chapter will provide a comprehensive overview of vibe coding applications across diverse industry verticals and their transformative impact on sector-specific challenges and opportunities. It will equip readers with the essential knowledge and strategic insights needed to understand how vibe coding methodologies adapt to unique industry requirements and operational contexts. By the end of this chapter, the readers will understand the evolutionary trajectory of vibe coding applications from experimental implementations to mature industry solutions that drive competitive advantage and operational excellence.

Rise of vibe coding applications

The emergence of vibe coding represents a fundamental shift in how software applications are typically built. It moves development towards intuitive and creative practices that align with human thought patterns and creative workflows. The rise of vibe coding applications stems from a growing recognition that the most innovative software emerges not from mechanical code production, but from environments that foster experimentation, encourage rapid iteration, and eliminate friction between creative ideas and their technical implementation. Modern developers increasingly seek tools that adapt to their thinking patterns rather than forcing them to conform to inflexible programming paradigms.

There are many vibe coding platforms available that enable the creation of vibe coding applications, with each tool offering distinctive strengths that enrich the creative development process. Vibe coding applications are intent-driven interfaces that turn natural language, sketches, and live data into functioning features. A defining trait of vibe coding applications is progressive formalization. Many vibe coding applications embed automation in their runtime, not just in the main environment. Collaboration features can be made first-class in vibe-coded applications. Shared canvases allow product managers, designers, analysts, and engineers to co-edit flows, prompts, and data views in real-time. Domain experts can attach domain rules directly to screens or steps, such as *clinical checklists* bound to intake forms or *supplier compliance clauses* attached to procurement steps.

Vibe coding applications compress the path from idea to impact by mixing freeform composition with guardrails, making them well-suited to domains that demand rapid iteration. As **artificial intelligence** (**AI**) models and vibe coding tools continue to evolve, these applications will become a default way to deliver complex software, ranging from internal tools to customer-facing experiences. Organizations that invest in adopting vibe coding tools today will compound speed, quality, and learning over time. In the next section, we will look at some of the examples of vibe coding applications in the healthcare industry.

Vibe coding applications in healthcare

Vibe coding represents a revolutionary shift in healthcare software development, where traditional programming gives way to natural language-driven creation. This approach allows healthcare professionals, from clinicians to researchers, to describe their needs in plain text, such as **`Analyze this genomic dataset`** or **`build a patient support app`**, and receive working software solutions within hours rather than months. The technology fundamentally bridges the gap between complex programming requirements and human intent, thus enabling domain experts who understand clinical workflows to directly create the tools they need, without traditional coding expertise. In healthcare, where speed and precision can directly impact patient outcomes, vibe coding accelerates development cycles while reducing dependency on technical teams and costly vendor contracts.

Vibe coding operates through an iterative cycle where users write descriptions, generate code, test functionality, and refine based on feedback, all of which is conducted in plain language rather than traditional programming syntax. This approach enables rapid prototyping with healthcare applications, often moving from concept to working prototype in less than a week, and complete solutions costing under $500 to test initially. This technology particularly excels in healthcare because it captures not just functional requirements but also the emotional tone and patient-centric design principles that are crucial for clinical environments.

The following *Figure 2.1* shows a patent management system developed using vibe coding prompts on *Lovable*[1]. The prompt used was **`Build a simple patent management system`**, and the vibe coding platform created a professional patient management system with a clean medical interface. This application has features such as a patient dashboard that allows viewing all patients with search and status filtering, edit patients' functionality that allows completing forms with medical info, emergency contacts, and allergies, and a patient details page that contains complete patient profiles with medical information. This system uses a professional healthcare color scheme and includes sample patient data to demonstrate functionality. Further changes can be made to this application using follow-up prompts as required. The figure is as follows:

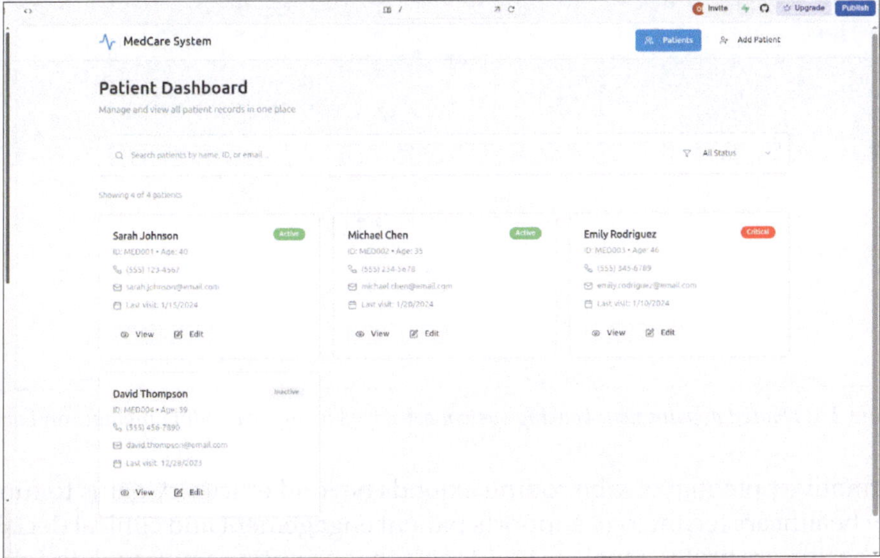

***Figure 2.1**: Patent management system developed using vibe coding prompts on Lovable*

1 **(https://lovable.dev/)**

Healthcare organizations are already implementing vibe coding across diverse clinical and administrative functions with measurable impact. In clinical education, educators have successfully created interactive learning tools such as blood sugar simulation platforms without requiring programming expertise. Patient engagement applications represent another significant use case where vibe coding enables the development of medication adherence apps, telemedicine interfaces, and digital chatbots that prioritize empathetic communication and human-centered design. Administrative applications include claims and billing automation systems, electronic health record onboarding flows, and patient navigation tools that emphasize emotional intelligence over purely functional interfaces. One notable example from *CareYaya* demonstrates how a caregiver group built a dementia symptom tracker in under 10 days using vibe coding, while *Counterforce Health* used vibe coding to develop an insurance denial appeal tool that reduced manual paperwork time by nearly half[2].

The following *Figure* 2.2 shows a dentist appointment booking system developed using vibe coding prompts on Lovable. The prompt used was **`Build a simple dentist appointment booking system`** and the vibe coding platform created a professional dentist appointment booking system with a medical-inspired design. The system features a complete booking flow with date and time selection, patient information collection, and confirmation. Further changes can be made to this application using follow-up prompts as required. The figure is as follows:

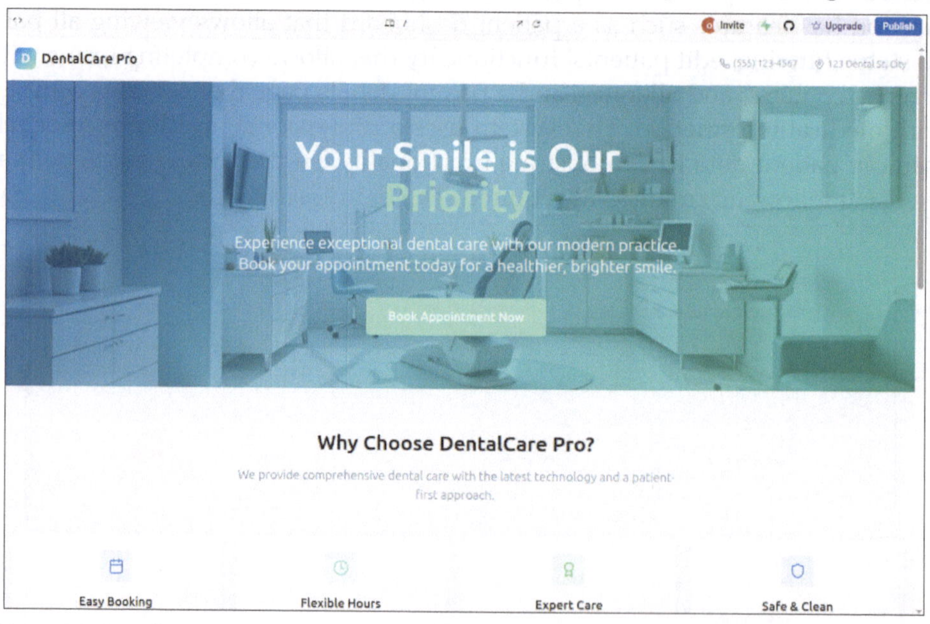

***Figure 2.2**: Dentist appointment booking system developed using vibe coding prompts on Lovable*

The transformative potential of vibe coding extends beyond efficiency gains to fundamentally reshape how healthcare technology supports patient engagement and clinical decision making. By enabling healthcare professionals to build tools that prioritize emotional design and patient

2 **(https://www.clarahealth.co/blog/vibe-coding-in-healthcare)**

empowerment, vibe coding applications can achieve higher user completion rates, reduced digital frustration, and improved treatment adherence. Clinical workflows benefit significantly as practitioners can rapidly prototype solutions for specific challenges they encounter daily. These solutions range from patient reminder systems that display encouraging messages to real-time clinical data dashboards that provide actionable insights without overwhelming users. Vibe coding ensures that the final solutions are more closely aligned with actual user needs because they are built by those who understand the clinical context intimately.

Vibe coding will democratize healthcare innovation by removing traditional barriers between clinical insight and technological implementation. It will potentially transform how digital health solutions are conceived and deployed. The healthcare industry is evolving towards more personalized care and emotionally intelligent digital tools. Vibe coding would enable faster innovation cycles, broader accessibility for non-technical healthcare professionals, and stronger emotional connections between patients and technology. Vibe coding's emphasis on rapid prototyping and iterative refinement aligns perfectly with healthcare's need for agile responses to emerging challenges, whether in patient care, regulatory compliance, or clinical research. However, this speed comes with significant risks, such as healthcare applications built through vibe coding must still meet stringent data privacy standards (such as HIPAA and GDPR), and AI-generated code that has not been rigorously audited could introduce critical vulnerabilities in systems handling sensitive patient data or life-critical workflows. Ensuring that clinical validation and security reviews remain non-negotiable checkpoints will be essential to responsibly harnessing vibe coding's potential in healthcare. Looking forward, the integration of vibe coding with existing healthcare infrastructure promises to accelerate the development of new health systems where clinical insights can be quickly transformed into functional tools that improve patient outcomes and operational efficiency. In the next section, we will look at some of the examples of vibe coding applications in the finance industry.

Vibe coding applications in finance

Vibe coding is a paradigm shift in financial technology development that allows financial professionals, from quantitative analysts to wealth managers, to describe their requirements in plain text, such as **`Build a risk assessment model`** or **`create a trading dashboard`**, and receive working software solutions within hours rather than months. This technology fundamentally transforms how financial institutions approach software development by removing traditional coding barriers. This enables domain experts who understand market dynamics to directly create the tools they need. In finance, where regulatory compliance, speed to market, and precision are paramount, vibe coding accelerates innovation cycles while reducing dependency on technical teams and development costs.

Vibe coding tools operate through an iterative cycle where financial professionals describe functionality, generate code, test compliance requirements, and refine based on regulatory feedback, which is all conducted in domain-specific financial language rather than traditional programming syntax. This approach enables rapid prototyping of financial applications with trading platforms and risk management tools to move from concept to working prototype in less than a week. It also reduces overall development costs, with complete solutions costing significantly less than traditional development approaches. Vibe coding excels in developing applications for finance because it captures not just functional requirements but also the regulatory compliance and risk management principles that are crucial for financial environments.

Financial institutions are already implementing vibe coding across diverse trading, risk management, and customer service functions with measurable impact. In algorithmic trading, employees have successfully created order routing logic simulations, backtesting frameworks, and market risk analysis tools without requiring programming expertise. Customer-facing applications represent another significant use case where vibe coding enables the development of wealth management platforms, AI-based savings advisors, and sophisticated chatbots that can handle complex financial queries. Internal operations benefit from automated compliance checking systems, **Know Your Customer** (**KYC**) flow simulations, and regulatory reporting tools that emphasize both efficiency and adherence to financial standards. Fintech startups have used vibe coding to rapidly prototype payment processing features, reducing development time from weeks to days while maintaining high security standards.

The following *Figure* 2.3 shows a trading platform developed using vibe coding prompts on v0 by Vercel[3]. The prompt used was `Build a simple trading platform` and the vibe coding platform created a trading platform that provides a complete trading experience with portfolio management, market data, and order placement capabilities. The trading platform covers portfolio monitoring, market analysis, position tracking, order execution, and transaction history, which is essentially all the core functionality needed for retail stock trading. The platform uses mock data for demonstration, but is structured to easily integrate with real trading **application programming interfaces** (**APIs**). All components are modular and reusable, following Next.js *15 best practices* with the App Router. Further changes can be made to this application using follow-up prompts as required. The figure is as follows:

3 **(https://v0.app/)**

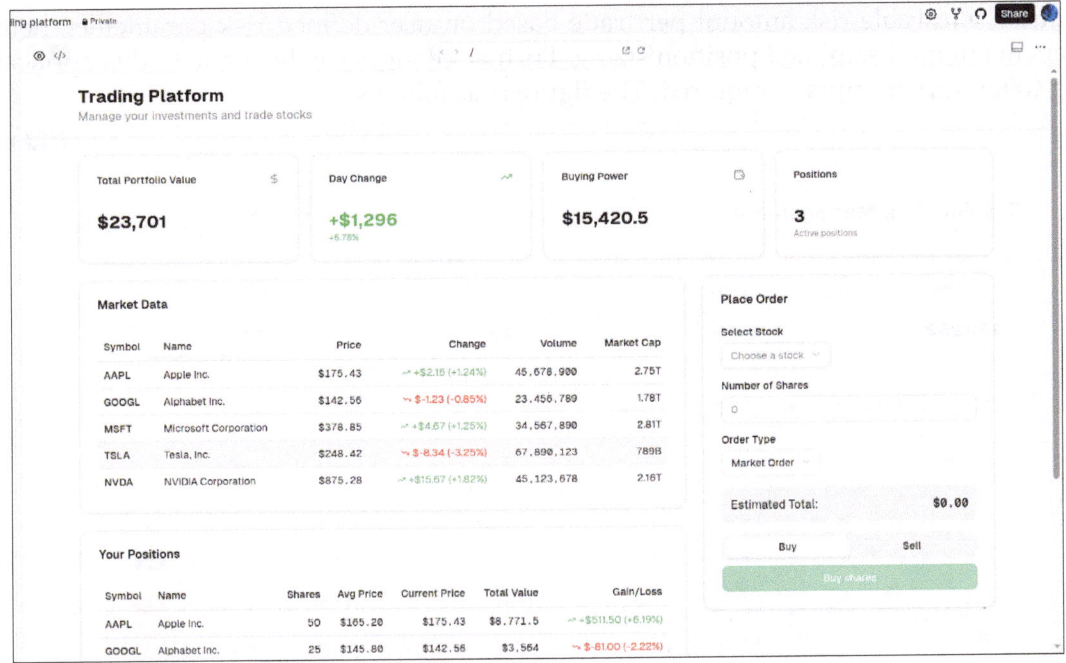

***Figure 2.3**: AI-generated image comparing vibe coders to traditional programmers*

The transformative potential of vibe coding fundamentally reshapes how financial technology supports trading, regulatory compliance, and risk management. By enabling financial professionals to build tools that incorporate banking standards and compliance requirements, vibe coding applications often achieve higher regulatory adherence while reducing manual oversight requirements. The technology allows for the creation of financial interfaces that communicate trust, security, and regulatory compliance, which are essential elements that traditional development approaches often struggle to implement consistently. Trading platforms and risk management systems benefit significantly as practitioners can rapidly prototype solutions for specific regulatory challenges they encounter daily. These include fraud detection algorithms with sophisticated pattern recognition to real-time compliance monitoring dashboards that provide actionable insights without overwhelming users. This approach ensures that final solutions are more closely aligned with actual regulatory requirements because they are built by those who understand the compliance context.

The following *Figure 2.4* shows a trading risk management system developed using vibe coding prompts on v0 by Vercel. The prompt used was **`Build a simple trading risk management application`**, and the vibe coding platform created a comprehensive trading risk management application with portfolio tracking, risk metrics, and position sizing tools. The application presents critical financial metrics, including total portfolio value, overall profit and loss performance, and portfolio risk as a percentage of the total account balance. Key performance indicators are displayed, showing account balance, risk per trade settings, and visual progress bars for portfolio risk assessment. The system calculates and displays the maximum allowable risk amount per trade based on user-defined risk parameters, helping traders maintain disciplined position sizing. Further changes can be made to this application using follow-up prompts as required. The figure is as follows:

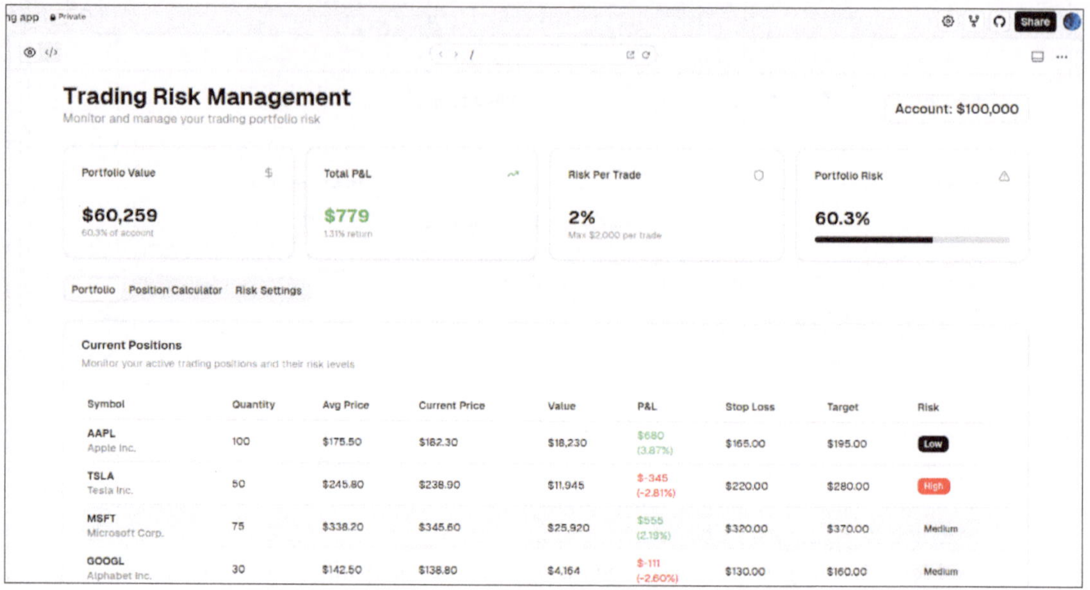

***Figure 2.4**: AI-generated image comparing vibe coders to traditional programmers*

Vibe coding is positioned to democratize financial innovation by removing traditional barriers between financial expertise and technological implementation. As the financial services sector evolves toward more personalized banking experiences and AI-driven decision-making tools, vibe coding will enable faster innovation cycles, broader accessibility for non-technical financial professionals, and stronger integration between human judgment and automated systems. Vibe coding's focus on rapid prototyping aligns well with finance's need for agile responses to market volatility, regulatory changes, and emerging financial products. Further, the integration of vibe coding with existing financial infrastructure promises to accelerate the development of adaptive trading systems where market insights can be quickly transformed into functional algorithms that improve performance and risk management while maintaining regulatory compliance. In the next section, we will look at some of the examples of vibe coding applications in the e-commerce industry.

Vibe coding applications in e-commerce

Vibe coding represents a transformative approach to e-commerce development where entrepreneurs and business owners describe their vision in plain English, and AI generates fully functional online stores and applications. This allows business owners, from startup founders to established retailers, to describe requirements such as **`Create a mobile-first fashion`**

`store` or **`Build a product recommendation system`** and receive a working e-commerce solution within hours rather than months. The technology fundamentally eliminates traditional barriers between business vision and technical implementation. This enables domain experts who understand market dynamics and customer behavior to directly create the digital experiences they need. In e-commerce, where speed to market, personalization, and user experience are critical competitive advantages, vibe coding accelerates innovation cycles while reducing dependency on technical teams.

Vibe coding systems operate through an iterative cycle where business owners describe their store concept, generate functional prototypes, test user flows, and refine based on customer feedback. This approach enables rapid prototyping of e-commerce platforms with complete online stores, often moving from concept to working deployment in less than a week, with the development costs significantly lower than traditional approaches. Vibe coding excels with e-commerce application development because it captures not just functional requirements but also the brand identity, visual aesthetics, and conversion optimization principles that are crucial for successful online retail experiences.

E-commerce businesses are already implementing vibe coding across diverse retail functions with measurable impact on speed and effectiveness. In-store creation, entrepreneurs have successfully built complete e-commerce platforms, including product catalogs, payment processing, inventory management, and mobile-responsive designs, without requiring programming expertise. Marketing applications represent another significant use case where vibe coding enables the rapid development of landing pages, promotional sites, interactive product demos, and personalized shopping experiences that can be quickly adapted to seasonal trends or campaign needs. Customer-facing applications benefit from AI-generated chatbots, recommendation engines, and dynamic merchandising systems that automatically adjust product placement based on real-time market trends and consumer behavior patterns.

The following *Figure 2.5* shows an e-commerce platform for selling clothes developed using vibe coding prompts on v0 by Vercel. The prompt used was **`Build a simple e-commerce platform for selling clothes`**, and the vibe coding platform created a simple e-commerce platform for selling clothes using Next.js with the App Router featuring a modern design, shopping cart functionality, and responsive layout. The application showcases a main section with featured products and category navigation, while the products page offers filtering by category and sorting options with a responsive grid layout. Individual product pages include detailed information, image galleries, size selection, and customer ratings. The platform consists of a fully functional shopping cart with quantity management, item removal, and order summary calculations, including tax. Additional features include a sticky navigation header with cart item count, a comprehensive footer with links, and notifications for user feedback when adding items to the cart. Further changes can be made to this application using follow-up prompts and integration options as required. The figure is as follows:

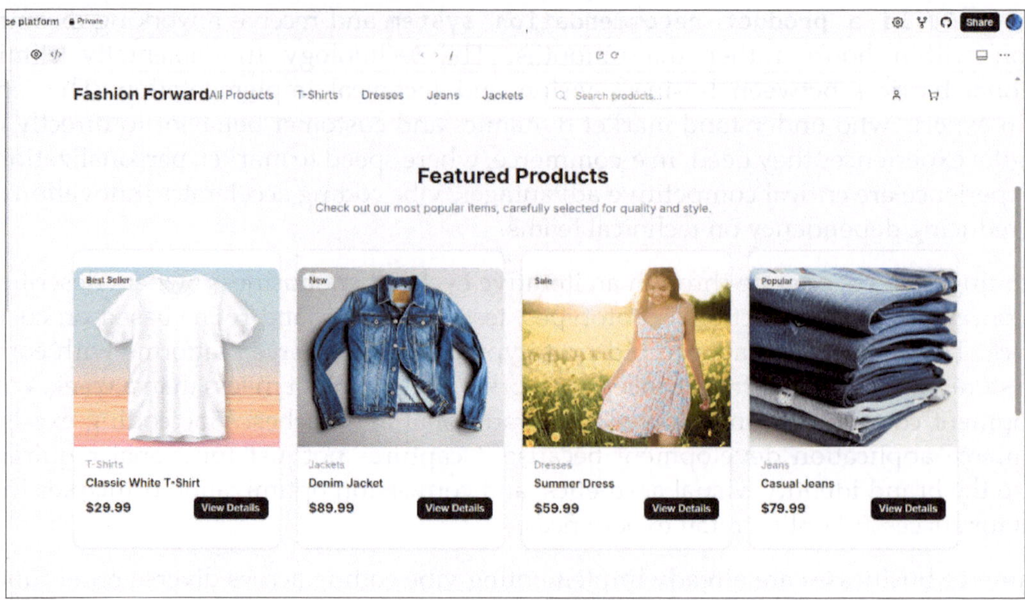

***Figure 2.5**: AI-generated image comparing vibe coders to traditional programmers*

The transformative potential of vibe coding reshapes how e-commerce platforms support customer engagement and conversion optimization. These applications often achieve higher performance metrics while reducing manual optimization requirements by enabling business owners to build stores that automatically incorporate best practices for user experience, mobile responsiveness, and conversion optimization. Vibe coding allows for the creation of retail interfaces that communicate brand personality, trust, and visual appeal, which are essential elements that traditional development approaches often struggle to implement consistently across all touchpoints. Dynamic merchandising systems benefit significantly as retailers can rapidly prototype solutions for specific market opportunities they encounter daily. These range from trend-responsive product displays to personalized shopping experiences that provide relevant recommendations without overwhelming users. This approach ensures that final solutions are more closely aligned with actual customer needs because they are built by those who understand the retail context and customer psychology intimately.

The following *Figure 2.6* shows an e-commerce inventory management system developed using vibe coding prompts on v0 by Vercel. The prompt used was to **`Build a simple e-commerce inventory management system`**, and the vibe coding platform created a complete application for managing products, stock levels, and basic inventory operations. This inventory management system provides a comprehensive dashboard with real-time statistics displaying total products, stock levels, low stock alerts, and inventory value in an intuitive card-based interface. Users can efficiently manage their product catalog through operations, such as adding new products with form validation, editing existing items with inline editing capabilities, and deleting products with safety confirmation dialogs. The system features intelligent stock level indicators that automatically categorize items as **`In Stock`**, **`Low Stock`**, or **`Out of Stock`** for quick inventory assessment. Further changes can be made to this application using follow-up prompts and integration options as required. The figure is as follows:

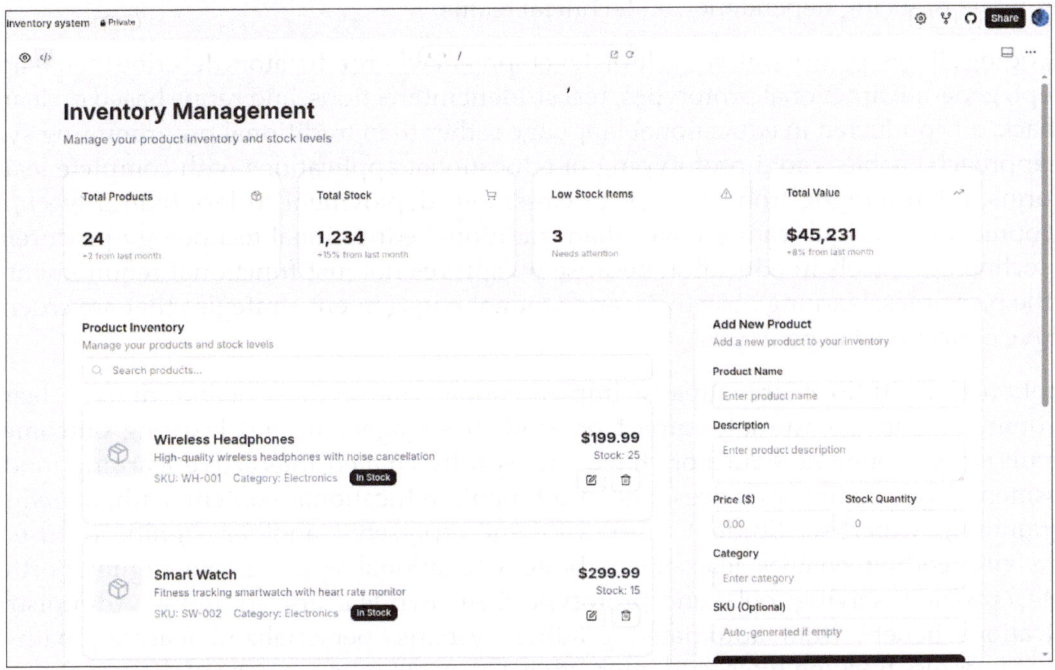

***Figure 2.6**: AI-generated image comparing vibe coders to traditional programmers*

Vibe coding is positioned to democratize e-commerce innovation by removing traditional barriers between business vision and technical implementation, potentially transforming how online retail solutions are conceived and deployed across the industry. As the e-commerce sector evolves toward more personalized shopping experiences and AI-driven customer interactions, vibe coding enables faster innovation cycles and broader accessibility for non-technical entrepreneurs. Vibe coding's emphasis on rapid prototyping and iterative refinement aligns perfectly with e-commerce's need for agile responses to market trends, seasonal demands, and emerging consumer behaviors. In the next section, we will look at some of the examples of vibe coding applications in the education sector.

Vibe coding applications in education

Vibe coding represents a paradigm shift in education and educational technology where educators can describe their learning objectives in natural language, and AI transforms these descriptions into functional educational applications and tools. This revolutionary approach allows teachers from elementary educators to university professors to express requirements such as **`Create an interactive math quiz`** or **`build a language learning game`**, and receive working educational software within hours rather than months. The technology enables educators who understand learning dynamics and student needs to directly create the digital experiences that enhance their teaching. In education, where engagement, personalization, and accessibility are critical for effective learning outcomes, vibe coding accelerates innovation cycles while reducing dependency on technical teams.

Vibe coding allows for an iterative cycle of development where educators describe their teaching concept, generate functional prototypes, test student interactions, and refine based on learning feedback, all conducted in educational language rather than traditional programming syntax. This approach enables rapid prototyping of educational applications with complete learning platforms, often moving from concept to classroom deployment in less than a week, with development costs significantly lower than traditional educational technology procurement. This technology excels in education because it captures not just functional requirements but also the principles, learning objectives, and student engagement strategies that are crucial for effective educational experiences.

Educational institutions are already implementing vibe coding across diverse learning environments with measurable impact on student engagement and learning outcomes. In curriculum development, educators have successfully created interactive learning modules, assessment tools, coding exercises, and multimedia educational content without requiring programming expertise. Student empowerment represents another significant use case where vibe coding enables learners to build educational apps, create digital portfolios, develop problem-solving tools, and prototype their own learning solutions. Administrative applications benefit from automated grading systems, personalized learning pathways, student progress tracking tools, and interactive classroom management platforms that can be quickly adapted to specific educational needs. Notable examples include Yale's *Coding with Kyle*[4] program, where **master of business administration** (**MBA**) students with no technical background create functional applications, and various high schools implement after-school clubs, where students solve community problems using AI-driven development.

The following *Figure 2.7* shows a comprehensive web education platform developed using vibe coding prompts on v0 by Vercel. The prompt used was **`Create a web education platform`**, and the vibe coding platform created a comprehensive web education platform with multiple pages, including a landing page, course catalog, course details, and student dashboard. This web education platform offers a comprehensive learning experience through four main sections. The **`Landing Page`** serves as an entry point with a showcase of featured courses with ratings and pricing, authentic student testimonials, and strategic call-to-action elements to drive enrollment. The **`Course Catalog`** provides a browsing experience with filtering and search capabilities, detailed course cards, and multiple sorting options. The **`Course Detail Page`** delivers in-depth information through a comprehensive overview, video preview, and student reviews. Finally, the **`Student Dashboard`** creates a personalized learning hub displaying individual progress statistics, course progress tracking, an achievement system to gamify learning, recent activity feeds, and seamless continuation of learning paths. Further changes can be made to this application using follow-up prompts and integration options as required. The figure is as follows:

---

4 (**https://som.yale.edu/story/2025/vibe-coding-how-ai-transforming-mba-experience-yale**)

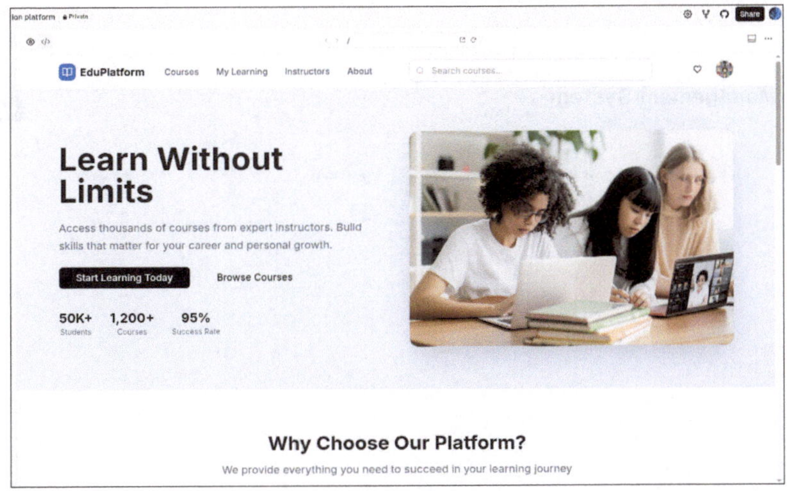

***Figure 2.7**: AI-generated image comparing vibe coders to traditional programmers*

Vibe coding fundamentally reshapes how educational technology supports student learning and teacher effectiveness. Vibe-coded educational applications often achieve higher completion rates and improved learning outcomes by enabling educators to build tools that automatically incorporate best practices for engagement, accessibility, and personalized learning. Vibe coding allows for the creation of educational interfaces that communicate clearly, inspire creativity, and adapt to individual learning styles, which are essential elements that traditional educational technology often struggles to implement consistently across diverse learning environments. Learning experiences benefit significantly, as educators can rapidly prototype solutions for specific challenges they encounter daily. These can range from adaptive assessment systems that provide immediate feedback to interactive simulations that help students visualize complex concepts without overwhelming them.

The following *Figure 2.8* shows a student management system developed using vibe coding prompts on v0 by Vercel. The prompt used was **`Create a student management system`**, and the vibe coding platform created a comprehensive student management system with a modern interface, featuring student registration, profile management, course tracking, and grade management. This student management system features a dashboard with key statistics, including total students, active enrollments, available courses, and **grade point average** (**GPA**), along with a complete student directory that supports search and filtering by name, email, status, and grade level. Users can add new students through a detailed form capturing personal information, contact details, academic status, and GPA, while also having the ability to edit existing student records or remove them from the system entirely. The application includes course management functionality where administrators can view, edit, and manage available courses with details such as course codes, credit hours, instructors, and current enrollment numbers. Further changes can be made to this application using follow-up prompts and integration options as required. The figure is as follows:

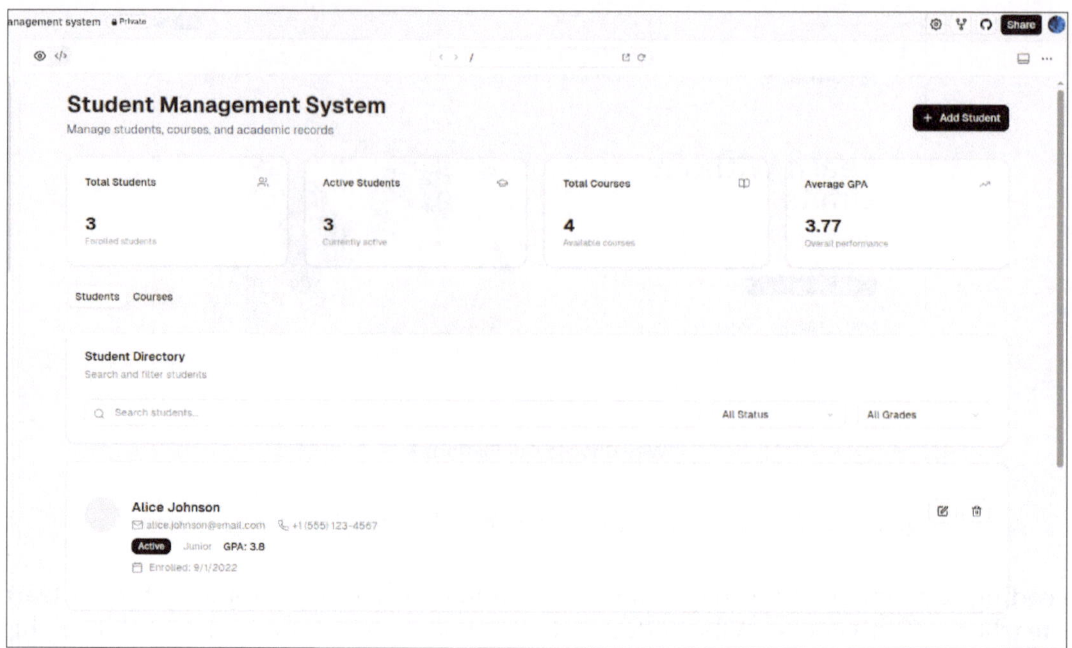

Figure 2.8: *AI-generated image comparing vibe coders to traditional programmers*

Vibe coding is positioned to democratize educational innovation by removing traditional barriers between expertise and technological implementation. Looking forward, the integration of vibe coding with existing educational infrastructure promises to accelerate the development of adaptive learning systems. Here, insights can be quickly transformed into functional educational tools that improve student engagement and academic achievement, while maintaining educational quality and accessibility standards across all learning environments. In the next section, we will look at some of the examples of vibe coding applications in the entertainment industry.

Vibe coding applications in entertainment

Vibe coding allows creators in the entertainment industry to describe their vision in natural language, and AI transforms these descriptions into functional entertainment applications, games, and multimedia experiences. This allows content creators from independent game developers to digital artists to express requirements, such as `Create an interactive story game` or `build a music visualization app`, and receive working entertainment software within hours rather than months. The technology eliminates traditional barriers between creative vision and technical implementation, enabling artists, filmmakers, musicians, and content creators who understand audience engagement and storytelling to directly create the digital experiences they want. In entertainment, where creativity, audience engagement, and time-to-market are critical competitive advantages, vibe coding accelerates content production cycles while reducing dependency on technical teams and development costs.

Vibe coding allows creators to describe their artistic concept, generate functional prototypes, test user interactions, and refine based on audience feedback, which is all conducted in creative language rather than traditional programming syntax. This approach enables rapid prototyping of entertainment applications with complete games, interactive media, and digital art tools. They often move from concept to working deployment in less than a week, with the development costs significantly lower than traditional software development. Vibe coding captures not just functional requirements but also the artistic vision, aesthetic principles, and audience engagement strategies that are crucial for successful entertainment experiences.

Entertainment and content creators are already implementing vibe coding across diverse creative domains with measurable impact on content quality and production speed. In game development, independent creators have successfully built interactive games, puzzle platforms, simulation experiences, and mobile entertainment apps without requiring extensive programming expertise. Digital art and media applications represent another significant use case where vibe coding enables the rapid development of visual effects tools, interactive installations, music applications, and multimedia presentations that can be quickly adapted to artistic trends or project requirements. Content creation benefits from AI-generated streaming tools, audience engagement platforms, social media applications, and creative automation systems that automatically enhance content production workflows based on real-time performance analytics and audience behavior patterns. Notable examples include creators building complete entertainment applications from scratch using only natural language prompts, with some projects achieving substantial user engagement within days of deployment.

The following *Figure* 2.9 shows a content hosting platform similar to Netflix developed using vibe coding prompts on v0 by Vercel. The prompt used was **`Create a content hosting platform similar to netflix`**, and the vibe coding platform created a content hosting platform with a comprehensive video player component with full controls, including play/pause, volume, progress tracking, skip functionality, and full-screen support. The application includes a full-featured streaming interface with a dark cinematic theme, a comprehensive user authentication system, a fully functional video player with controls, a complete admin dashboard for content management, and detailed user profiles with watch history and personal watchlists. The platform is ready for deployment and can be easily upgraded with real database integration and video streaming services as needed. Further changes can be made to this application using follow-up prompts and integration options as required. The figure is as follows:

Figure 2.9: AI-generated image comparing vibe coders to traditional programmers

Vibe coding fundamentally reshapes how entertainment technology supports audience interaction and creative expression. By enabling creators to build entertainment platforms that automatically incorporate best practices for user engagement, visual appeal, and interactive design, vibe-coded entertainment applications often achieve higher user retention and engagement metrics while reducing manual optimization requirements. Vibe coding allows for the creation of entertainment interfaces that communicate artistic vision and interactive appeal, which are essential elements that traditional development approaches often struggle to implement consistently across all creative touchpoints. Creative workflows benefit significantly as artists can rapidly prototype solutions for specific artistic challenges they encounter daily. These range from interactive storytelling platforms that adapt to user choices to real-time performance tools that provide immersive experiences without overwhelming audiences. This approach ensures that final entertainment solutions are more closely aligned with actual audience needs because they are built by those who understand the creative context and audience intimately.

The following *Figure 2.10* shows a single-player Mario game with all the classic features developed using vibe coding prompts on *Bolt.new*[5]. The prompt used was **`Create a single player Mario game`**, and the vibe coding platform created a fully playable Mario game with smooth controls, enemies, collectibles, and multiple levels. The game features smooth character movement with proper physics, enemy AI, collectible coins, multiple challenging levels, and a complete scoring system. The visual design captures the iconic Mario style with pixel-perfect character sprites, detailed platform textures, and smooth animations that bring the classic platformer experience to life. Further changes can be made to this application using follow-up prompts as required. The figure is as follows:

5 (**https://bolt.new/**)

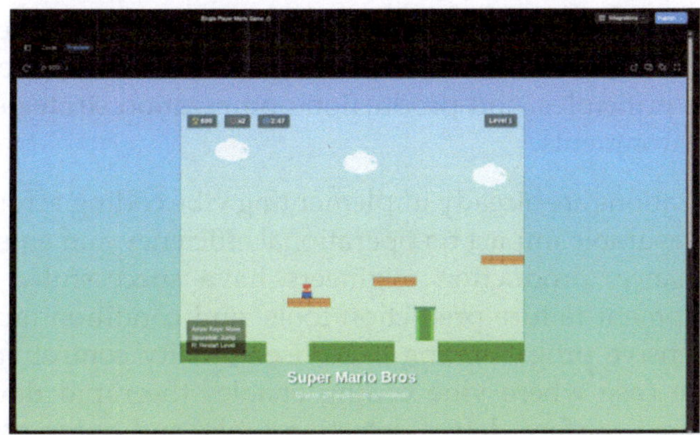

***Figure 2.10**: AI-generated image comparing vibe coders to traditional programmers*

Vibe coding is positioned to democratize entertainment innovation by removing traditional barriers between creative vision and technical implementation. This can potentially transform how entertainment solutions are conceived and deployed across the industry. Vibe coding enables faster creative cycles, broader accessibility for non-technical creators, and stronger integration between human creativity and automated production optimization systems. Looking forward, the integration of vibe coding with existing entertainment infrastructure promises to accelerate the development of creative systems where artistic insights can be quickly transformed into functional entertainment experiences. In the next section, we will look at some of the examples of vibe coding applications in the manufacturing industry.

Vibe coding applications in manufacturing

Vibe coding represents a transformative approach to manufacturing software development where manufacturing employees describe their operational needs in natural language, and AI generates functional manufacturing applications and automation tools. This allows manufacturing professionals, from production managers to quality engineers, to express requirements such as `Build a monitoring dashboard for machine temperatures` or `create an equipment failure prediction system`, and receive working industrial software within hours rather than months. Vibe coding fundamentally eliminates traditional barriers between operational expertise and technical implementation, enabling manufacturing professionals who understand production workflows and equipment behavior to directly create the digital solutions they need for optimizing processes. In manufacturing, where equipment uptime, quality control, and operational efficiency are critical competitive advantages, vibe coding accelerates development cycles while reducing dependency on technical teams and costly industrial software procurement.

Vibe coding allows manufacturing employees to describe their operational concept, generate functional prototypes, test equipment integrations, and refine based on performance feedback. This approach enables rapid prototyping of manufacturing applications with monitoring systems, quality control tools, and predictive maintenance platforms, often moving from concept to factory deployment in less than a week. Vibe coding excels in manufacturing because it captures not just functional requirements but also the operational safety standards, regulatory compliance principles, and production optimization strategies that are crucial for effective industrial environments.

Manufacturing organizations are already implementing vibe coding across diverse production environments with measurable impact on operational efficiency and equipment performance. In predictive maintenance, production engineers have successfully created sensor data analysis systems, equipment failure prediction tools, and condition monitoring dashboards without requiring extensive programming expertise. Quality control applications represent another significant use case where vibe coding enables the rapid development of vision-based inspection systems, surface defect detection tools, and automated quality assurance platforms that can be quickly adapted to specific product requirements. Notable examples include production managers using simple commands like **`Detect surface defects on product X using camera feeds`** to generate complete quality inspection systems, with some implementations achieving significant reductions in manual inspection time while improving defect detection accuracy.

The following *Figure 2.11* shows a steel manufacturing quality control system developed using vibe coding prompts on Bolt.new. The prompt used was **`Create simple quality control system for steel manufacturing`**, and the vibe coding platform created a steel manufacturing quality control system with industrial design and robust functionality. The system includes a real-time dashboard with quality metrics, comprehensive batch management, detailed inspection forms covering all major testing areas, and advanced reporting capabilities with data visualization. Further changes can be made to this application using follow-up prompts and integration options as required. The figure is as follows:

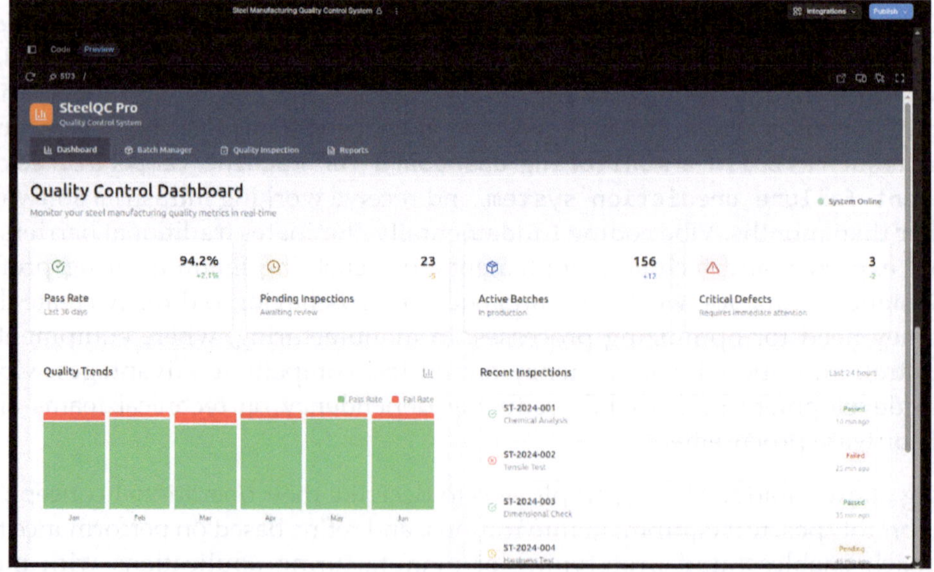

***Figure 2.11**: AI-generated image comparing vibe coders to traditional programmers*

The transformative potential of vibe coding extends beyond mere efficiency gains to fundamentally reshape how manufacturing technology supports operational decision-making and process optimization. By enabling production personnel to build systems that automatically incorporate best practices for equipment monitoring, quality assurance, and production optimization, vibe-coded manufacturing applications often achieve higher operational performance metrics while reducing manual oversight requirements. Vibe coding allows for the creation of manufacturing interfaces that communicate critical production data, safety alerts, and performance insights that are essential elements that traditional industrial software often struggles to implement consistently across all production environments. Production workflows benefit significantly as operators can rapidly prototype solutions for specific manufacturing challenges they encounter daily. These range from real-time equipment monitoring systems that provide early warning alerts to automated inventory management platforms that optimize material flow without disrupting production schedules.

The following *Figure 2.12* shows a car manufacturing process control system developed using vibe coding prompts on *Replit*[6]. The prompt used was **`Create a car manufacturing process control system`**, and the vibe coding platform created a car manufacturing process control system with real-time monitoring and management capabilities for automotive production operations. The dashboard displays key production metrics, including daily vehicle output, overall efficiency, quality rate, and active issues tracking. The system monitors three production lines with real-time status indicators showing operational state, production speed, temperature readings, and efficiency percentages. Quality control features track multiple checkpoints, including body weld integrity, paint quality, engine mounting, and electrical systems. Equipment status monitoring covers robotic arms, conveyor belts, control units, and **heating, ventilation, and air conditioning** (HVAC) systems with uptime percentages and maintenance scheduling. Further changes can be made to this application using follow-up prompts and integration options as required. The figure is as follows:

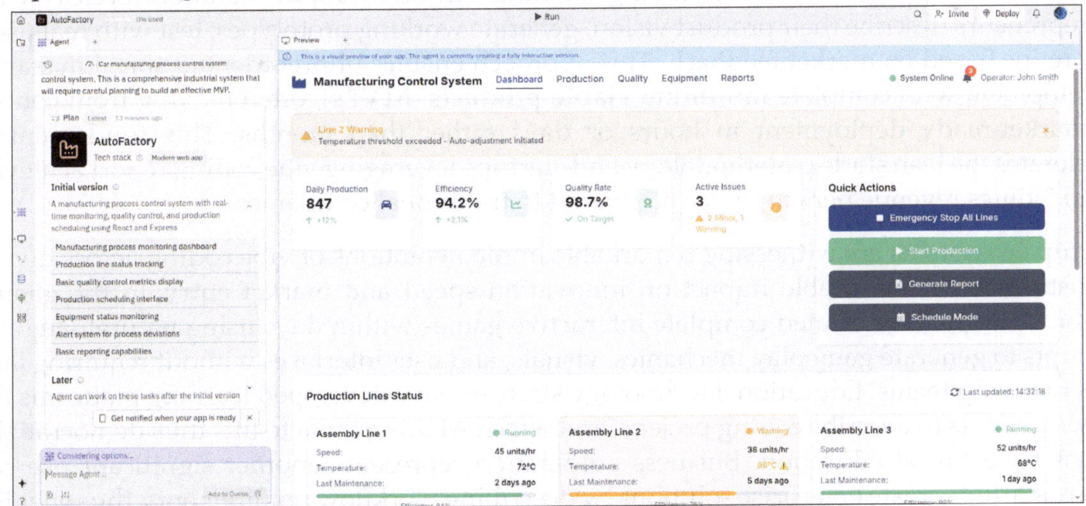

***Figure 2.12**: AI-generated image comparing vibe coders to traditional programmers*

6 **(https://replit.com/)**

Vibe coding is positioned to democratize manufacturing innovation by removing traditional barriers between operational expertise and technical implementation. This can potentially transform how industrial solutions are conceived and deployed across the manufacturing sector. As the manufacturing industry evolves toward Industry 4.0 principles and smart factory implementations, vibe coding enables faster innovation cycles, broader accessibility for non-technical manufacturing personnel, and stronger integration between human operational knowledge and automated production optimization systems. The technology's emphasis on rapid prototyping and iterative refinement aligns perfectly with manufacturing's need for agile responses to production demands, equipment changes, and emerging operational challenges. In the next section, we will look at some of the examples of vibe coding applications in startup ecosystems.

Vibe coding applications in start-up ecosystems

Vibe coding represents a revolutionary shift for startup ecosystems where entrepreneurs can describe their business ideas in natural language, and AI transforms these descriptions into functional applications and digital products. This approach fundamentally changes the traditional startup formation model by eliminating the barrier between having a great idea and possessing technical implementation skills. Previously, non-technical founders faced months of delay to recruit technical talent with significant equity dilution and high burn rates before generating any revenue. With vibe coding, entrepreneurs can gain immediate development capability and can build initial prototypes within days with minimal equity dilution and achieve faster paths to revenue through reduced development costs.

Vibe coding employs sophisticated AI-powered tools such as Replit, v0, Lovable, and others that translate plain language descriptions into functional code, allowing founders to achieve AI-generated applications. Vibe coding operates through rapid iteration cycles where entrepreneurs describe their product vision, generate working prototypes, test with real users, and refine based on market feedback. This approach enables unprecedented speed in startup development with complete **minimum viable products** (**MVPs**), often moving from concept to market-ready deployment in hours or days rather than months. This fundamentally accelerates the lean startup methodology and startups leveraging vibe coding report achieving up to 5 times revenue per employee compared to traditional companies.

Startup ecosystems are witnessing remarkable implementations of vibe coding across diverse industries with measurable impact on innovation speed and market entry. In the gaming sector, startups have created complete interactive games within days using natural language prompts to generate gameplay mechanics, visuals, and user interfaces without requiring large programming teams. Educational technology startups have developed learning platforms that allow students to describe coding projects and watch AI bring them to life, thus democratizing access to technical education. Business automation represents another significant use case where startups create enterprise solutions by describing workflow requirements, thus enabling non-technical users to generate custom automation tools that save organizations time and money.

The following *Figure 2.13* shows an MVP for a business process automation platform developed using vibe coding prompts on Replit. The prompt used was **`Create an MVP for a business process automation platform`**, and the vibe coding platform business process automation platform that allows users to design, manage, and execute automated workflows through an intuitive visual interface. The platform features a sophisticated drag-and-drop workflow builder with a component library containing trigger nodes (such as manual execution, scheduled tasks, and webhook endpoints) and action nodes (such as email notifications, API calls, data processing operations, and conditional logic branching). Users can easily configure each component through a detailed properties panel that provides node-specific settings like cron expressions for schedulers, **Simple Mail Transfer Protocol** (**SMTP**) configurations for emails, **Hypertext Transfer Protocol** (**HTTP**) parameters for API calls, and conditional operators for decision logic. The system includes pre-built workflow templates for standard business processes, such as approval workflows and notification systems, enabling rapid deployment of standard automation patterns. The platform offers extensive customization through a settings interface covering user profiles, email server configuration, webhook security settings, notification preferences, and system-wide execution parameters. Further changes can be made to this application using follow-up prompts and integration options as required. The figure is as follows:

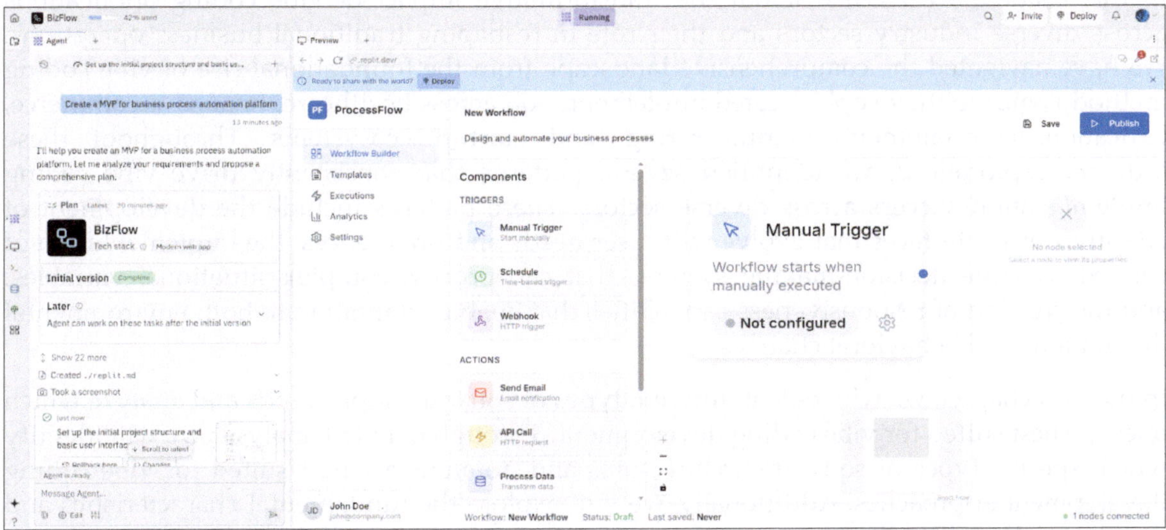

***Figure 2.13**: AI-generated image comparing vibe coders to traditional programmers*

Vibe coding fundamentally reshapes competitive dynamics within startup ecosystems. By enabling rapid experimentation and lower costs for testing new ideas, vibe coding allows startups to place smaller bets instead of committing to expensive and long-term development cycles. This shift forces the market to compete on business model innovation and execution rather than technical complexity, as defensive modes built on programming barriers become harder to defend. Startups can now test multiple product directions simultaneously and validate product market fit with real users in weeks rather than quarters. Startups can also pivot quickly, based on market feedback, without burning through significant runway. Vibe coding particularly benefits cash-strapped startups by enabling parallel experiments and rapid iteration cycles that would have been prohibitively expensive using traditional development approaches, thus fundamentally changing the risk profile of startup innovation.

Vibe coding is positioned to completely transform startup ecosystems by democratizing innovation and removing traditional barriers between business vision and technical execution. As the startup landscape evolves toward AI-first business models and rapid iteration cycles, vibe coding enables broader entrepreneurial participation, faster market validation, and more efficient capital deployment across the innovation ecosystem. Vibe coding's emphasis on natural language development aligns perfectly with startup needs for agility, cost efficiency, and speed to market, which allows entrepreneurs to focus on solving real problems rather than technical implementation challenges. Looking forward, the integration of vibe coding with startup innovation promises to accelerate the development of a new generation of AI native companies where business insights can be rapidly transformed into market-ready products.

Conclusion

In this chapter, we learned about the transformative impact of vibe coding applications across diverse industry sectors and their role in reshaping traditional business operations. We have navigated the comprehensive landscape from the foundational rise of vibe coding methodologies to their sophisticated implementation across healthcare, finance, e-commerce, education, entertainment, manufacturing, and startup ecosystems. Throughout these industry explorations, we identified several patterns that consistently drive vibe coding implementation success across diverse sectors. These patterns include the development of adaptive user interfaces that evolve with user needs and preferences, the implementation of context-sensitive decision-making systems that can process complex situational variables, and the creation of responsiveness capabilities that enable adaptation to both environmental fluctuations and behavioral changes.

In the next chapter, we will look at different types of software applications and analyze which ones are best suited for vibe coding development. Through detailed analysis, we will identify which specific types of software architectures and domains are best suited for vibe coding development approaches. Additionally, we will explore the fundamental characteristics and architectural qualities that make certain software types ideal candidates for prompt-driven development methodologies, including their tolerance for iterative refinement, the nature of their user feedback loops, and the flexibility of their underlying frameworks.

Further readings

There are lots of online resources to help the readers improve their learning on vibe coding applications. The following *Table 2.1* lists some of the best resources to further enhance the understanding of vibe coding applications in different industries:

Resource name	Link
The Rise of Vibe Coding—How It's Changing the Future of Software Development	**https://mimo.org/blog/the-rise-of-vibe-coding**
The rise of vibe coding: Why architecture still matters in the age of AI agents	**https://vfunction.com/blog/vibe-coding-architecture-ai-agents/**
The Rise of Vibe Coding: How AI is Changing Development	**https://www.index.dev/blog/vibe-coding-ai-development**
The rise of 'vibe coding'	**https://theweek.com/tech/the-rise-of-vibe-coding**
The Rise of Vibe Coding: Why Describing Software Is the New Way to Build It	**https://element451.com/blog/the-rise-of-vibe-coding-why-describing-software-is-the-new-way-to-build-it**
Vibe coding: a new paradigm for biomedical software development	**https://pmc.ncbi.nlm.nih.gov/articles/PMC12217882/**
Building with Words: Vibe Coding in Healthcare	**https://www.clarahealth.co/blog/vibe-coding-in-healthcare**
Is Vibe Coding in Life Sciences Driving a More Empathetic Future? These 6 Use Cases Say Yes	**https://hexaware.com/blogs/is-vibe-coding-in-life-sciences-driving-a-more-empathetic-future-these-6-use-cases-say-yes/**
'Vibe Coding' is accelerating healthcare innovation and transforming lives	**https://www.wral.com/business/technology/vibe-coding-healthcare-innovation-march-2025/**
Top Use Cases for Enterprise Vibe Coding in Healthcare	**https://www.superblocks.com/blog/enterprise-vibe-coding-in-healthcare**
Beyond the Blueprint: Vibe Coding the Future of Life Sciences	**https://www.cognizant.com/de/de/insights/blog/articles/coding-by-feel-vibe-coding-life-sciences**
The Rise of "Vibe Coding"—Risks and Opportunities for Insurance Executives	**https://www.xceedance.com/the-rise-of-vibe-coding-risks-and-opportunities-for-insurance-executives/**
Can You Trust Vibe Coding to Build Your Next Trading Tool?	**https://www.financemagnates.com/trending/can-you-trust-vibe-coding-to-build-your-next-trading-tool/**
Vibe Coding an E-commerce App with Prisma MCP and Next.js	**https://www.prisma.io/blog/vibe-coding-with-prisma-mcp-and-nextjs**
Vibe Code Your Way to Commerce with PayPal and Replit	**https://developer.paypal.com/community/blog/vibe-coding/**

Resource name	Link
Benefits of Vibe Coding With AI tools: Hype or Trend?	**https://nix-united.com/blog/vibe-coding-use-cases-benefits/**
Build an Online Store in Minutes with Hostinger Horizons & Vibe Coding	**https://analyticsindiamag.com/ai-highlights/build-an-online-store-in-minutes-with-hostinger-horizons-vibe-coding/**
How Can Vibe Coding Transform Programming Education?	**https://cacm.acm.org/blogcacm/how-can-vibe-coding-transform-programming-education/**
Vibe Coding for Students: Unlocking Your Creativity With AI	**https://girlswhocode.com/news/vibecodingforstudents**
Rethinking Coding Education: Teaching the Next Generation in a Vibe Coding World	**https://www.nucamp.co/blog/vibe-coding-rethinking-coding-education-teaching-the-next-generation-in-a-vibe-coding-world**
How 'Vibe Coding' is Reshaping Education in Computer Science and Software Development	**https://www.arsturn.com/blog/how-vibe-coding-is-reshaping-education**
Vibe Coding in Education: Preparing Students for 2025 Tech Careers	**https://fueler.io/blog/vibe-coding-in-education-preparing-students-tech-careers**
How Can Educational Institutions Integrate Vibe Coding into Their Curricula?	**https://www.dhiwise.com/post/educational-institutions-integrate-vibe-coding-into-curricula**
Vibe Coding Impact on Education and Trickle AI's Role	**https://content.trickle.so/blog/vibe-coding-impact-on-education-and-trickle-ais-role**
The Ultimate Guide to Vibe Coding Games with Three.js and Cursor in 2025	**https://webtech.tools/the-ultimate-guide-to-vibe-coding-games-in-2025**
Vibe-Coding Applications in Manufacturing: A Game Changer	**https://praxie.com/vibe-coding-applications-in-manufacturing/**
Vibe Coding: How Natural Language Programming is Changing Manufacturing Software Development	**https://www.automationworld.com/analytics/article/55300106/vibe-coding-how-natural-language-programming-is-changing-manufacturing-software-development**
Success Stories: Real-World Applications of "Vibe Coding" by Emerging Startups	**https://www.arsturn.com/blog/success-stories-real-world-applications-of-vibe-coding-by-emerging-startups**
Vibe Coding: The Future of Building Software (Without Writing Code Like a Caveman)	**https://www.siddharthbharath.com/vibe-coding/**

Resource name	Link
How 'Vibe Coding' Is Creating A New AI Economy	**https://www.forbes.com/sites/kolawolesamueladebayo/2025/08/04/how-vibe-coding-is-creating-a-new-ai-economy/**
"Vibe coding" surges as a quarter of Y Combinator startups now get AI to write their code	**https://explodingtopics.com/blog/vibe-coding**

***Table 2.1**: Vibe coding applications in different industries*

Questions

1. Why did vibe coding applications become popular?
2. How did AI enable the development of vibe-coded applications?
3. What are vibe coding platforms?
4. What are the different vibe coding applications in healthcare?
5. How are healthcare organizations implementing vibe coding?
6. Why will vibe coding democratize healthcare innovation?
7. What are the different vibe coding applications in finance?
8. How are financial institutions implementing vibe coding?
9. What are the advantages of using vibe coding for e-commerce?
10. How does vibe coding reshape the education sector?
11. What are the main use cases for vibe coding for teachers and students?
12. How can vibe coding help with game development?
13. What are the advantages of using vibe coding tools by creative professionals?
14. What are the main applications of vibe coding in manufacturing?
15. Why are manufacturing organizations implementing vibe coding?
16. How does vibe coding help entrepreneurs?
17. Why are startups rapidly adopting vibe coding?
18. How can a user create an MVP for their business idea using vibe coding?

Join our Discord space

Join our Discord workspace for latest updates, offers, tech happenings around the world, new releases, and sessions with the authors:

https://discord.bpbonline.com

Chapter 3

Types of Software Suitable for Vibe Coding

Introduction

Vibe coding has the potential to revolutionize software development by transforming how applications are conceptualized, designed, and deployed across diverse technological domains. In web development, it enables rapid creation of responsive interfaces and dynamic user experiences through iterative visual refinement. In contrast, mobile development leverages it for cross-platform solutions that adapt seamlessly to varying device contexts and user interactions. Data-driven applications benefit from intuitive dashboard creation and real-time analytics visualization that evolves based on stakeholder feedback and emerging insights. Automation and workflow systems utilize vibe coding for building adaptive tools that optimize processes through continuous refinement and user-driven adjustments. Database architecture implementations create flexible schema designs and management interfaces that respond to changing data requirements and access patterns. The blockchain ecosystem employs it for decentralized application development with smart contracts that iterate rapidly based on community governance and security considerations. Game development studios harness vibe coding for prototyping mechanics, designing interactive systems, and creating immersive experiences that evolve through playtesting feedback loops. The developer community particularly benefits from compressed development cycles, enabling experimental features and market-responsive iterations that would traditionally require extensive planning phases. This evolution spans from prototype stage experimentation to production-grade solutions that fundamentally reshape how software architectures are conceived, validated, and deployed across technical disciplines.

Structure

In this chapter, we will cover the following topics:

- Web applications and responsive interfaces
- Mobile app development and cross-platform solutions
- Data visualization and analytics dashboards
- Automation tools and workflow systems

- Database design and management systems
- Blockchain and decentralized application development
- Game development

Objectives

This chapter will provide a comprehensive analysis of software categories and patterns that align optimally with vibe coding methodologies. It will equip readers with the analytical frameworks and insights needed to identify which application types benefit most from prompt-driven development approaches. By the end of this chapter, the readers will understand the characteristics and technical requirements that make certain software domains ideal candidates for vibe coding implementation. Additionally, the readers will master the evaluation criteria for assessing software suitability based on iteration tolerance, feedback loop dynamics, and framework flexibility. Further, you will develop proficiency in recognizing structural patterns across web applications, mobile platforms, data systems, automation tools, database architectures, blockchain implementations, and game engines that maximize vibe coding effectiveness. Finally, the readers will acquire comprehensive knowledge of specific considerations and technical constraints. This will enable them to make informed decisions about when to leverage vibe coding approaches while optimizing the balance between rapid iteration capabilities and architectural robustness in their software selection and design processes.

Web applications and responsive interfaces

Web applications are one of the most successful domains for vibe coding implementation because they offer an ideal balance of complexity and standardization that **artificial intelligence** (**AI**)-powered tools can effectively handle. The structured nature of web technologies, combined with well-established patterns and frameworks, makes web development particularly suited to vibe coding. Unlike specialized domains that require deep domain expertise or highly novel approaches, web development operates within a relatively mature ecosystem where common patterns, best practices, and architectural decisions have been extensively documented and refined over decades of evolution.

The standardization in web technologies provides AI tools with a rich foundation of predictable patterns and conventions to draw upon. **HyperText Markup Language** (**HTML**), **Cascading Style Sheets** (**CSS**), and JavaScript follow consistent syntactic rules and semantic structures that AI models can readily parse and generate. Popular frameworks like React, Vue, Angular, and their associated ecosystems have established clear conventions for component architecture, state management, and application organization. This standardization means that when an AI system encounters a web development task, it can leverage its training on millions of similar code examples to make informed decisions about structure, naming conventions, and implementation approaches that align with development standards.

The modular nature of web development also aligns well with AI-driven workflows. Web applications naturally decompose into discrete and testable components such as individual **user interface** (**UI**) elements, **application programming interface** (**API**) endpoints, database schemas, and service layers, each with clear interfaces and responsibilities. This modularity allows AI tools to focus on well-defined problems rather than attempting to solve monolithic challenges. When building a user interface, the AI system can concentrate on creating a single component with clear behavior and then iterate on that component in isolation before integrating it into the larger application architecture.

The following *Figure 3.1* illustrates the collaborative workflow between AI tools and web development technologies that makes vibe coding particularly effective in the web domain. At the center of the process is an AI tool that generates code by leveraging the standardized ecosystem of web technologies. The diagram shows how the AI draws upon the structured foundation of HTML, CSS, and JavaScript, along with established frameworks like React, Vue, and Angular, to create cohesive web applications. The flow from AI-generated code to the final web application demonstrates the modular approach that makes web development suitable for vibe coding. The iterative feedback loop captures the collaborative refinement process that makes AI-driven web development so effective. This cycle represents how developers can observe the visual and functional results of AI-generated code, then provide specific feedback or adjustments that guide the AI toward better solutions. The figure is as follows:

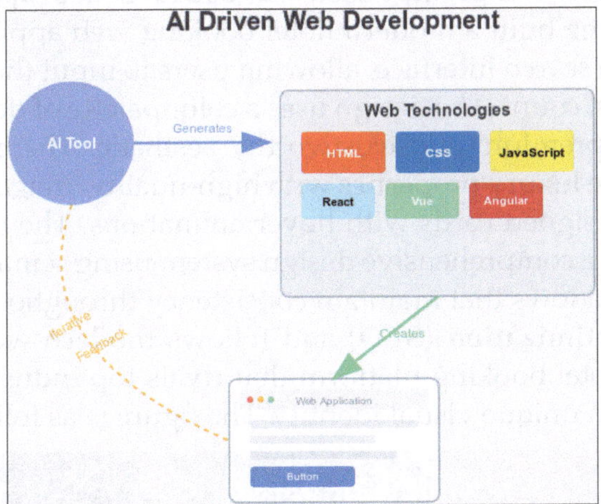

***Figure 3.1**: AI-generated image comparing vibe coders to traditional programmers*

Vibe coding tools excel at generating responsive user interfaces that adapt seamlessly across different devices and screen sizes. The AI can interpret design requirements described in natural language and translate them into pixel-perfect implementations with proper semantic HTML structure. The visual nature of web interfaces allows vibe coding tools to provide real-time previews and iterative refinement capabilities. Developers can describe layout modifications, color schemes, and typography changes, and watch as the AI implements these changes instantly. This immediate feedback loop significantly accelerates the design-to-implementation process.

Latest vibe coding platforms seamlessly integrate frontend development with backend services. They handle user authentication, database connections, and API integrations automatically. Vibe coding tools like Lovable integrate with Supabase for backend functionality, while others connect with various cloud services and databases to create complete web applications without requiring deep technical knowledge of server-side architecture. The platforms handle complex aspects like state management, routing, and data flow between frontend and backend components, allowing developers to focus on business logic and user experience rather than technical implementation details. This abstraction enables rapid development of sophisticated web applications that would traditionally require months of development time.

Vibe coding tools also implement responsive design principles using modern CSS techniques like flexbox, grid layouts, and media queries. These tools understand the importance of mobile-first design and create interfaces that work effectively across desktop, tablet, and mobile devices without requiring separate implementations for each platform. The tools can generate progressive web app features, including offline functionality, push notifications, and app-like experiences that bridge the gap between traditional websites and native mobile applications. This capability is particularly valuable for businesses looking to provide consistent user experiences across all digital touchpoints.

The following *Figure 3.2* shows a modern hotel booking web application developed using vibe coding prompts on Lovable. The prompt used was **`Build a Web application for booking hotels`** and the vibe coding built a modern hotel booking web application. It features a full-screen hero section with a search interface, allowing users to input their destination, check-in/check-out dates, and guest count. The design uses a color palette of deep ocean blue and warm gold accents, creating a premium and trustworthy aesthetic. There is also a featured hotel showcase displaying three luxury properties with high-quality images, ratings, amenities, and pricing information in designed cards with hover animations. The entire application is fully responsive and built with a comprehensive design system using semantic color tokens, custom gradients, and elegant shadows that maintain consistency throughout. The interface includes proper **search engine optimization** (**SEO**) and follows modern web design best practices, creating a professional hotel booking platform that rivals top industry sites like *Booking.com* while maintaining its own unique visual identity. The figure is as follows:

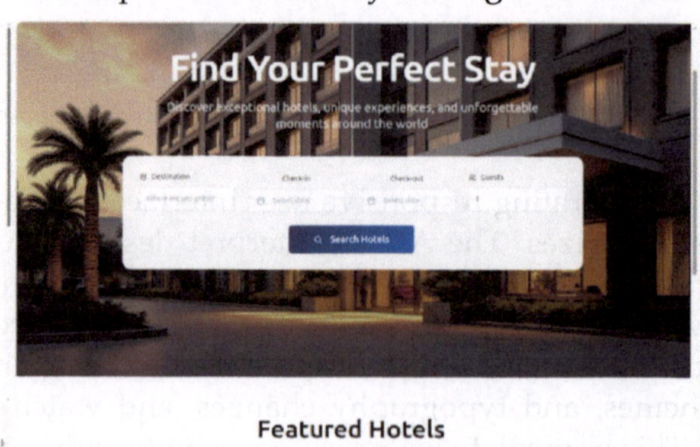

Figure 3.2: *A modern hotel booking web application*

The extensive documentation and community resources surrounding web technologies also create an environment where AI systems can access vast amounts of contextual knowledge about implementation patterns, common pitfalls, and optimization strategies. Stack Overflow Discussions, GitHub repositories, official documentation, and tutorial content provide AI models with exposure to both successful implementations and debugging approaches for virtually every conceivable web development scenario. This wealth of training data enables AI systems not just to generate syntactically correct code but also to make architectural decisions that reflect real-world experience and community wisdom. In the next section, we will look at the development of mobile applications and cross-platform solutions using vibe coding tools.

Mobile app development and cross-platform solutions

Vibe coding platforms excel with cross-platform frameworks like *React Native* and *Flutter*, enabling developers to create applications that run natively on both *iOS* and *Android* from a single codebase. Vibe coding tools can interpret functional requirements and generate appropriate code for navigation patterns, UI components, and platform-specific integrations while maintaining native performance characteristics. The AI can understand platform-specific design guidelines and can automatically implement Material Design principles for Android and Human Interface Guidelines for iOS applications. This ensures that applications feel native to each platform while maintaining code efficiency through cross-platform development approaches.

Advanced vibe coding systems demonstrate a sophisticated understanding of mobile architecture patterns and can automatically implement state management solutions like *Redux* or *MobX* for React Native applications. These platforms can generate complete application architecture, including proper folder structures, dependency injection configurations, and testing frameworks, while ensuring adherence to established architectural principles. The AI can also analyze user requirements and suggest optimal patterns for data flow, component hierarchy, and performance optimization strategies specific to mobile environments.

Device capability integration represents another strength of vibe coding platforms in mobile development, where AI can generate code for accessing native device features like cameras, **global positioning system** (**GPS**), accelerometers, and biometric authentication systems. Specialised vibe coding systems understand the complexity of permissions management across different operating system versions and can automatically generate appropriate permission request flows and fallback mechanisms. This includes generating platform-specific code for features that require native implementations while maintaining cross-platform compatibility through appropriate abstraction layers.

The following *Figure 3.3* shows a mobile networking event app designed for Tech Summit 2025, developed using vibe coding prompts on Lovable. The prompt used was `Create a mobile app for a very large networking event`, and the vibe coding built a complete mobile app with features such as a home dashboard that displays the event's **quick response (QR)** code pass for quick connections, real-time statistics showing total attendees and personal connections, along with upcoming session highlights. The schedule section in the app provides a complete 3-day agenda organized by day, allowing users to browse keynotes, workshops, panels, and networking sessions with details about time, location, speakers, and expected attendance. The attendees directory offers a searchable database of all conference participants, filterable by name, company, or skills, with separate views for all attendees and established connections. The connections feature manages networking relationships with tabs for connection requests and confirmed connections, including messaging capabilities and detailed professional profiles with tags like *AI, ML, Leadership*, etc. Finally, the profile section displays the user's professional information, interests, event statistics, achievements, and social media links, which are all accessible through an intuitive bottom navigation bar designed for mobile interaction. The figure is as follows:

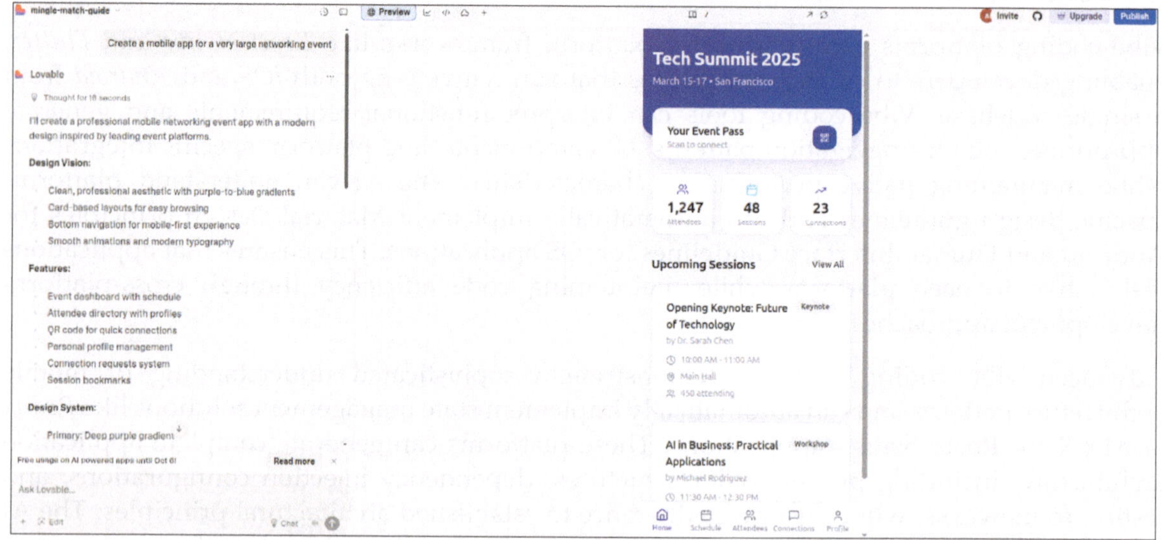

***Figure 3.3:** A mobile networking event app designed for Tech Summit 2025*

Vibe coding tools can help with performance optimization in mobile applications, and they can analyze code patterns and suggest improvements for memory management, battery efficiency, and rendering performance. The AI understands mobile-specific constraints like limited processing power and memory. This enables it to automatically implement lazy loading patterns, image optimization strategies, and efficient data caching mechanisms. Some of the vibe coding platforms can detect potential performance bottlenecks and suggest alternatives like virtualized lists for large datasets or optimized animation libraries for smooth user interactions.

App store deployment and distribution workflows are streamlined through vibe coding platforms that can generate appropriate build configurations, signing certificates management, and continuous integration pipelines for both iOS App Store and Google Play Store submissions. The AI understands the complex requirements for app store approval processes and automatically generates necessary metadata, privacy policy templates, and compliance documentation. This includes configuration of automated testing suites, crash reporting integration, and analytics setup to ensure applications meet production-ready standards.

Responsive design adaptation across various screen sizes and device orientations can be handled intelligently by vibe coding systems, and it can generate flexible UI layouts that work seamlessly across phones, tablets, and foldable devices. The AI can understand the nuances of different screen sizes and aspect ratios and implement appropriate scaling strategies and breakpoint systems. This ensures consistent user experiences across the diverse ecosystem of mobile devices while optimizing interface elements for touch interactions and accessibility requirements.

API integration and data synchronization capabilities can be enhanced using vibe coding platforms through the generation of networking layers, offline data management, and real-time synchronization systems. The AI can interpret API documentation and generate appropriate service layers with error handling, retry mechanisms, and data validation logic. This includes the implementation of offline-first architectures with local database solutions like SQLite, ensuring applications remain functional even with poor network connectivity.

Security implementation in mobile applications can be addressed comprehensively by vibe coding tools. These tools can generate secure authentication flows, data encryption mechanisms, and secure storage solutions for sensitive information. The AI can understand mobile-specific security concerns like certificate pinning, root detection, and secure communication protocols, and automatically implement industry-standard security practices. This includes the generation of secure key management systems, biometric authentication integration, and compliance with mobile security frameworks like the **Open Worldwide Application Security Project** (**OWASP**) Mobile Security standards. In the next section, we will look at the development of data visualizations and analytics dashboards using vibe coding tools.

Data visualization and analytics dashboards

Vibe coding tools can create interactive dashboards that combine multiple data sources and visualization types into cohesive analytical interfaces. The AI can interpret requirements for charts, graphs, tables, and other data presentation components and automatically select appropriate visualization types based on the nature of the data and the analytical goals. Vibe coding platforms can also handle complex aspects of dashboard development, including real-time data updates, filtering mechanisms, and interactive drill-down capabilities. Users can describe their data analysis needs in natural language, and the AI generates appropriate dashboard layouts with proper data binding and update mechanisms.

Modern vibe coding platforms can connect to various data sources such as **Structured Query Language** (**SQL**) databases, NoSQL systems, APIs, **comma-separated values** (**CSV**) files, and cloud-based data warehouses. The AI understands how to structure queries, handle data transformations, and manage real-time data feeds to keep dashboards current and accurate.

The tools can automatically generate data processing pipelines that clean, transform, and aggregate data before visualization. This includes handling missing data, calculating derived metrics, and implementing proper caching mechanisms to ensure dashboard performance remains optimal even with large datasets.

The following *Figure 3.4* shows a sales analytics dashboard with AI-powered forecasting capabilities developed using vibe coding prompts on Lovable. The prompt used was **`Build analytics dashboard for sales forecast and integrate this with sql database and prediction models`**, and the vibe coding built a sales analytics dashboard that combines real-time data visualization with AI-powered forecasting capabilities. At its core, the dashboard provides essential **key performance index** (**KPI**) metrics, including total sales tracking, growth rate analysis, average sale calculations, and transaction counts. These are displayed through interactive cards with color-coded trend indicators showing positive or negative performance changes. Users can view detailed transaction data through a sortable data grid that organizes sales records by date, amount, product category, and region, making it easy to identify patterns and drill down into specific segments. The AI-powered forecasting engine leverages Google Gemini to generate 6-month sales predictions at the click of a button. The AI analyzes historical sales patterns, seasonality trends, and growth rates to produce forecasts accompanied by confidence level indicators to help users understand prediction reliability. The figure is as follows:

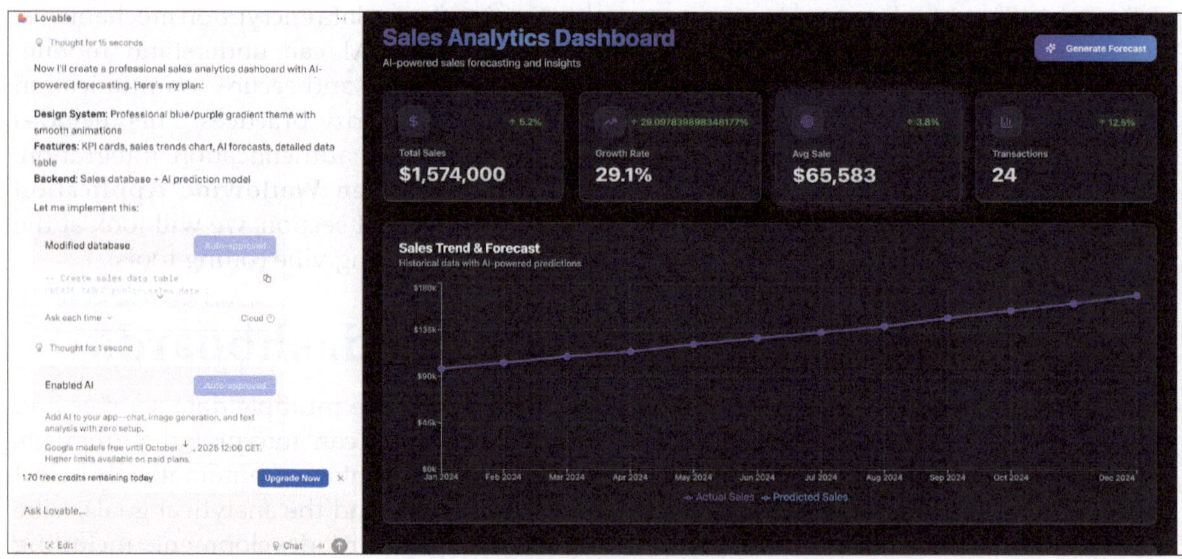

Figure 3.4: *A sales analytics dashboard with AI-powered forecasting capabilities*

Vibe coding platforms can incorporate statistical analysis directly into dashboard visualizations and create predictive analytics interfaces that go beyond simple data presentation. The AI tools can generate code for trend analysis, forecasting models, and anomaly detection algorithms. Vibe coding tools can also implement performance optimization strategies to handle enterprise-scale analytics dashboards that process millions of data points without compromising user experience or system responsiveness. In the next section, we will look at the development of automation tools and workflow systems using vibe coding tools.

Automation tools and workflow systems

Automation tools and workflow systems benefit tremendously from vibe coding approaches because these applications typically follow logical patterns and rule-based structures that AI can effectively interpret and implement. The ability to describe complex business processes in natural language and have them translated into functional automation systems represents one of the most practical applications of vibe coding. Vibe coding platforms excel at creating workflow automation systems that can handle complex business processes involving multiple steps, conditional logic, and integration with various external systems. The AI can interpret descriptions of business rules and translate them into functional workflow engines with proper error handling and monitoring capabilities. Vibe coding platforms can generate approval workflows, document processing systems, and task management applications that integrate with existing business systems. The AI understands common workflow patterns like sequential processing, parallel execution, and conditional branching, and can implement these concepts without requiring detailed technical specifications. Event-driven architecture implementation is a particular strength of vibe coding platforms in automation systems. Here, the AI can generate event handling mechanisms that respond to triggers from various sources, including database changes, file uploads, API calls, and scheduled time intervals.

Vibe coding tools can seamlessly handle integration with third-party services and APIs, and these tools can interpret API documentation and generate appropriate connector modules for popular business applications like Salesforce, Microsoft Office 365, Slack, and various cloud storage services. These tools understand how to implement proper authentication flows, rate limiting, and error handling for external integrations while maintaining data consistency across different systems. This includes automatic generation of webhook handlers, OAuth implementations, and data transformation layers that ensure smooth communication between disparate business systems.

The following *Figure 3.5* shows a workflow automation for payroll process using QuickBooks API developed using vibe coding prompts on *Replit*[1]. The prompt used was **`Build a workflow automation for payroll process using Quickbooks API with time based schedule and retrieving employee time data and calculating payroll`**. The vibe coding tool built a complete payroll automation system that streamlines the user's payroll processing using QuickBooks integration. The system features three specialized tools working together, where one retrieves employee time tracking data from QuickBooks, another calculates payroll, including regular hours, overtime at a 1.5 times rate, and a twenty percent tax deduction, and a final tool that submits the processed payroll back to QuickBooks. These tools are orchestrated through an automated workflow that runs on a biweekly schedule, executing at 9 AM on the first and fifteenth of each month in the Los Angeles timezone by default. The workflow operates completely automatically once published, fetching employee hours from the previous fourteen-day period, performing all necessary payroll calculations with detailed breakdowns

1 (**https://replit.com/**)

for each employee, and submitting the finalized payroll data to QuickBooks with a unique batch ID for tracking. The figure is as follows:

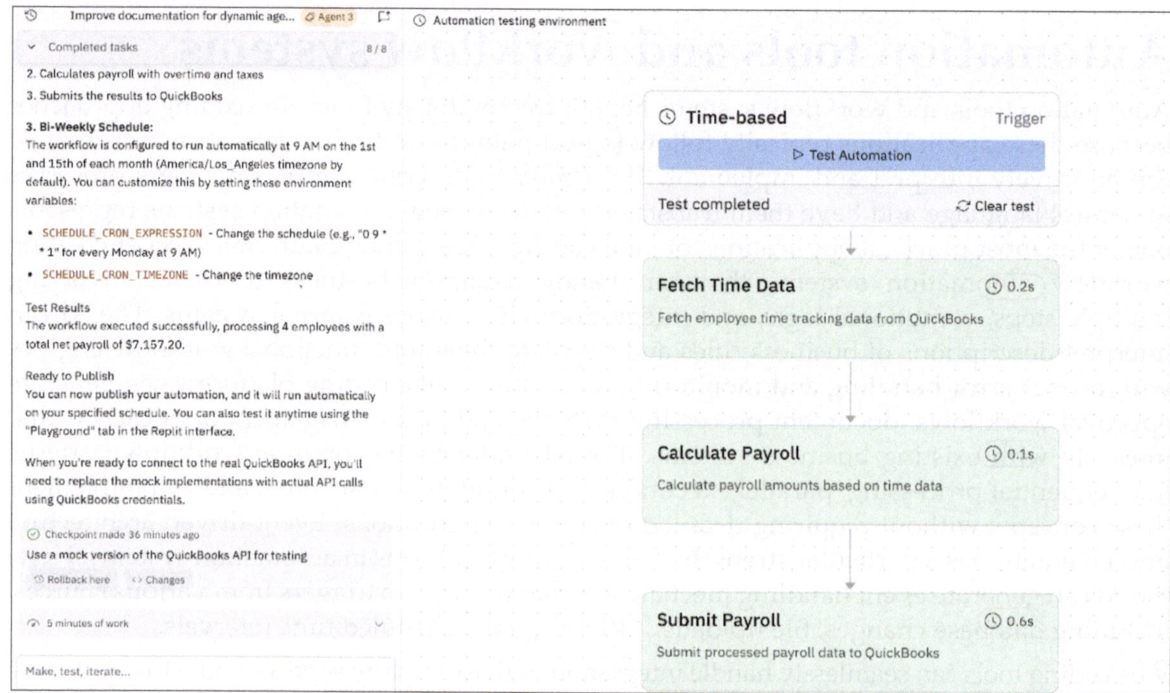

Figure 3.5: A workflow automation for payroll process using QuickBooks API

Vibe coding platforms can generate advanced conditional logic, creating sophisticated rule engines that can handle complex business scenarios with multiple variables, weighted scoring systems, and dynamic rule modification capabilities. These tools can interpret natural language descriptions of business logic and translate them into efficient decision-making algorithms that can be easily modified without requiring technical expertise. These systems can also include proper audit trails, version control for rule changes, and testing frameworks that allow business users to validate rule modifications before deployment to production environments.

Scalability and load management features can be implemented by vibe coding tools to ensure automation workflows can handle enterprise-scale processing requirements while maintaining optimal performance and resource utilization. The user can ask the tools to generate distributed processing architectures, auto scaling mechanisms, and load balancing strategies that adapt to varying workload demands without manual intervention. In the next section, we will look at the development of database management and migration systems using vibe coding tools.

Database design and management systems

Vibe coding tools revolutionize database schema generation by using AI and **large language models** (**LLM**) to analyze application requirements and automatically create normalized database structures that follow industry best practices. These systems can interpret natural language descriptions of data relationships and generate comprehensive entity relationship diagrams complete with primary keys, foreign keys, and appropriate constraints that maintain data integrity. The AI-driven development approach ensures that schemas are properly normalized to eliminate redundant data while maintaining performance considerations. As applications evolve, vibe coding tools can modify existing schemas and propose structural changes that accommodate new features without breaking existing functionality or compromising data consistency.

The query optimization capabilities of vibe coding tools extend far beyond traditional database management approaches by using machine learning algorithms to analyze query patterns and suggest optimal execution plans. These systems can automatically identify bottlenecks in complex joins, subqueries, and aggregations. The AI models can further be used to continuously monitor query performance across different workloads and dynamically adjust optimization strategies based on real-time usage patterns and data distribution changes. These tools can also predict future performance issues by analyzing query trends and proactively suggest schema modifications, index additions, or partitioning strategies before performance degradation occurs.

Modern vibe coding tools excel at creating sophisticated data access layers that seamlessly integrate with popular **Object Relational Mapping** (**ORM**) frameworks and API architectures. These systems can generate type-safe database models, repository patterns, and data transfer objects that maintain consistency between database schemas and application code. The vibe coding development approach ensures that data access patterns are optimized for specific use cases. Additionally, these tools can be used to generate comprehensive unit tests for data access components, ensuring that database interactions are thoroughly validated and maintain backward compatibility during schema updates.

Database migration management through vibe coding tools provides significant automation opportunities. These tools can analyze schema differences between versions and generate migration scripts that safely transform data while preserving data integrity and business logic constraints. The AI models can be used to detect potential migration issues, such as data type conflicts or constraint violations, and suggest remediation strategies before deployment. Version control integration allows teams to track schema changes alongside application code with automatic rollback capabilities that can restore previous database states in case of deployment failures. The tools also generate comprehensive migration documentation, including impact assessments and rollback procedures for each schema change.

The following *Figure 3.6* shows an SQL to MongoDB migration tool developed using vibe coding prompts on *Bolt AI builder*[2]. The prompt used was **`Create a data migration tool to move data from SQL database to MangoDB`**. In response, the vibe coding tool built an SQL to MongoDB migration tool that enables flexible and configurable data transfer from SQL databases such as PostgreSQL to MongoDB with efficient handling of various table and collection structures. Key features of this tool include configuration management for both database connections, robust SQL and MongoDB clients for data retrieval and document

2 (**https://bolt.new/**)

insertion, and a batch processing migration orchestrator for optimal performance. The system has an executable migration script and a user-friendly interface for setting up database connections and viewing available tables. The tool also offers refresh capabilities to list tables, ensuring an up-to-date migration workflow while maintaining clear error messaging for database connection issues. The figure is as follows:

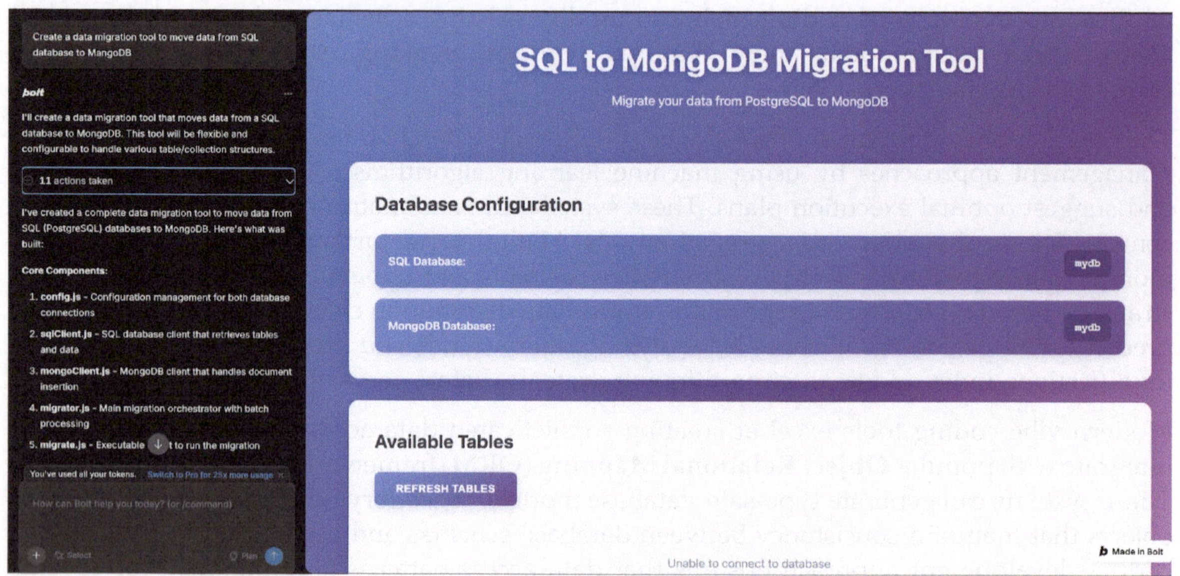

Figure 3.6: An SQL to MongoDB migration tool

Vibe coding tools can also be used for database backup and recovery procedures by implementing intelligent scheduling and monitoring systems that adapt to usage patterns and business requirements. These systems can automatically determine optimal backup frequencies based on transaction volumes, data criticality, and recovery time objectives. Advanced performance monitoring capabilities with vibe coding tools can provide comprehensive visibility into database operations through intelligent alerting and diagnostic systems.

Security implementation through vibe coding tools encompasses comprehensive access control, data encryption, and compliance monitoring that adapts to evolving regulatory requirements. These tools can automatically generate role-based access control policies, implement field-level encryption for sensitive data, and create audit trails that meet industry-specific compliance standards. In the next section, we will look at the development of blockchain and decentralized applications using vibe coding tools.

Blockchain and decentralized application development

Vibe coding tools excel at generating sophisticated smart contracts by translating business logic descriptions into secure, gas-optimized Solidity, Rust, or other blockchain-specific programming languages. These platforms can automatically implement common contract patterns such as **Ethereum Request for Comment** (**ERC**)-20 tokens, ERC-721 **non-fungible tokens** (**NFT**), multi-signature wallets, and **decentralized autonomous organization** (**DAO**) governance structures based on natural language specifications. These tools can understand blockchain-specific requirements, such as gas optimization and proper access control mechanisms, and generate smart contracts that follow established security best practices. Further, vibe coding tools can create deployment scripts, migration procedures, and contract verification processes that streamline the path from development to deployment.

The frontend development capabilities of vibe coding tools can help with decentralized application creation. These tools can automatically generate responsive web interfaces that seamlessly interact with blockchain networks. These tools analyze smart contract **application binary interface** (**ABI**) and automatically create user-friendly interfaces with wallet connection logic, transaction signing workflows, and real-time blockchain state updates. Vibe coding tools can understand different blockchain interaction patterns and can implement appropriate error handling for common scenarios such as insufficient gas fees, network congestion, and transaction failures.

The following *Figure 3.7* shows a prototype of a blockchain-based decentralized social network, which can be deployed on the Ethereum platform, developed using vibe coding prompts on Replit. The prompt used was **`Create a blockchain based decentralised social network on Ethereum`**, and the vibe coding tool built a prototype of a blockchain-based decentralized social network. This can be deployed on the Ethereum platform, leveraging Web3 integration to enable secure posting, following, and interactive content features. Users need to authenticate with a Web3 wallet such as MetaMask, ensuring true decentralization and privacy. The system utilizes Ethereum smart contracts to store posts and user relationships directly on the blockchain. Its core functionality includes creating and publishing posts, viewing blockchain-based feeds, browsing basic user profiles with wallet addresses, and engaging with posts through on-chain likes and interactions. The network features a modern Web3-enabled UI, giving users real-time feedback on blockchain transactions and integrating robust support for posting, following, and social activity in a decentralized environment. The figure is as follows:

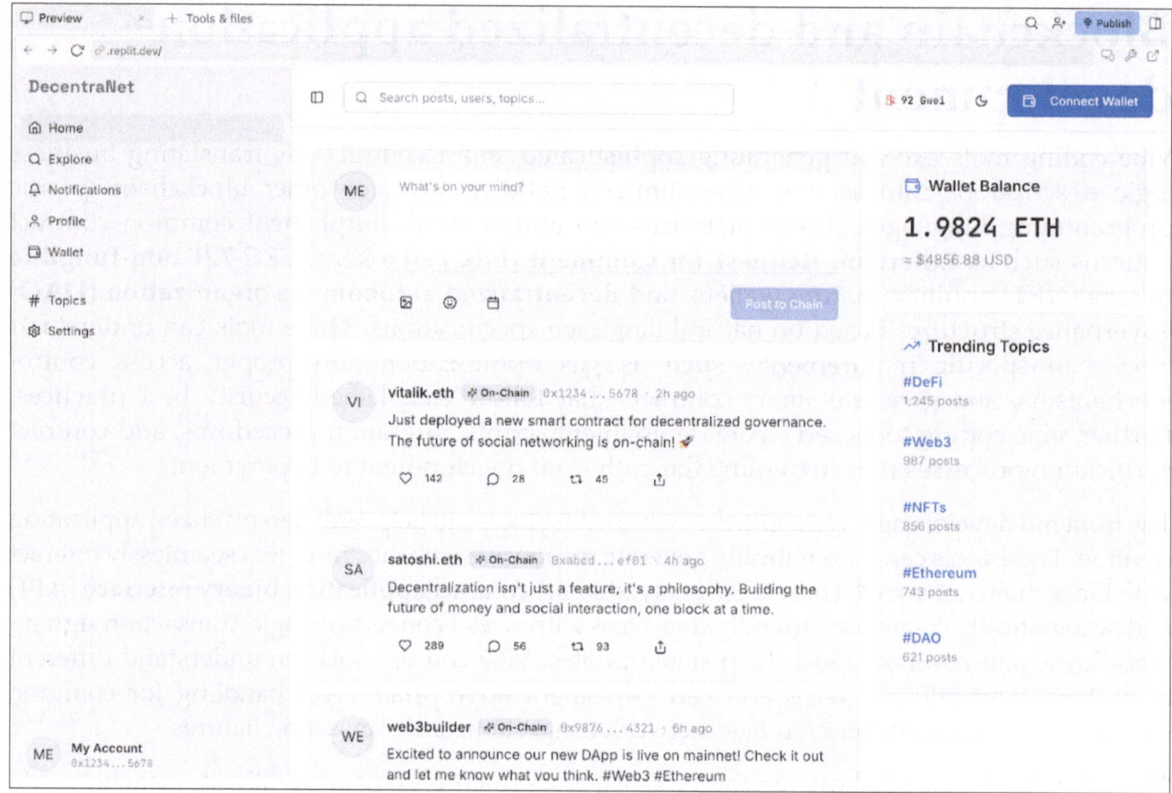

Figure 3.7: *A prototype of a blockchain-based decentralized social network*

Vibe coding tools are also capable of creating cross-chain code that enables seamless asset transfers and communication between different blockchain networks. These systems can automatically generate bridge contracts, relay mechanisms, and cross-chain protocols that can facilitate interoperability between major blockchain ecosystems. Vibe coding platforms also excel at implementing complex tokenomics models and automated market-making systems through intelligent contract generation and liquidity management tools. The security analysis capabilities of vibe coding tools provide comprehensive vulnerability detection and automated auditing systems that ensure smart contract safety before deployment. These systems can identify common security vulnerabilities such as reentrancy attacks, integer overflows, access control issues, and front-running vulnerabilities through sophisticated static analysis and formal verification methods.

Vibe coding tools revolutionize NFT platform development by automatically generating comprehensive marketplace infrastructure, minting systems, and digital asset management capabilities. These systems can create sophisticated NFT contracts with advanced features such as royalty distribution, dynamic metadata updates, composable traits, and utility token integration based on project specifications. The **decentralized finance** (**DeFi**) protocol generation capabilities of vibe coding platforms enable the creation of sophisticated financial instruments and yield generation mechanisms through automated smart contract development. These systems can implement lending and borrowing protocols, derivatives trading platforms, and synthetic asset systems that compete with established DeFi protocols. In the next section, we will look at the development of different types of games using vibe coding tools.

Game development

Vibe coding revolutionizes game development by enabling developers to create functional game prototypes within hours through natural language descriptions of desired mechanics and gameplay systems. These tools can translate high-level game concepts, such as **`2D grid based and turn based sci-fi strategy game`**, into fully playable experiences with resource management, battle systems, and AI opponents without requiring manual code implementation. The iterative nature of vibe coding allows developers to rapidly experiment with different game mechanics, adjusting rules, balancing systems, and implementing new features through conversational prompts rather than traditional programming workflows.

The 3D graphics capabilities of vibe coding tools have made JavaScript libraries like Three.js popular for browser-based game development. The AI can generate complex scenes, lighting systems, and interactive 3D environments through simple natural language prompts. These systems can automatically create game assets, including spacecraft models, terrain systems, particle effects, and environmental elements that would traditionally require specialized 3D modeling skills. Vibe coding tools also excel at generating sophisticated game state management systems that handle complex gameplay mechanics, including turn-based systems, resource tracking, and multi-layered game logic.

The following *Figure 3.8* shows an immersive first-person shooter game, featuring a fully 3D first-person perspective developed using vibe coding prompts on Lovable. The prompt used was **`Create a single player first person shooter game`** and the vibe coding tool built the immersive first person shooter game with a futuristic aesthetic. It features a fully 3D first-person perspective, where players navigate the environment using the keyboard, with aiming using the mouse. The core mechanics include weapon usage, click-to-shoot with hit detection, and enemy targets that actively spawn in the arena. The game tracks vital stats such as health, ammo, and score, displaying them through a glowing overlay that fits the sci-fi theme. A start screen provides intuitive instructions before gameplay begins, and the entire design draws from a palette of neon accents, dark environments, and futuristic monospace fonts. Built with Three.js and React Three Fiber, the game incorporates smooth animations, glowing effects, and offers players opportunities for customization and expansion in future versions, such as new weapons, enemies, or backend integration for persistent leaderboards. The figure is as follows:

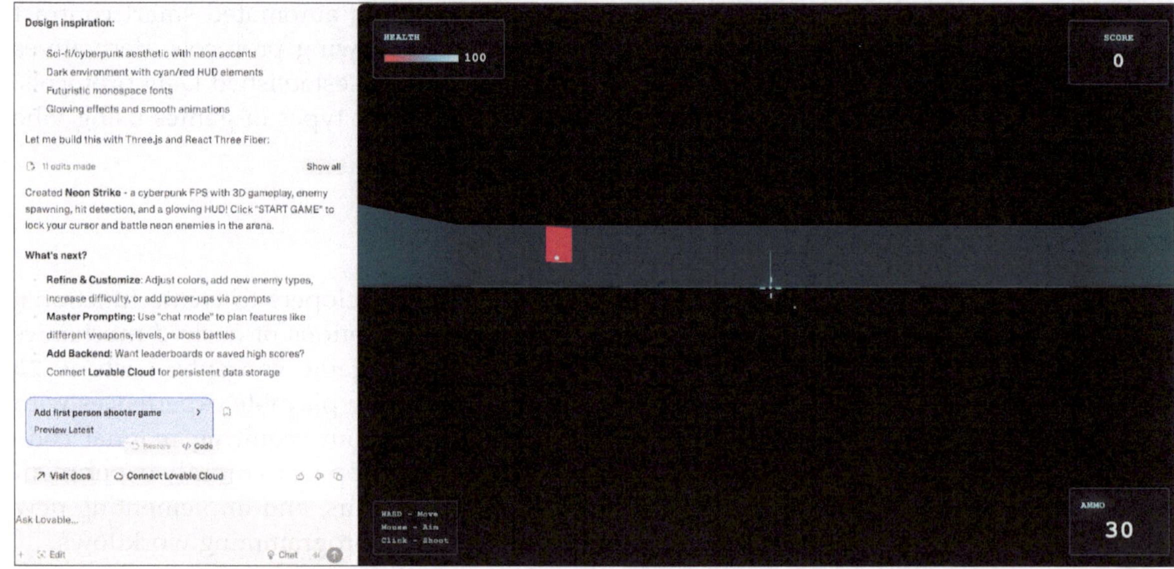

Figure 3.8: *A first-person shooter game featuring a fully 3D first-person perspective*

Modern vibe coding platforms can also create multiplayer game experiences through networking code generation and real-time synchronization systems. These tools can implement WebSocket connections, player matchmaking systems, and synchronized game state management that enables seamless multiplayer interactions. These tools understand common multiplayer patterns and can generate appropriate conflict resolution mechanisms, lag compensation, and network optimization strategies that ensure smooth gameplay across different connection qualities. These tools can also generate comprehensive player management features, including authentication, leaderboards, and social interaction mechanisms that enhance multiplayer engagement.

Conclusion

In this chapter, the diverse software categories and patterns that align with vibe coding methodologies have been discussed. We have navigated through web applications, mobile platforms, data visualization systems, automation tools, database architectures, blockchain implementations, and game development domains to identify their suitability for prompt-driven development. The key characteristics of iteration tolerance, feedback loop responsiveness, and framework flexibility can help developers determine which software types benefit most from vibe coding approaches. We have looked at the architectural qualities and technical requirements across different domains with their varying degrees of compatibility, paving the way for strategic application of vibe coding in appropriate contexts.

In the next chapter, the essential AI models, platforms, and tools that power vibe coding development will be discussed. We will examine different AI vibe coding platforms, their strengths and use cases, and provide practical guidance on selecting the right tools for your projects while addressing crucial considerations like version control and UI/ **user experience** (**UX**) design in AI-assisted development.

Further readings

There are a lot of online resources to help readers improve their learning on different types of software application development using vibe coding tools. The following *Table 3.1* lists some of the best resources to enhance further understanding of the types of software suitable for vibe coding:

Resource name	Link
A Structured Workflow for "Vibe Coding" Full-Stack Apps	**https://dev.to/wasp/a-structured-workflow-for-vibe-coding-full-stack-apps-352l**
My experience AI vibe coding a complete web application from scratch	**https://techhub.iodigital.com/articles/my-experience-ai-vibe-coding-a-complete-web-application-from-scratch**
How to build a web app using vibe coding and natural language prompts	**https://graphite.dev/guides/vibe-coding-web-app**
Vibe Coding: The Future of Seamless User Experiences in Web Development	**https://www.weblineindia.com/blog/vibe-coding-future-of-user-experience/**
I Took a Popular Vibe Coding Course and Built a Sample App	**https://dev.to/atsushiambo/i-took-a-popular-vibe-coding-course-and-built-a-sample-app-3124**
How to Vibe Code Cross-Platform Mobile Apps with Bolt	**https://medium.com/data-science-collective/how-to-vibe-code-cross-platform-mobile-apps-with-bolt-80e48b46b9aa**
Vibe Coding a Kotlin Multiplatform App	**https://proandroiddev.com/vibe-coding-a-kotlin-multiplatform-app-08195f9a6b62**
My First Experience Building a Mobile App with Vibe Coding	**https://www.linkedin.com/pulse/my-first-experience-building-mobile-app-vibe-coding--ohvwf/**
Vibe Coding in Data Analysis Function: Vibe Data Analysis Is In	**https://powerdrill.ai/blog/vibe-coding-in-data-analysis-fuction-vibe-analytics-is-in**
What Vibe Coding Gets Wrong (and Why Vibe Analytics is Better)	**https://plotly.com/blog/vibe-coding-gets-wrong-vibe-analytics-better/**

Resource name	Link
Vibe Analytics: Vibe Coding's New Cousin Unlocks Insights	**https://sloanreview.mit.edu/article/vibe-analytics-vibe-codings-new-cousin-unlocks-insights/**
Vibe Data Analysis > Vibe Coding: Create your own AI Data Analyst	**https://medium.com/@gal.peretz/vibe-data-analysis-vibe-coding-create-your-own-ai-data-analyst-734401fd581f**
Introduction: Building Dashboards with Next.js + Vibe Coding	**https://www.squadbase.dev/en/ebooks/nextjs-bi-claude-code**
Build dashboards & visualize data with AI	**https://replit.com/usecases/dashboards-data-visualization**
Vibe Automation: The Next Evolution of AI-Native Automation	**https://beam.ai/agentic-insights/vibe-automating-the-next-evolution-of-ai-driven-automation**
Automation Tools for Vibe Coding	**https://vibecoder.me/categories/automation**
From Vibe Coding Platforms to Vibe Ops: Reshaping Software Development	**https://www.hsc.com/resources/blog/vibe-coding-platforms/**
Vibe Automation: The Future of Business Processes with AI Agents	**https://beam.ai/lp/vibe-automation**
The Great Vibe Coding Experiment - How I Built 15 Projects with AI in My Spare Time	**https://www.stephanmiller.com/the-great-vibe-coding-experiment/**
Vibe Automation: making business processes conversational	**https://maisa.ai/agentic-insights/vibe-automation/**
How Vibe Coding Simplifies Data Preprocessing	**https://www.newline.co/@zaoyang/how-vibe-coding-simplifies-data-preprocessing--f711ad85**
Engineering Productivity with Vibe Coding: Reimagining the Software Delivery Playbook	**https://www.relanto.ai/resources/blog/engineering-productivity-with-vibe-coding-reimagining-the-software-delivery-playbook**
Vibe Coding: Software Development and Test Automation with LLMs and AI	**https://naveenautomationlabs.medium.com/vibe-coding-software-development-and-test-automation-with-llms-and-ai-2416db06d131**
A Practical Guide to Getting Stuff Done with Vibe Coding	**https://www.observeinc.com/blog/practical-guide-getting-stuff-done-with-vibe-coding**
Vibe coding with a database in the sandbox	**https://electric-sql.com/blog/2025/06/05/database-in-the-sandbox**

Resource name	Link
This is how I'm going to Vibe Code from now on - Schema-First.	**https://dev.to/deanius/this-is-how-im-going-to-vibe-code-from-now-on-schema-first-p5g**
The Future of Blockchain Building: Vibe Coding and the Rise of AI-Generated Code	**https://medium.com/@cryptorescuesquad/the-future-of-blockchain-building-vibe-coding-and-the-rise-of-ai-generated-code-204f23cd6b3d**
Vibe Coding: Revolutionizing Software Development with AI Agents	**https://www.blockchainappfactory.com/blog/vibe-coding-with-ai-agents/**
Vibe Coding: Infusing Creativity and Intuition into Smart Contract Development	**https://blog.blockmagnates.com/vibe-coding-infusing-creativity-and-intuition-into-smart-contract-development-cd627a802c92**
Blockchain App Builder	**https://replit.com/build/blockchain-app-builder**
Building a working Game in an hour: My Experience with Vibe Coding	**https://medium.com/agileinsider/building-a-working-game-in-a-single-afternoon-my-experience-with-vibe-coding-8a5a02ddcabd**
VibeGame: Exploring Vibe Coding Games	**https://huggingface.co/blog/vibegame**
I Vibe Coded a Game That Attracted 10k+ Players In a Single Weekend	**https://generativeai.pub/i-vibe-coded-a-game-that-attracted-10k-players-in-a-single-weekend-6cff508bad58**

Table 3.1: *Online resources on types of software suitable for vibe coding*

Questions

- How can you build web applications using vibe coding?
- What are the main advantages of developing web applications using vibe coding?
- How do vibe coding tools help with rapid prototyping?
- Why is vibe coding particularly suitable for developing web interfaces?
- How can vibe coding create responsive interfaces?
- What are the advantages of using vibe coding for mobile application development?
- How does vibe coding create cross-platform applications?
- What are the different types of mobile applications supported with vibe coding?

- How can a data analytics dashboard be built with vibe coding?
- What are the advantages of using vibe coding for analytics dashboards?
- What makes vibe coding particularly suitable for data analytics?
- How can workflow automations be built with vibe coding?
- What are the advantages of vibe coding tools for building automation tools?
- Why is vibe coding well placed to build integration with third-party services?
- How can you build workflow automation for the payroll process?
- What are the prompts required to build an SQL to MongoDB migration tool?
- What are the different security implementations supported by vibe coding tools?
- How can vibe coding tools help with decentralized application development?
- What are the advantages of using vibe coding tools for Web3 development?
- Why does vibe coding revolutionize game development?
- What are the limitations of vibe coding tools for game development?

Join our Discord space

Join our Discord workspace for latest updates, offers, tech happenings around the world, new releases, and sessions with the authors:

https://discord.bpbonline.com

CHAPTER 4

AI Models, Tools and Practices for Vibe Coding

Introduction

The transformative power of vibe coding emerges through sophisticated AI models, specialized platforms and refined practices that translate creative intent into functional reality. Leading vibe coding platforms have evolved into comprehensive ecosystems where natural language interfaces, multimodal understanding and iterative generation capabilities converge to enable seamless development workflows using latest language models trained on vast repositories of code, documentation and design patterns. These platforms represent a fundamental shift in software creation moving beyond traditional syntax driven programming toward collaborative human AI partnerships where developers articulate intentions while AI systems handle implementation intricacies. Understanding the capabilities, limitations and optimal usage patterns of these tools becomes essential for maximizing productivity while maintaining code quality and system reliability across diverse application domains. This chapter explores the landscape of vibe coding tools through detailed examination of platform architectures, underlying AI models and practical implementation strategies that drive effective development outcomes.

Structure

In this chapter, we will cover the following topics:

- Overview of leading vibe coding platforms
- Analysis of different vibe coding systems
- AI models used in vibe coding tools
- Internal workings of vibe coding tools
- Best practices for using vibe coding tools
- Model context protocol connectors with vibe coding

Objectives

This chapter will provide a comprehensive overview of vibe coding tools, platforms, and underlying AI technologies that enable AI-driven software development across diverse application scenarios. It will equip you with the essential knowledge and technical insights needed to understand how different vibe coding systems use advanced language models, implement sophisticated code generation mechanisms, and integrate with development workflows through standardized protocols. By the end of this chapter, you will understand the architectural foundations of leading vibe coding platforms, the comparative strengths of various AI models powering these tools, and the best practices that maximize development efficiency while ensuring code quality and maintainability in production environments.

Overview of leading vibe coding platforms

Vibe coding has created an entire ecosystem of sophisticated platforms that democratize software creation while maintaining the power and flexibility needed for complex development tasks. The leading vibe coding platforms today combine advanced AI models trained on billions of lines of code with intuitive interfaces that allow both technical and non-technical users to materialize their vision through conversation rather than syntax. The vibe coding ecosystem has evolved into several distinct tiers, each serving different use cases and skill levels.

At the forefront are conversational AI platforms like *Claude, ChatGPT, Gemini,* and *Grok,* which enable real-time code generation through natural language dialogue. These platforms understand context, maintain conversation history, and can iterate on solutions based on user feedback, which makes them ideal for both rapid prototyping and production development. Beyond conversational AI platforms, specialized development environments have emerged that integrate AI assistance directly into the coding workflow or generate working applications through prompts.

GenMB (https://genmb.com/) is a powerful vibe coding platform built to generate complete production-ready full-stack applications from a single natural language prompt. The platform automatically provisions databases, choosing between Firestore (NoSQL) or PostgreSQL (relational) based on the application's needs, and includes built-in authentication, database operations, API generation, and real-time listeners. GenMB integrates seamlessly with over 45 plugins, including Stripe for payments, Supabase for database management, and Clerk for authentication, and supports multiple front-end frameworks, including Vanilla JS, React, React with TypeScript, and Vue. Users interact with GenMB through a prompt-driven interface, refining their application iteratively with the help of an AI Code Healer that automatically detects and fixes errors such as missing imports, syntax issues, type mismatches, and API integration problems. Unlike many tools that lock users into proprietary ecosystems, GenMB provides full source code access with zero lock-in, meaning users own their code and can export it anywhere, making it equally appealing to non-technical founders and experienced developers who want to take the code further.

Several robust applications have been built using GenMB, showcasing its capabilities across diverse and demanding use cases. A multi-user project management tool was developed featuring real-time task synchronization, role-based access control, file upload management, and push notifications, which are all built with GenMB capabilities. An e-commerce store, complete with a product catalog, shopping cart, Stripe checkout integration, and an order management dashboard, was assembled as a Vue-powered installable mobile web application. GenMB has also enabled the creation of a customer support portal with live chat, ticket prioritization, file attachments, team collaboration tools, and an analytics dashboard demonstrating the platform's ability to handle enterprise-grade requirements without any manual backend setup or DevOps configuration.

Figure 4.1 shows the GenMB (**https://genmb.com/**) interface, where you can specify your requirements to build applications and websites:

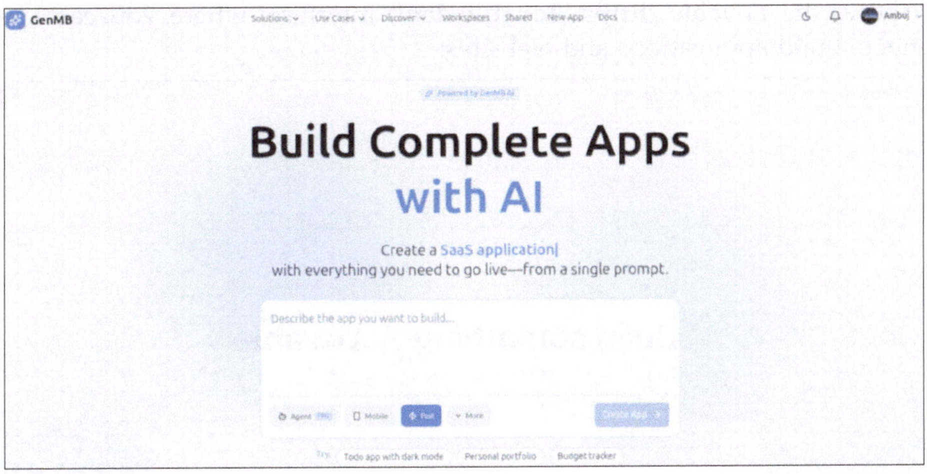

***Figure 4.1**: GenMB interface, where you can specify your ideas to build complete applications*

Lovable (**https://lovable.dev/**) is one of the most popular vibe coding platforms, distinguished by its ability to build full-stack web applications from natural language prompts. The platform interprets user descriptions and automatically generates the necessary frontend code, backend logic, and database setup, and integrates seamlessly with essential services like Supabase for database management, Stripe for payments, and GitHub for version control. Users interact with Lovable through an intuitive chat interface, describing features and making refinements in an iterative cycle until their application is ready for one-click deployment. This dramatically accelerates development timelines and makes app creation accessible to non-coders, founders, and designers. Unlike many no-code tools that lock users into proprietary systems, Lovable generates editable code that users own and can export to GitHub, offering both simplicity for beginners and control for experienced developers who want to extend their applications. This unique combination of speed, accessibility, and code ownership has made Lovable popular among startups and entrepreneurs looking to quickly validate their ideas and build functional MVPs without extensive technical knowledge or development teams.

Several popular applications have been developed using the Lovable vibe coding tool, which demonstrates its capabilities across diverse use cases. Lovable has many users who are leveraging its AI-driven tools to create professional-grade applications significantly faster than traditional development methods. Some of the popular applications that are built using Lovable include a healthcare solution that utilizes artificial intelligence for skin analysis and detection, an AI storyteller that creates personalized coloring books for children, and a tool that offers users the ability to upload WhatsApp chat exports and receive beautiful insights about their conversations, including emoji usage patterns and chat statistics. Lovable has also enabled the development of productivity tools that can allow users to store and track all their warranties in one centralized location, a tool that provides instant conversion of invoice PDFs into Excel spreadsheets, and an AI-powered stock discovery tool that makes investment research more accessible to everyday traders.

Figure 4.2 shows the Lovable (**https://lovable.dev/**) interface, where you can specify your requirements to build applications and websites:

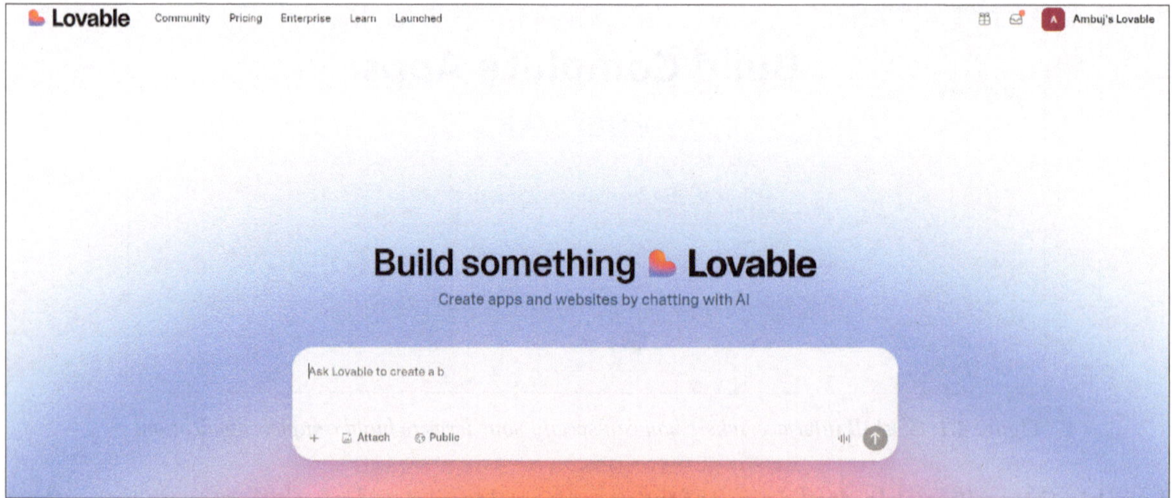

***Figure 4.2**: Lovable interface where you can specify your requirements to build applications*

Bolt (**https://bolt.new/**) revolutionizes application development by operating entirely within the browser, eliminating the friction of local environment setup that traditionally slows down development workflows. Built on powerful LLM models such as Anthropic's Claude, Bolt provides users with a chat-based interface where they can build full-stack applications by simply describing what they want. The AI generates code, creates file structures, and installs dependencies in real-time. The platform's significant advantage lies in its AI's comprehensive control over the entire development stack, from installing packages to running servers, which streamlines the development process and reduces the complexity traditionally associated with application development. Bolt also features AI-powered debugging capabilities that can automatically identify errors and suggest or apply fixes, accelerating the entire build-to-deploy process and allowing users to maintain focus on creative problem-solving rather than technical troubleshooting. The platform has become particularly valuable for users who need to quickly prototype ideas, experiment with new technologies, or collaborate with team members without the overhead of environment configuration and dependency management.

Figure 4.3 shows the Bolt (**https://bolt.new/**) interface, where you can specify your project requirements and get applications and websites developed with AI:

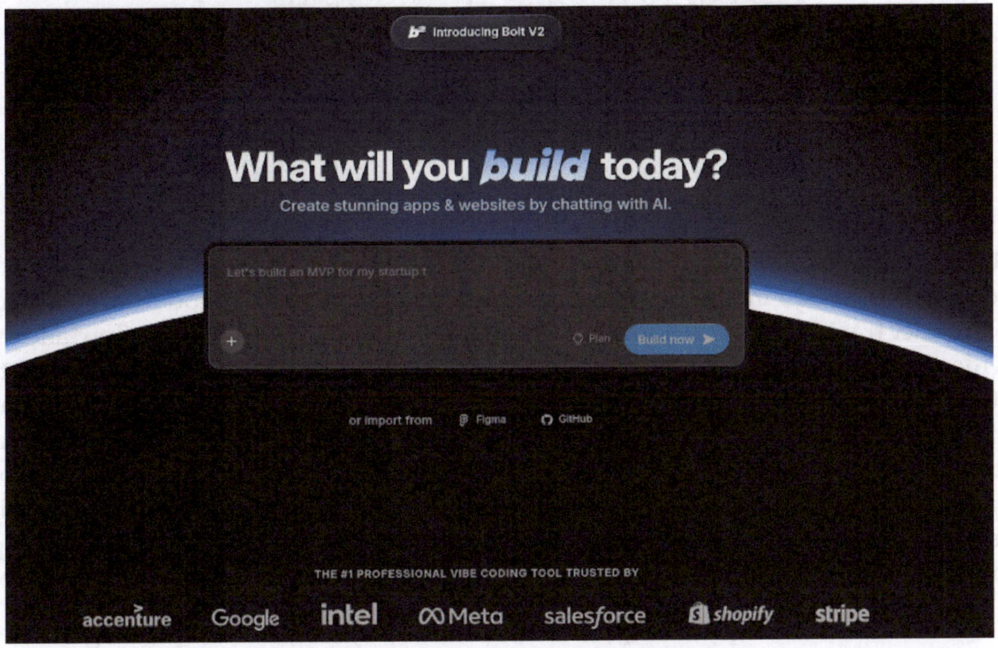

Figure 4.3: *Bolt interface to build applications*

The **Replit** (**https://replit.com/**) platform has established itself as a cloud-based **integrated development environment** (**IDE**) that incorporates sophisticated AI agents with unique planning capabilities that set it apart from other vibe coding platforms. Replit's AI assistant engages in a comprehensive planning phase where it asks clarifying questions to better understand user requirements before generating code, leading to more accurate implementations and reducing the iterations needed to achieve desired functionality. The platform supports an extensive range of technology stacks and provides a complete environment for building, testing, and deploying applications, including advanced features like database controls and user authentication systems. Replit's real-time collaboration features make it particularly suitable for development teams, while its built-in security scanner helps ensure code quality and security compliance. The platform's end-to-end cloud-based approach eliminates the complexity of local development environment setup and maintenance, making it an ideal choice for developers who want to focus on building applications rather than managing infrastructure and development tools.

Figure 4.4 shows the Replit (**https://replit.com/**) interface, where you get suggestions or write a prompt to build applications based on your requirements:

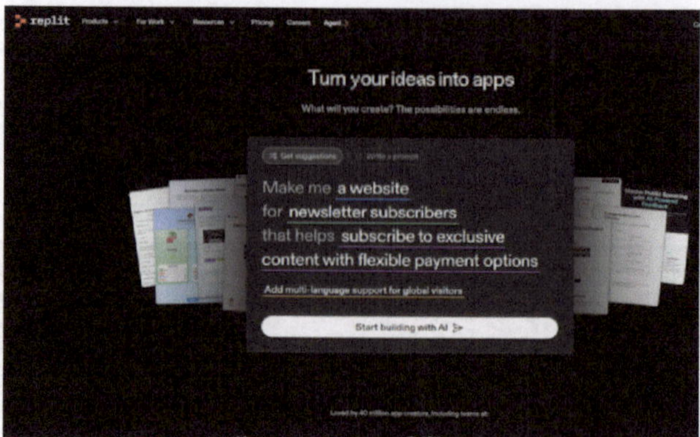

Figure 4.4: Replit interface to build applications

V0 (**https://v0.app/**) by Vercel focuses on generative AI for user interface creation, transforming text prompts and design mockups into production-ready code using modern frameworks like NextJS (a React framework) and Tailwind CSS. The platform's iterative workflow allows users to provide prompts and receive multiple UI variations, which they can then select, customize, and refine through continued conversation. The v0's core strength lies in its ability to rapidly generate production-ready UI code that follows industry best practices, making it an invaluable tool for designers and product managers who need to turn mockups into functional components without deep coding knowledge. The generated code maintains high standards of modularity and cleanliness based on established best practices, which makes it easy for developers to integrate v0's outputs into larger projects and maintain code quality standards.

Figure 4.5 shows the V0 (**https://v0.app/**) interface, where you can start building with a single prompt and no coding is required:

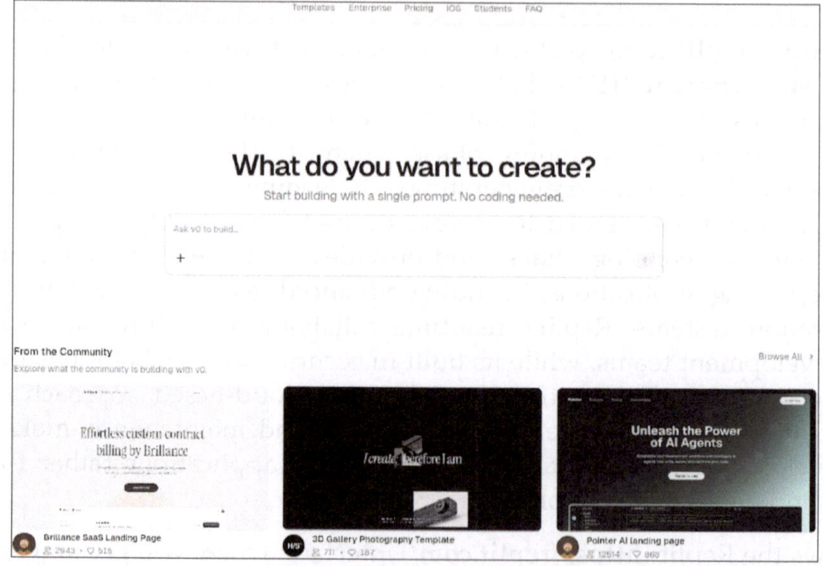

Figure 4.5: V0 interface to build applications

Autonomous AI software engineers represent a paradigm shift in how software is conceptualized, designed, and implemented. Platforms like **Claude Code** show this evolution by demonstrating the ability to understand high-level project goals, architect appropriate solutions, write comprehensive codebases, and iterate on implementations with minimal human intervention. This autonomy extends beyond simple code generation to encompass decision-making about technology stacks, design patterns, and architectural approaches that traditionally required experienced developers. The integration of autonomous AI engineers into vibe coding workflows creates a synergistic relationship where human creativity and machine execution complement each other seamlessly. Developers can focus on articulating their vision, defining user experiences, and making strategic product decisions while the AI handles the intricate technical implementation details.

Claude Code (**https://www.claude.com/product/claude-code**) can handle entire projects end-to-end, managing multiple files simultaneously, understanding complex dependencies, and maintaining coherent architecture across diverse components. The platform can refactor legacy code, optimize performance bottlenecks, implement security best practices, and even write comprehensive documentation and tests without explicit instructions for each task. This holistic approach transforms development from a series of discrete coding tasks into a collaborative dialogue where developers express what they want to achieve and the AI determines the optimal path to implementation. The system learns from each interaction and builds up contextual understanding that enables increasingly sophisticated solutions.

Figure 4.6 shows Claude Code that allows you to run multiple coding tasks in the cloud seamlessly between browser, terminal, or mobile:

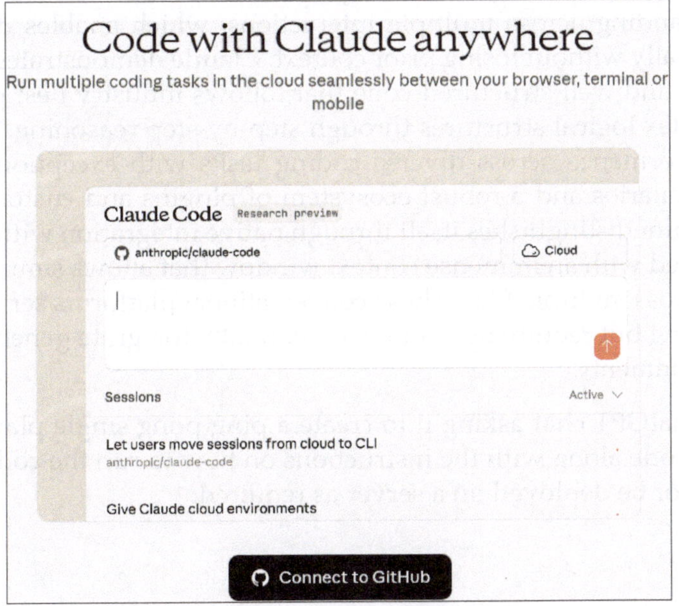

Figure 4.6*: Claude Code platform*

The implications for development productivity and accessibility are profound. Autonomous AI engineers democratize software creation by lowering the technical barriers to entry, enabling domain experts without extensive programming backgrounds to bring their ideas to life. Simultaneously, they amplify the capabilities of experienced developers by handling routine implementation work, allowing them to tackle more complex problems and explore innovative solutions. Looking forward, autonomous AI software engineers will likely evolve toward even greater independence, handling not just implementation but also requirements analysis, user research, and strategic technical planning. This evolution positions vibe coding as the dominant development paradigm for the next generation of software creation, where the speed of thought becomes the primary constraint on innovation rather than technical implementation complexity.

Analysis of different vibe coding systems

The vibe coding ecosystem encompasses diverse platforms that vary significantly in their architecture, target users, and implementation approaches. Understanding these differences enables developers to select appropriate tools for specific use cases and project requirements. The primary differentiation factors include the underlying AI models employed, the degree of automation versus human control, the scope of development supported, and the execution environment architecture.

Conversational AI platforms like Claude, ChatGPT, Gemini, and Grok operate as general-purpose code generation assistants that excel at rapid prototyping and iterative development through natural language dialogue. These platforms maintain conversation history and contextual understanding across multiple interactions, which enables developers to refine solutions incrementally without losing prior context. Claude demonstrates particular strength in generating clean and well-structured code that follows industry best practices and excels at explaining complex logical structures through step-by-step reasoning. ChatGPT offers the most balanced performance across diverse coding tasks with exceptional speed in simple problem-solving scenarios and a robust ecosystem of plugins and custom GPTs that extend its capabilities. Gemini distinguishes itself through native integration with Google Search and Workspace, combined with an immense context window that allows simultaneous analysis of entire codebases across multiple files. These conversational platforms serve as excellent entry points for vibe coding but require developers to manually integrate generated code into their development environments.

Figure 4.7 shows ChatGPT chat asking it to create a ping pong single player game. ChatGPT then generates the code along with the instructions on how to run the code, and the code can be executed locally or be deployed on a server as required:

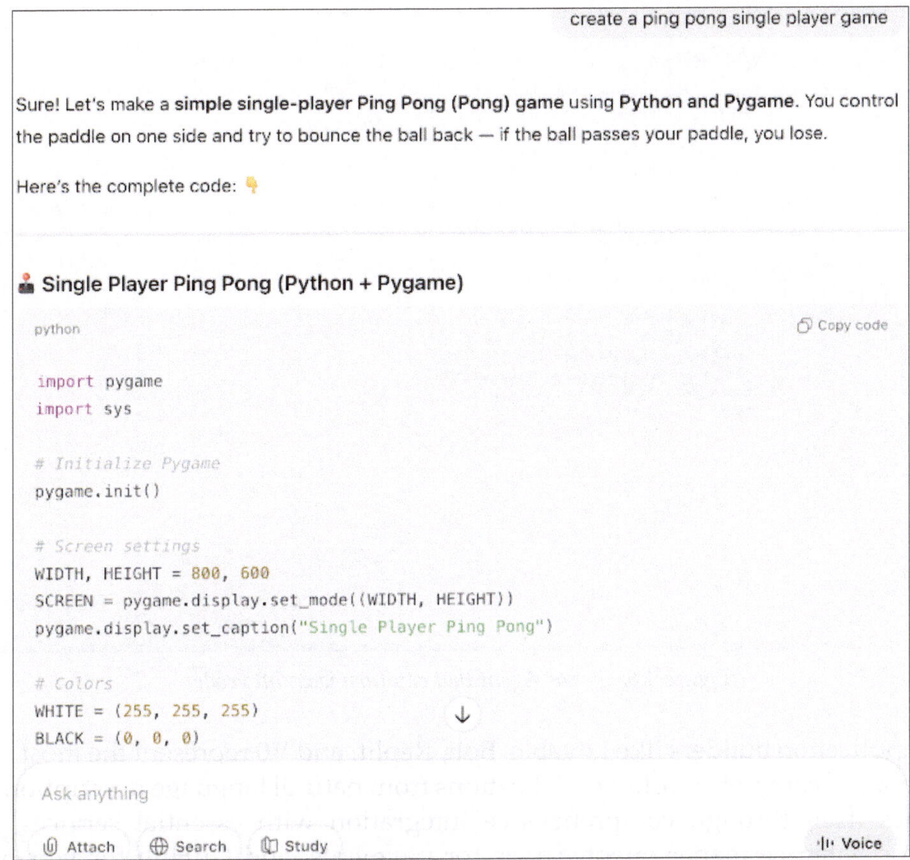

Figure 4.7: ChatGPT chat to create a ping pong single player game

Integrated development environments with AI assistance represent a more sophisticated tier that embeds intelligent code generation directly into traditional development workflows. GitHub Copilot pioneered this category by providing context-aware autocomplete-style suggestions that range from single lines to entire functions within IDEs like *VS Code*. Cursor advances this paradigm by combining IDE functionality with conversational AI and sophisticated context management through customizable rules files that shape how the AI assistant responds to developer needs. These platforms maintain awareness of the entire project structure, including dependencies, file relationships, and coding patterns, which enables more coherent suggestions that integrate seamlessly with existing code. The primary advantage of IDE-integrated tools lies in their ability to understand project-specific context and conventions while maintaining developer control over the final implementation.

Figure 4.8 shows the Cursor Agent that can turn ideas into code and offers human-AI collaboration that are orders of magnitude more effective than any developer alone:

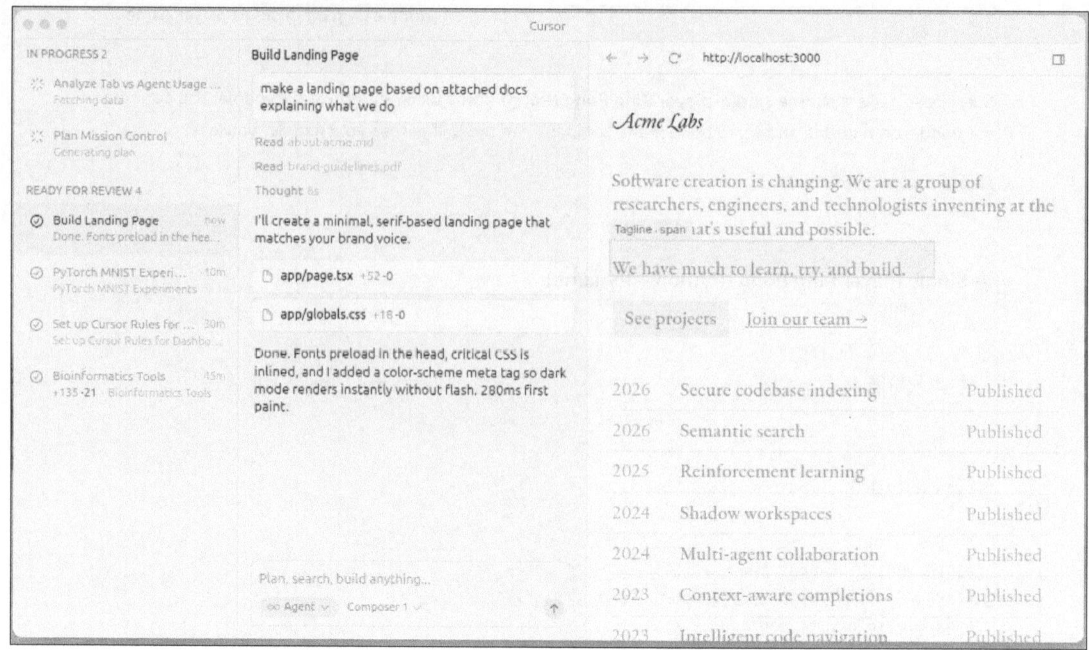

Figure 4.8: *Cursor Agent that can turn ideas into code*

Full-stack application builders like Lovable, Bolt, Replit, and V0 represent the most automated tier by generating complete working applications from natural language descriptions. Lovable distinguishes itself through comprehensive integration with essential services, including Supabase for database management, Stripe for payments, and GitHub for version control, which dramatically accelerates the path from concept to deployed application. Bolt operates entirely within the browser and eliminates local environment setup friction while providing AI-powered debugging capabilities that automatically identify errors and suggest fixes. Replit incorporates sophisticated AI agents with planning capabilities that ask clarifying questions before generating code, which leads to more accurate implementations and fewer iteration cycles. V0 specializes in user interface creation and transforms text prompts and design mockups into production-ready React and Next.js components with Tailwind CSS styling. These platforms democratize software creation by enabling non-technical users to build functional applications, but may sacrifice fine-grained control compared to IDE-integrated tools.

Figure 4.9 illustrates the vibe coding ecosystem that progresses from manual control on the left to full automation on the right and represents the varying degrees of human oversight versus AI autonomy across different platform categories. The first tier represents conversational AI platforms that serve as the entry point into vibe coding by offering rapid prototyping capabilities through natural language dialogue, but require users to manually integrate generated code into their projects. The second tier shows IDE integration tools like *GitHub Copilot* and *Cursor,* which embed AI assistance directly into development environments. The third tier shows full-stack builders such as Lovable, Bolt, Replit, and V0, which generate complete working applications from natural language descriptions with minimal setup required. These platforms democratize software creation for non-technical users. The fourth tier represents autonomous AI engineers such as Claude Code that handle end-to-end project management, including architecture decisions, comprehensive code generation, and iterative refinement with minimal human intervention.

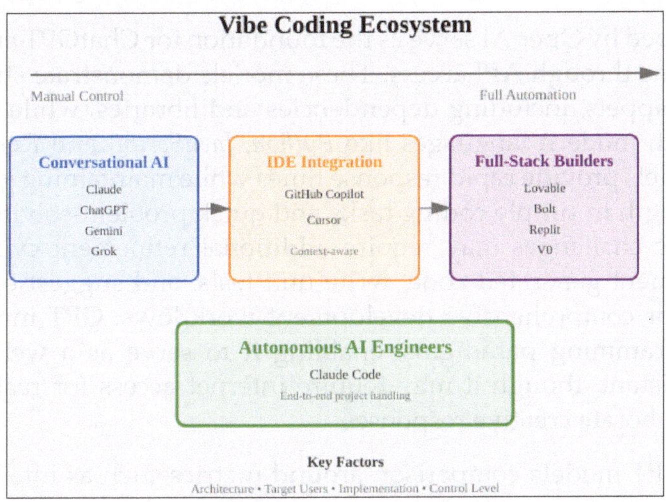

***Figure 4.9**: Vibe coding ecosystem*

The evolution toward autonomous AI software engineers represents the frontier of vibe coding, where systems can understand high-level project goals, architect solutions, write comprehensive codebases, and iterate on implementations with minimal human intervention. These systems extend beyond simple code generation to encompass decision-making about technology stacks, design patterns, and architectural approaches that traditionally required experienced developers. Claude Code exemplifies this category by handling entire projects end-to-end with the ability to manage multiple files simultaneously, understand complex dependencies, refactor legacy code, optimize performance bottlenecks, and write comprehensive documentation and tests without explicit instructions for each task. The integration of autonomous AI engineers creates a synergistic relationship where human creativity and machine execution complement each other, with developers focusing on articulating vision and making strategic product decisions while the AI handles intricate technical implementation details.

AI models used in vibe coding tools

The foundation of vibe coding platforms rests on advanced large language models trained on billions of lines of code across diverse programming languages and frameworks. These models employ transformer architectures that process entire sequences of text simultaneously, rather than word by word, allowing the model to grasp how any word or token relates to every other word in context. Think of it like reading a whole sentence at once instead of one letter at a time, and the model can instantly connect a variable defined at the top of a file to how it is used fifty lines later. This enables transformers to understand both natural human language and formal programming languages through sophisticated pattern recognition and contextual understanding developed during extensive training phases. The choice of underlying AI model significantly impacts code generation quality, reasoning capabilities, debugging effectiveness, and the types of tasks where a vibe coding tool excels.

GPT models developed by OpenAI serve as the foundation for ChatGPT and power numerous vibe coding platforms through API access. These models demonstrate strong capabilities for interpreting code snippets, including dependencies and libraries, while generating reusable functions across both modern languages like *Python, JavaScript,* and *Rust,* as well as legacy languages. GPT models provide rapid response times while maintaining good accuracy levels, with particular strength in simple coding tasks and quick problem-solving scenarios, though complex algorithmic challenges may require additional refinement cycles. The model can automatically document generated code, write unit tests, and suggest optimizations, which makes it valuable for comprehensive development workflows. GPT models broad training across diverse programming paradigms, enabling it to serve as a well-balanced, general-purpose coding assistant, though it may require internet access for real-time data and can occasionally over-elaborate creative responses.

Figure 4.10 shows GPT models comparison around metrics such as intelligence, speed, cost, context size, and supported input/output types:

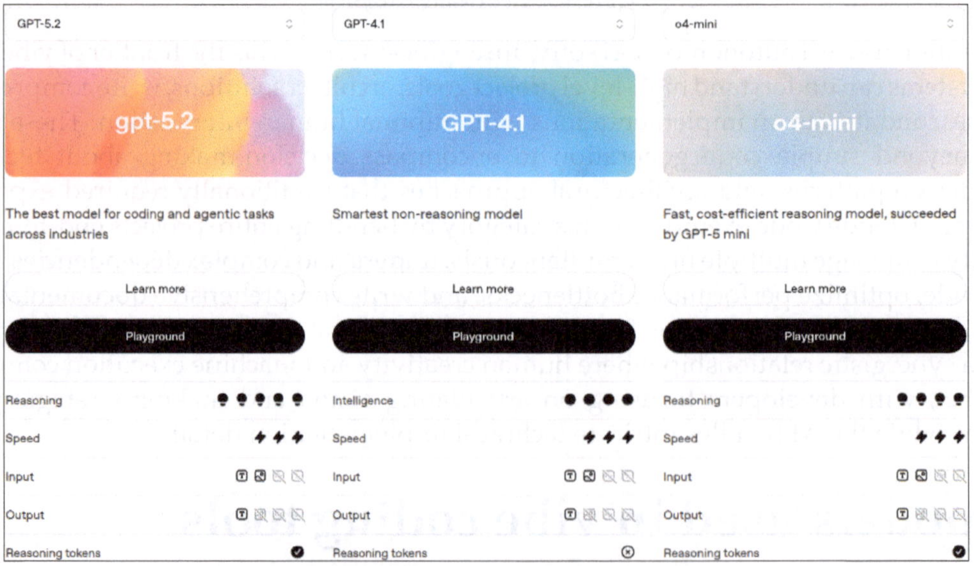

Figure 4.10: GPT models comparison

Claude models developed by Anthropic have emerged as particularly effective models for vibe coding applications, with many practitioners considering Claude as the optimal choice for most coding use cases. Claude excels at providing clear and detailed explanations with an exceptional understanding of complex structures such as recursive algorithms or distributed systems, which makes it excellent for deep debugging and code analysis. The model's step-by-step reasoning capabilities improve understanding of complex logical structures and lead to more accurate implementations with fewer iterations required to achieve working solutions. Claude demonstrates particular strength in generating well-structured code that follows industry best practices and captures writing style more effectively than competing models when provided with examples. The deliberate approach to code generation results in higher initial accuracy, though response times may be slower than other models for simple tasks. Claude's core strength lies in refactoring and debugging tasks where clarity and correctness are paramount.

Figure 4.11 shows different Claude models compared with their capabilities and cost structure:

Latest models comparison

Feature	Claude Opus 4.6	Claude Sonnet 4.6	Claude Haiku 4.5
Description	The most intelligent model for building agents and coding	The best combination of speed and intelligence	The fastest model with near-frontier intelligence
Claude API ID	`claude-opus-4-6`	`claude-sonnet-4-6`	`claude-haiku-4-5-20251001`
Claude API alias	`claude-opus-4-6`	`claude-sonnet-4-6`	`claude-haiku-4-5`
AWS Bedrock ID	`anthropic.claude-opus-4-6-v1`	`anthropic.claude-sonnet-4-6`	`anthropic.claude-haiku-4-5-20251001-v1:0`
GCP Vertex AI ID	`claude-opus-4-6`	`claude-sonnet-4-6`	`claude-haiku-4-5@20251001`
Pricing[1]	$5 / input MTok $25 / output MTok	$3 / input MTok $15 / output MTok	$1 / input MTok $5 / output MTok
Extended thinking	Yes	Yes	Yes
Adaptive thinking	Yes	Yes	No

***Figure 4.11**: Claude models comparisons*

Gemini models developed by Google bring unique capabilities through their immense context window that allows analysis of entire codebases and identification of broader architectural issues while maintaining consistency across multiple files. This massive context capacity enables the model to handle large-scale projects more effectively than competitors by understanding relationships and dependencies across thousands of lines of code simultaneously. Gemini benefits from direct integration with *Google Search* and *Workspace,* which enables access to real-time information and native multimodal capabilities that process text, images, video, and audio. The model excels in factual accuracy and proves particularly valuable for projects within the Google ecosystem, including Android development, Firebase integration, and App Engine deployment. However, Gemini can demonstrate lower accuracy with less common programming languages like Ruby or Perl and with niche frameworks compared to more widely used technologies.

Figure 4.12 shows different Gemini models compared with their capabilities and advantages:

Featured Gemini models

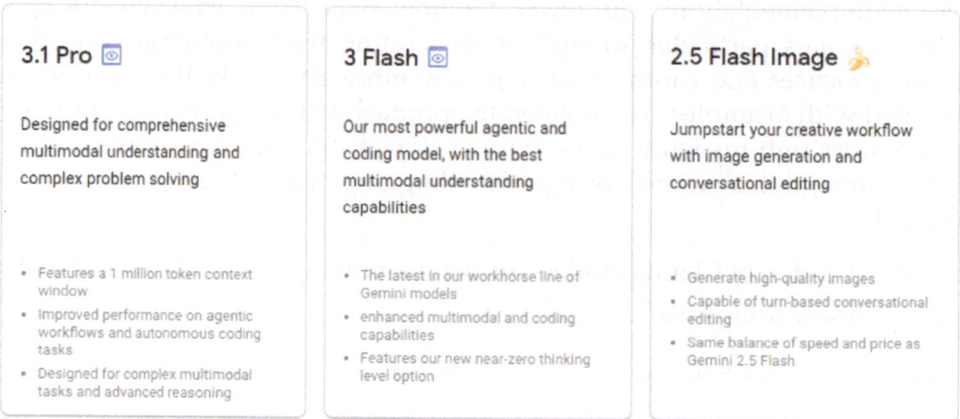

***Figure 4.12**: Gemini models comparisons*

Grok models developed by xAI have evolved into some of the most advanced **large language models** (**LLMs**) and are particularly effective for reasoning, coding, and real-time data integration. Their design philosophy balances large computational scale with grounded reasoning and multimodal understanding, which makes Grok a highly adaptive model for vibe coding applications. Grok models are proficient across *TypeScript, Python, Java, Rust, C++,* and *Go* with native Python execution capabilities that enable real-time simulation and verification of outputs. Grok stands out for its real-time internet awareness, explainable reasoning modes, and large context processing. Unlike the spontaneous creativity of GPT or the deliberate precision of Claude, Grok embodies an adaptive, reasoning-centric approach that balances freeform exploration with computational structure, making it highly suitable for both code understanding and live system orchestration in complex environments.

Figure 4.13 shows the capabilities of Grok models, and these models can create rich documents, write code, and have the most real-time search capabilities of any AI model:

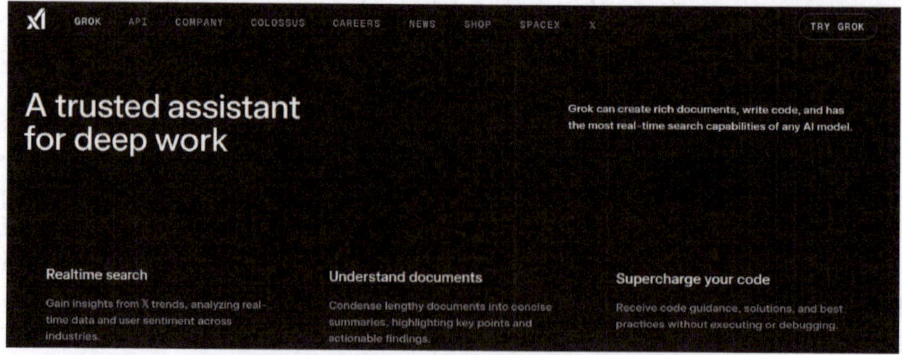

***Figure 4.13**: Capabilities of Grok models*

Specialized coding models have emerged that focus exclusively on code generation and understanding rather than general-purpose language tasks. For example, Replit's Agent models demonstrate exceptional abilities by thinking deeply through every layer of prompts, which can make it feel slower but often results in cleaner and more structured implementations. These specialized models sometimes outperform general-purpose LLMs on code-specific benchmarks and tasks by dedicating their entire training capacity to understanding programming languages, software architecture patterns, and development best practices. The evolution of code-specific models represents a maturation of the field where purpose-built architectures optimized for software development tasks can achieve superior performance compared to adapted general-purpose language models.

The architectural foundation of these models relies on transformer neural networks that employ self-attention mechanisms, which is a process where the model scores how strongly each word or token should *pay attention* to every other token in the sequence, letting it capture long-range dependencies like matching an opening function call to its closing logic hundreds of lines later. Pre-training occurs on massive datasets including open-source code repositories, technical documentation, Stack Overflow discussions, and programming tutorials, which enables models to learn syntax, semantics, common patterns, and best practices across programming languages. Post-training techniques, including instruction tuning, reinforcement learning from human feedback, and supervised fine-tuning, further align model outputs with developer expectations and preferences, which involves teaching the model not just to predict code but to produce code a human would actually want.

Some implementations incorporate **retrieval augmented generation** (**RAG**) architectures that combine the parametric memory of pretrained language models, such as knowledge baked in during training, with access to live external knowledge sources through neural retrievers. Think of it as the difference between a developer working purely from memory versus one who can instantly look up the latest documents mid-conversation. RAG systems fetch relevant code examples, documentation, and API specifications during generation, which grounds model outputs in factual information and enables updating knowledge without retraining the entire model. This hybrid approach proves particularly valuable for code generation, where accuracy and adherence to current API specifications are critical.

Internal workings of vibe coding tools

Vibe coding platforms operate through sophisticated multi-stage pipelines that transform natural language intent into executable code while maintaining contextual awareness across development sessions. Understanding the internal mechanisms that enable these systems reveals both their capabilities and limitations, which inform effective usage strategies and help developers optimize their workflows. The core architecture encompasses prompt processing, context engineering, code generation, execution feedback loops, iterative refinement mechanisms, and memory management.

The **prompt processing** stage begins when users articulate requirements in natural language, which the system must interpret to extract actionable intent. Advanced platforms employ hybrid matching strategies that combine keyword matching, pattern recognition, semantic understanding through embeddings, and LLM-based inference to map user intent to specific development actions. Sophisticated systems implement multi-strategy approaches that allocate confidence weights across different matching techniques, including keyword matching for direct command recognition, pattern matching for common phrase structures, semantic matching to understand meaning beyond literal words, and LLM-based matching for ambiguous requests. When confidence falls below thresholds, systems automatically ask for user confirmation to prevent executing incorrect commands, which serves as a critical safeguard against misinterpretation. The prompt processing phase translates informal user intent into structured instructions that guide subsequent generation stages with context, constraints, and examples that shape model outputs.

Context engineering represents the most critical component determining vibe coding effectiveness, as models must assemble relevant information from exponentially large candidate sets within limited context windows. The vibe coding system orchestrates multiple information sources, including system instructions defining the task, codebase contents with source code and API interfaces, database schemas and persistent data, domain knowledge encompassing documentation and best practices, tool definitions for compilers and testing frameworks, historical interaction memory from multi turn dialogues and current task queues with execution status. The optimization challenge involves identifying context orchestration strategies that maximize generation quality subject to context length constraints, which platforms address through sophisticated retrieval, filtering, and ranking algorithms. For example, Cursor implements this through customizable rules files that establish global preferences and persona patterns, which narrow the scope of AI responses to align with project conventions and developer preferences. Replit's planning capable AI agents engage in clarifying questions before code generation to better understand requirements and retrieve relevant context, which leads to more accurate initial implementations.

The **code generation** process follows an autoregressive architecture where models produce code token by token with each generation step conditioned on previously generated tokens and dynamically assembled context. The conditional generation probability at each step incorporates the current instruction, retrieved project context, execution environment state, and partial code generated thus far. Some systems employ RAG architectures that combine knowledge from pre-training with access to external datastores. During generation, the retriever component fetches relevant code snippets, documentation, and examples based on semantic similarity to the current task, which grounds outputs in factual information and enables the system to reference up-to-date APIs and libraries. The generator component then conditions its output on both the retrieved context and the base language model's knowledge to produce code that adheres to project conventions and leverages appropriate libraries. This hybrid approach can improve factual accuracy and reduce hallucinations compared to pure parametric generation.

Execution feedback systems create closed-loop systems where generated code runs in isolated environments and produces signals that inform subsequent iterations. Compiler feedback provides immediate syntax and type error detection, along with static analysis warnings that identify potential issues before runtime. Execution feedback includes unit test results, integration test outcomes, runtime errors, and exception traces that reveal functional correctness issues. Browser-based platforms like Bolt execute code entirely within sandboxed environments, which eliminates local setup requirements while enabling real-time preview of application behavior. Container technologies and cloud-based execution platforms provide security isolation that prevents generated code from affecting development machines while supporting reproducible execution across different environments. Some platforms incorporate AI-powered debugging where the same language model analyzes error messages and execution traces to propose fixes automatically. This automated debugging capability accelerates iteration cycles by identifying root causes and generating corrective code without requiring developers to manually diagnose issues.

The **iterative refinement** loop embodies the core philosophy of vibe coding, where human developers guide systems toward project objectives through continuous feedback rather than comprehensive upfront specification. The process follows a decision process where human evaluation provides rewards, project constraints define transitions, and the AI agent executes requirements within these boundaries. Each iteration produces outputs that humans evaluate with acceptance decisions that determine whether code meets requirements and feedback signals that specify necessary corrections or new requirements. The system supports three modes of evolution, including full acceptance that terminates the iteration loop when code fully satisfies user requirements, local refinement, where the agent revises rejected portions based on specific feedback, and requirement expansion, where humans introduce new constraints or features that expand the task space. Iterative refinement captures vibe coding's dynamic nature, where the requirements do not need to be completely specified initially but are progressively defined through interactive exploration. This multi-stage optimization process enables subsequent task expansion where each development phase builds upon previous stages with increasing instruction sets that preserve earlier decisions while incorporating new requirements.

The **memory management** subsystem maintains conversation context across development sessions, enabling the AI to remember decisions, patterns, and preferences that inform future generations. Short-term memory preserves dialogue history within current sessions, allowing models to reference earlier exchanges and maintain logical consistency across related code modifications. Long-term memory architectures store design decisions, architectural patterns, and project conventions that persist across sessions, which enables the system to maintain consistent coding styles and respect established patterns even after conversation resets. Some platforms implement hierarchical memory systems that separate task-specific context from project-level knowledge and developer preferences, which optimizes context window usage by retrieving only relevant information for each generation step. For example, ChatGPT's memory feature shows this capability by automatically retaining user preferences and past interactions, which creates personalized experiences that anticipate developer needs.

Figure 4.14 illustrates the vibe coding architecture as a six-stage architecture that transforms natural language requirements into executable code through continuous feedback loops. The process begins when user input enters the Prompt Processing stage, where intent is extracted through multi-strategy matching techniques, then flows to Context Engineering, which assembles relevant information from multiple sources, including codebases, documentation, schemas, APIs, and interaction history. This assembled context feeds into the Code Generation stage, where models produce code token-by-token, potentially enhanced with RAG retrieval. The generated code then enters Execution Feedback, where it runs in isolated environments to produce compiler errors, test results, and runtime signals that inform quality assessment. These signals flow into Iterative Refinement, where human evaluation determines whether to accept the code, request local modifications, or expand requirements. Throughout this entire pipeline, Memory Management maintains both short-term dialogue context and long-term project conventions that persist across sessions, feeding learned preferences back into the context assembly process. This illustration emphasizes that vibe coding is fundamentally a closed-loop system where human guidance continuously steers AI execution through iterative cycles rather than comprehensive upfront specifications, with context sources serving as the knowledge foundation that grounds all generation attempts.

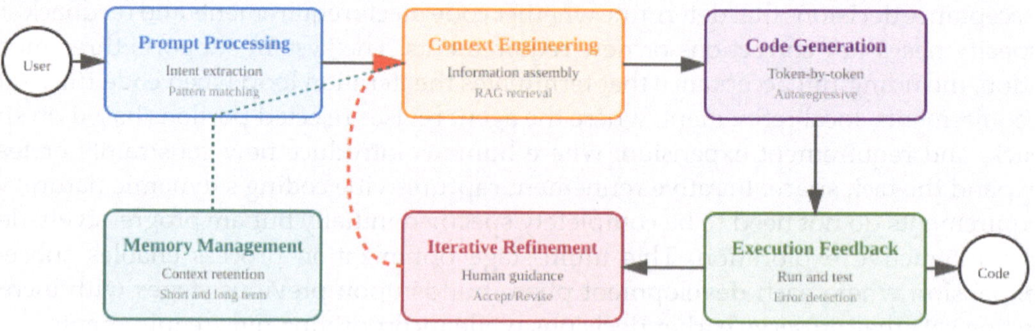

Figure 4.14: *Vibe coding architecture*

The multi-stage pipeline architecture underlying vibe coding platforms reveals a sophisticated orchestration of complementary technologies that work in concert to bridge the gap between human intent and machine execution. Each component from prompt processing and context engineering through code generation, execution feedback, iterative refinement, and memory management addresses specific challenges in translating natural language into functional software while maintaining coherence across development sessions. The effectiveness of vibe coding depends critically on the synergy between these stages. Understanding these internal mechanisms is essential to optimizing workflows by recognizing when to provide additional context, how to structure prompts for better intent extraction, and when iterative refinement offers advantages over comprehensive upfront specification.

Best practices for using vibe coding tools

Effective use of vibe coding tools requires systematic approaches that balance AI capabilities with human oversight to produce maintainable, secure, and functionally correct software. While vibe coding tools dramatically accelerate development timelines, their optimal usage demands structured workflows and disciplined practices rather than ad-hoc prompt engineering. The following best practices synthesize insights from experienced users and represent proven strategies for maximizing productivity while minimizing common pitfalls.

Pre-development planning establishes the foundation for successful vibe coding by providing clear specifications that guide AI code generation. Creating a comprehensive **Product Requirements Document** (**PRD**) before writing any code forces users to articulate what the application should do, who it serves, and how it functions, which reduces ambiguous instructions that lead to incorrect implementations. The PRD should define technologies underlying each function, along with their purpose, define user flows and edge cases, and establish project milestone stages that serve as a compass during the build phase. This upfront investment in planning dramatically improves the quality of generated code by providing precise requirements that reduce the iteration cycles needed to achieve working solutions.

Incremental development through focused prompts represents the most critical practice for successful vibe coding, as attempts to build entire applications in a single prompt can produce messy, incomplete, or fragile code. Users should decompose complex projects into logical slices such as user authentication, database schema, specific features, and integrations, then prompt for one slice at a time. Each focused prompt produces code that is easier to assess, test, and iterate while creating modular components that facilitate future evolution. Another important rule is to avoid multiple unrelated changes in a single prompt, as this can introduce more problems than it fixes. Users must resist the temptation to jump ahead to future features before completing current steps since installing dependencies or services prematurely can create reference errors. Experienced vibe coders emphasize that prompting for small features while keeping applications modular prevents the context issues that arise when files grow large and become difficult for AI models to manage effectively.

Prompt engineering with explicit context, constraints, and examples dramatically improves code quality by providing AI models with clear boundaries that shape their responses. Effective vibe coding prompts include three components, which are context describing the application domain and architecture, constraints specifying technology stack, coding style, performance requirements, and security limits, and examples demonstrating expected input output behavior or implementation patterns. A well-structured prompt might state, `I am building a REST API for a bookstore, use TypeScript with REST naming conventions, implement error handling and unit tests, for example GET /books?author= will filter books by author` which provides comprehensive guidance that reduces ambiguity. Some vibe coding practitioners add statements like, `You are free to add any functionality that you think will be necessary for this project`, at the end of prompts, which opens the model's creative freedom and often surfaces smart enhancements that developers might not have considered. Global rules configured at the project or account level establish overarching preferences, including naming conventions, linting standards, and comment formats that persist across all iterations, which ensures consistency without repeating instructions in every prompt.

Application review and testing remain essential despite AI generation, as models can produce code with subtle bugs, security vulnerabilities, or logic errors that only reveal themselves during execution. Users must understand generated code before accepting changes, looking for obvious red flags, checking that implementations match expectations, and verifying that new features do not break existing functionality. Running comprehensive tests after each code modification can help catch regressions early, before they cascade into larger problems. The review process should specifically examine error handling, input validation, authentication checks, SQL injection prevention, and other security-critical aspects since AI models may forget to implement these safeguards unless explicitly prompted. It is recommended to treat AI-generated code as pull requests requiring thorough review and approval before merging, rather than blindly accepting outputs, which maintains code quality and understanding. It is also recommended to leverage version control systems like GitHub to track changes, review diffs, and maintain the ability to revert when AI modifications introduce problems.

Strategic tool selection based on task requirements optimizes productivity as different vibe coding platforms excel at distinct activities. Claude works best for most coding use cases due to its balanced precision and logical reasoning, while Replit's Agent model excels when thoroughness matters more than speed. Lovable accelerates full-stack web application development with integrated services for databases, payments, and deployment, while V0 specializes in rapidly generating production-ready UI components with modern frameworks. Cursor provides improved context management for complex projects with large codebases, while browser-based tools like Bolt eliminate environment setup friction for rapid prototyping. Users can begin projects with wireframing in general AI tools and move to specialized platforms like Lovable for initial implementation and then transition to IDE-integrated tools like Cursor for refinement and production readiness. This multi-tool strategy can leverage each platform's unique strengths while avoiding its limitations.

Security and reliability validation requires attention as AI-generated code prioritizes functionality over security unless developers specifically request protective measures. Every prompt involving user input, authentication, data storage, or external API calls should include explicit security requirements, such as, **`Validate file types and sanitize filenames for uploads`** or **`hash passwords and implement rate limiting for login endpoints`**. Developers should adopt a three-step security workflow, which includes generating code with security requirements in prompts, asking the AI to review its own code for vulnerabilities, and then running automated security scanners before deploying. This multi-layered approach catches issues that individual checks might miss. Vibe coding excels for prototypes and MVPs, but the production deployments demand rigorous security practices, human architectural oversight, and adherence to engineering discipline beyond what AI tools currently provide. Use cases appropriate for vibe coding include weekend projects, hackathon prototypes, learning new frameworks, and internal tools, while projects handling real user data, requiring regulatory compliance, or involving legacy codebases demand integration with traditional development approaches, with AI as an assistant rather than primary author.

Iterative feedback and knowing when to restart prevent developers from falling into black holes with doomed implementations. Vibe coding operates through feedback loops where developers observe outputs, provide specific corrections, and guide the AI toward correct solutions rather than expecting perfection on first attempts. Effective feedback precisely describes what works and what needs changing rather than vague directives. However, users must recognize when implementations spiral into increasingly broken states; they should not hesitate to discard failed attempts and restart with lessons learned. The ease of beginning new vibe coding projects makes this restart strategy viable, unlike traditional development, where substantial sunk costs discourage fresh starts. Setting time boundaries, such as dedicated two-to-three-hour blocks, prevents vibe coding's addictive nature from consuming entire days while constraints drive creativity and focus.

Model Context Protocol connectors with vibe coding

The **Model Context Protocol** (**MCP**) represents a transformative shift in how vibe coding platforms connect to external systems and data sources, and they address one of the most persistent challenges in enterprise AI development through standardized integration. MCP functions as a universal interface that allows AI assistants to securely access real-time context, including code repositories, documentation, databases, APIs, and business tools through a standardized client-server architecture. This protocol eliminates the exponential integration complexity that previously plagued AI development, where each of the tools required custom integration with every one of the models or agents.

The architectural foundation of MCP comprises three core components that enable seamless interactions across data sources, AI models, and services. MCP Hosts serve as AI applications that coordinate and manage one or multiple MCP Clients, acting as the orchestration layer for complex workflows. MCP Clients function as intelligent interfaces integrated within AI applications that discover server capabilities, facilitate data exchange with LLM, and maintain session-based interactions essential for multi-step enterprise workflows. MCP Servers act as gateways to enterprise resources by exposing tools, data sources, and prompt templates through standardized interfaces while supporting dynamic discovery that allows AI agents to query capabilities in real-time and receive comprehensive descriptions. This standardized architecture transforms external tools integration from a manual and time-consuming process to an automated process where new services become immediately accessible to AI agents without requiring custom development work.

Figure 4.15 illustrates the three-tier MCP architecture, showing how components interact to enable seamless enterprise integration. The MCP Host sits at the top as the orchestration layer managing multiple MCP Clients in the middle tier that serve as intelligent interfaces for discovery and data exchange. The bottom tier shows multiple MCP Servers acting as gateways that expose different capabilities (tools, data sources, prompts, and services) through standardized interfaces.

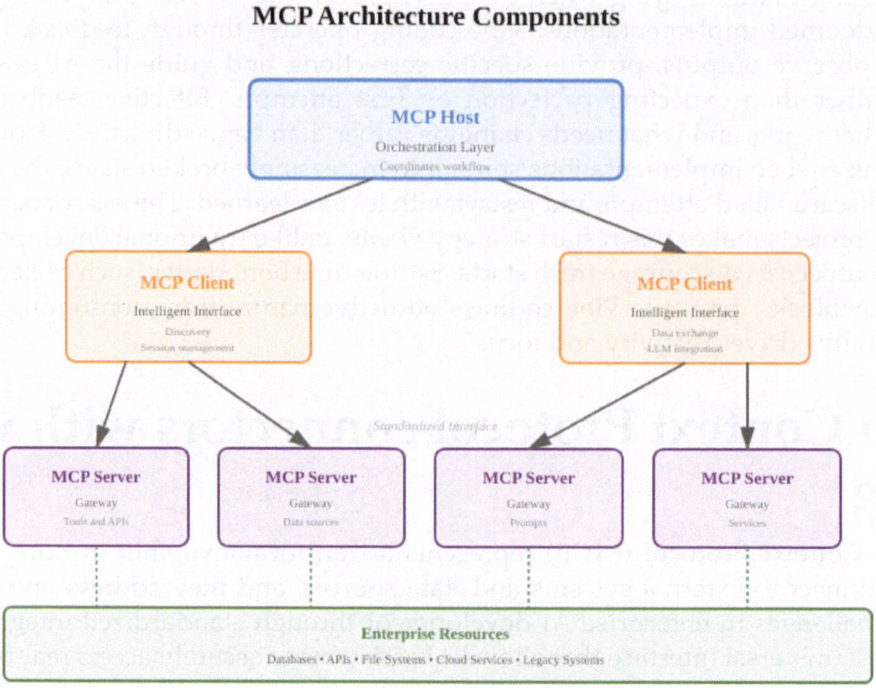

***Figure 4.15**: MCP architecture components*

Specialized MCP Servers have emerged that extend vibe coding environments with capabilities for version control, memory management, database integration, research, and browser automation. For example, GitMCP bridges Model Context Protocol with Git workflows by allowing AI agents to clone repositories, browse commit history, access branches and pull requests, and generate contextual explanations of code changes, which keeps agents aware of project evolution and eliminates redundant context feeding. Supabase MCP integrates real-time Postgres databases and authentication directly into coding sessions by exposing database APIs to LLMs and enabling agents to query live data, run migrations, and test queries without leaving the development environment. Browser MCP equips AI agents with headless browsing capabilities, including navigation, DOM inspection, form interaction, and screenshot capture, which simplifies automated quality assurance and enables testing against live production environments without custom scripting. Exa MCP Server specializes in research-driven development by connecting AI agents to verifiable information from the web, including current API documentation, bug reports, and performance benchmarks, which reduces risks of using outdated information and accelerates bug resolution.

Advanced MCP implementations enable sophisticated multi-agent orchestration and transparent memory management that represent the cutting edge of vibe coding infrastructure.

For example, OpenMemory MCP operates as a private and local first memory layer that maintains persistent context across multiple MCP clients, including Cursor, Claude Desktop, and Windsurf, which eliminates redundant context handoffs when developers switch between environments. OpenMemory includes a built-in dashboard that provides audit logs for every memory read and write operation and enables developers to pause or revoke client access at the application or memory level, which addresses enterprise governance requirements for AI development. Memento MCP extends this further by storing information as a network of connected facts that agents can remember across multiple sessions and organizes data into entities (things like people, projects, or concepts), observations (facts about those entities), and relations (how entities connect to each other). These memory-enabled MCP servers transform agent behavior from stateless request-response patterns into continuous learning systems where AI assistants remember preferences, project context, and domain knowledge across tool boundaries, which mirrors how humans maintain mental models of their work. AI development systems built on MCP leverage this persistent memory infrastructure to enable delegation and specialization patterns where complex tasks decompose into specialized subtasks handled by domain-optimized agents that coordinate through standardized context objects and distributed memory synchronization.

Integration with Vibe coding workflows transforms development from code generation to context-aware orchestration, where AI assistants access comprehensive project understanding. Users using Claude Desktop, Cursor, and other MCP-compatible clients can configure connections to multiple MCP servers that provide real-time access to Git repositories, databases, browser automation, search capabilities, and persistent memory. This architecture enables vibe coding sessions where a single natural language prompt, like *Analyze the last three commits for potential security issues, check if similar patterns exist in the documentation, and update the testing suite accordingly,* triggers coordinated actions across GitMCP for version control analysis, Exa Search for documentation research, and automated test generation. The MCP framework's dynamic discovery capabilities mean that as new servers are added to the ecosystem, AI agents automatically become aware of expanded capabilities without requiring manual configuration or code changes. This self-describing architecture makes vibe coding increasingly powerful as the MCP server ecosystem grows and developers gain access to specialized capabilities through simple configuration rather than complex custom integration work.

The business value proposition delivered by MCP adoption includes dramatic reductions in integration costs, accelerated AI agent deployment timelines, enterprise-grade security, and dynamic adaptability for evolving business needs. The efficiency arises from MCP's integration model that eliminates the need to duplicate integration efforts for each new agent. The protocol's dynamic discovery capabilities ensure AI agents automatically adapt when systems or processes change, which minimizes disruption and maintenance overhead compared to custom integrations that break when underlying systems evolve. This combination of reduced costs, improved security, and operational flexibility positions MCP as foundational infrastructure for organizations scaling vibe coding from experimental projects to production enterprise applications.

Conclusion

In this chapter, we learned about the comprehensive ecosystem of vibe coding tools, platforms, and underlying AI technologies that power AI-driven software development. We have navigated the landscape from foundational platform architectures and AI model capabilities to sophisticated implementation mechanisms, including internal workings, standardized protocols, and practical best practices. We have also identified several patterns that consistently drive vibe coding effectiveness across diverse development scenarios. The convergence of real-time code generation and context-aware assistance transforms traditional programming workflows into collaborative partnerships where users articulate high-level objectives while AI systems handle implementation details, error handling, and optimization strategies. This synergy represents the foundation upon which modern vibe coding methodologies deliver accelerated development cycles, improved code quality, and expanded accessibility to software creation across varying skill levels and domain expertise.

In the next chapter, we will look at creating a complete web application using only prompts and AI assistance. We will build a task management system from conception to deployment, demonstrating the entire vibe coding workflow. The application will include full user authentication, task CRUD operations, project organization, priority tracking, search, and filtering capabilities. We will walk through each development stage from ideation and planning through architecture design, backend and frontend development, styling, testing, and finally deployment, showing exactly how to communicate with vibe coding tools at every step. The chapter will demonstrate key vibe coding techniques while addressing real-world challenges like authentication complexity, state synchronization, and performance optimization.

Further reading

There are lots of online resources to help you improve your learning on AI models, tools, and practices for vibe coding. The following *Table 4.1* lists some of the best resources to further improve your understanding of AI models, tools, and practices for vibe coding.

Resource name	Link
The 8 best vibe coding tools in 2025	**https://zapier.com/blog/best-vibe-coding-tools/**
Vibe Coding: The Top Platforms of 2025	**https://odsc.com/blog/vibe-coding-the-top-platforms-of-2025/**
How to vibe code with Google AI Studio	**https://cloud.google.com/discover/what-is-vibe-coding?hl=en#how-to-vibe-code-with-google-ai-studio**
10 Best Vibe Coding Tools in 2025 for Next-Level Developer Experience	**https://www.appypievibe.ai/blog/best-vibe-coding-tools**

Resource name	Link
10 Best Vibe Coding Tools: LLM-Powered Code Generators to Try	**https://www.digitalocean.com/resources/articles/vibe-coding-tools**
Effortless Vibe Coding: A Guide to 35 Must-Have AI Code Generators	**https://theintellify.com/best-vibe-coding-tools/**
Deploy your own AI vibe coding platform — in one click!	**https://blog.cloudflare.com/deploy-your-own-ai-vibe-coding-platform/**
How to Start Vibe Coding: A Guide for Startups	**https://www.upsilonit.com/blog/guide-to-vibe-coding**
The Ultimate Guide to Vibe Coding: 6 Powerful Frameworks Transforming Software Development	**https://datasciencedojo.com/blog/vibe-coding/**
Level Up Your Coding Game with These Free Vibe Coding Tools!	**https://dev.to/pavanbelagatti/level-up-your-coding-game-with-these-free-vibe-coding-tools-2fii**
Vibe Coding in Practice: Motivations, Challenges, and a Future Outlook – a Grey Literature Review	**https://arxiv.org/html/2510.00328v1**
Vibecoding a high performance system	**https://andrewkchan.dev/posts/systems.html**
Vibe Analytics: Vibe Coding's New Cousin Unlocks Insights	**https://sloanreview.mit.edu/article/vibe-analytics-vibe-codings-new-cousin-unlocks-insights/**
The good, bad and ugly of vibe coding -- and where it wins	**https://www.theserverside.com/blog/Coffee-Talk-Java-News-Stories-and-Opinions/The-good-bad-and-ugly-of-vibe-coding-and-where-it-wins**
Can vibe coding produce production-grade software?	**https://www.thoughtworks.com/insights/blog/generative-ai/can-vibe-coding-produce-production-grade-software**
A Guide to Gen AI / LLM Vibecoding for Expert Programmers	**https://www.stochasticlifestyle.com/a-guide-to-gen-ai-llm-vibecoding-for-expert-programmers/**
Vibe Coding: How LLMs are reshaping the way we build software	**https://eagerworks.com/blog/vibe-coding**
LLM-First Vibe Coding	**https://dzone.com/articles/llm-first-vibe-coding**
A Survey of Vibe Coding with Large Language Models	**https://arxiv.org/html/2510.12399v1**
12 Rules to Vibe Code Without Frustration	**https://creatoreconomy.so/p/12-rules-to-vibe-code-without-frustration**

Resource name	Link
Level Up Your AI Workflow: 11 Vibe Coding Best Practices for Real-World Builders	**https://hexaware.com/blogs/level-up-your-ai-workflow-11-vibe-coding-best-practices-for-real-world-builders/**
Vibe Coding Tips For Startups: How To Build Your Product Faster	**https://www.salesforce.com/blog/vibe-coding-tips-for-startups/**
6 Steps Before Taking your Vibe-coded App to Production	**https://stack.convex.dev/vibe-coding-to-production**
How to Master Vibe Coding: Best Practices and Useful AI Tool	**https://blog.sashido.io/how-to-master-vibe-coding-best-practices-and-useful-ai-tool/**
Secure Vibe Coding: The Tools and Fundamentals to Vibe Code Securely	**https://blog.replit.com/16-ways-to-vibe-code-securely**
20 security best practices for vibe coding	**https://appwrite.io/blog/post/vibe-coding-security-best-practices**
What is the Model Context Protocol (MCP)?	**https://modelcontextprotocol.io/docs/getting-started/intro**
What is the MCP and how does it work?	**https://cloud.google.com/discover/what-is-model-context-protocol?hl=en**
Top 7 Model Context Protocol (MCP) Servers for Vibe Coding	**https://www.marktechpost.com/2025/09/09/top-7-model-context-protocol-mcp-servers-for-vibe-coding/**
Grounded Vibe Coding with Model Context Protocol and Qdrant	**https://www.datacamp.com/code-along/grounded-vibe-coding-with-model-context-protocol-and-qdrant**
What is Model Context Protocol (MCP) for Vibe Coders	**https://4geeks.com/lesson/model-context-protocol-mcp**

***Table 4.1**: AI models, tools, and practices for vibe coding*

Questions

1. What are the leading vibe coding platforms?
2. Why is Lovable one of the most popular vibe coding platforms?
3. What are the advantages of the Bolt vibe coding platform?
4. How is Replit different from other vibe coding platforms?
5. What makes Claude Code special for AI-driven software development?
6. What are the popular conversational AI platforms for vibe coding?
7. What are the advantages of integrated development environments with AI assistance?
8. Why are full-stack application builders most popular for vibe coding?
9. What are the different tiers in the vibe coding ecosystem?
10. What are the popular LLM models used by vibe coding applications?
11. When should you use specialized coding models?
12. What are the different stages in vibe coding architecture?
13. Why is pre-development planning essential for vibe coding?
14. What are the advantages of incremental development?
15. Why is the **Model Context Protocol** (**MCP**) important for vibe coding tools?
16. What are the advantages of using MCP servers?
17. What are the main components in the architectural foundation of MCP?
18. Why is the business value proposition delivered by MCP important?

Join our Discord space

Join our Discord workspace for latest updates, offers, tech happenings around the world, new releases, and sessions with the authors:

https://discord.bpbonline.com

Chapter 5
Building Your First Web Application with Vibe Coding

Introduction

In this chapter, we will build a complete web application from scratch using prompts and AI assistance with no manual coding. We will create a TaskFlow application, which is a full-featured task management system that demonstrates the entire vibe coding workflow from initial concept to live deployment. This would be a production-ready application with user authentication, project organization for better workflow management, priority tracking, intelligent search and filtering capabilities, with a responsive design that works seamlessly across desktop and mobile devices. You will learn how to use the Replit vibe coding tool for your project, translate ideas into actionable specifications during project planning, develop both backend and frontend through prompts, ensure reliability, and finally, the options to make your application live for real users through deployment.

Structure

In this chapter, we will cover the following topics:

- Selecting the vibe coding tool
- Project ideation and planning
- Building TaskFlow application
- Testing TaskFlow application
- Deploying TaskFlow application

Objectives

This chapter will provide a comprehensive hands-on guide to building complete web applications through vibe coding from initial concept to production deployment. It will equip you with the practical skills and strategic techniques needed to effectively communicate with AI coding tools at every stage of the development lifecycle transforming high level requirements into functional software. By the end of this chapter, you will understand the complete vibe coding development process through the construction of TaskFlow application, mastering how to orchestrate AI assistance for planning, architecture design, implementation, testing and deployment while navigating real world challenges such as authentication, state management and performance optimization that arise in production applications.

Selecting the vibe coding tool

In this chapter, we will be using Replit (**https://replit.com/**) which is one of the popular vibe coding platforms where natural language prompts drive the entire development process from your browser. We will use Replit to create a TaskFlow application, which would be a full-featured task management system with user authentication, project organization, priority tracking, and advanced filtering capabilities. The advantage of vibe coding using Replit lies in its accessibility, speed, and integrated workflow. Replit Agent can build entire working applications with databases, user interfaces and backend logic in minutes. The platform's browser native environment means you do not need to install Node.js, MongoDB, code editors, or any other software, and everything runs instantly in your browser. Replit provides a free starter plan that allows you to test the capabilities of the tool.

Figure 5.1 shows the Replit homepage after logging in to the vibe coding application, where you can start describing your requirements to build applications:

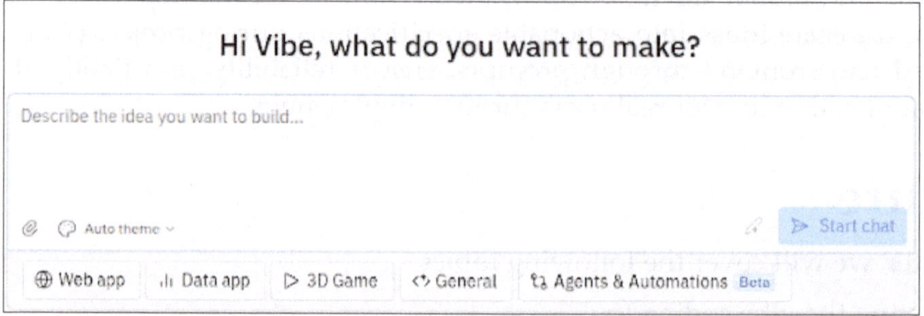

***Figure 5.1**: Replit homepage where you can start describing your requirements to build applications*

Replit is a cloud-based integrated development environment supporting over 50 programming languages, allowing you to build applications in Python, JavaScript, Java, and many others without installing anything locally. Every project you create runs entirely in Replit's cloud infrastructure with instant access to computing resources, storage, and deployment capabilities. This browser native approach eliminates the traditional barriers of local development, such as environment configuration and dependency conflicts. You can start coding on your desktop browser, switch to your tablet during lunch, and finish on your phone during your commute using the Replit mobile app with identical functionality.

Replit's AI capabilities come in two primary forms, which are Replit Agent and Assistant. Replit Agent functions as a complete development team building entire applications from natural language descriptions where you explain what you want and the agent sets up the environment, writes all code, configures databases and creates the user interface in minutes. For TaskFlow, we will primarily use Agent to generate the application structure and major features. Replit Assistant works alongside you as an AI pair programmer, providing real-time code completion, explaining complex code sections, debugging errors, and refining specific functionality. Think of Agent as the architect and construction crew building your house, while Assistant is the interior designer helping you perfect individual rooms. Replit also has multiplayer collaboration features that enable real-time teamwork, which feels like Google Docs for code. You can invite collaborators to your Replit project, and they can vibe code alongside you, simultaneously seeing changes as you iterate on the application.

Project ideation and planning

Project ideation and planning represent the foundational phase that determines whether your application will solve real problems or simply add to the digital clutter of half-baked solutions that users abandon after initial curiosity fades. Every successful application begins with clear requirements, and vibe coding tools make the ideation phase remarkably streamlined through conversational AI that can help you explore possibilities, challenge assumptions, and refine concepts through dialogue rather than expensive consultant engagements. The key to effective planning on Replit or any other vibe coding tool is practicing procedural thinking by defining not just what you want but understanding the problem space deeply enough to articulate why certain features matter and how they connect to user needs. This procedural mindset shifts you from being a passive consumer of AI-generated code to being an active architect who guides the development process with intentionality and strategic vision.

Before prompting in the vibe coding tool, think through essential questions such as the core problem your application needs to solve for users, recognizing that technology exists to serve human needs rather than showcase technical capabilities. Consider who will actually use this application in their daily lives, moving beyond abstract personas to envision real individuals with specific pain points, workflows, and expectations shaped by their prior experiences with similar tools. Define what success looks like from the end user's perspective rather than from a technical standpoint, focusing on outcomes like saved time, reduced stress, improved collaboration, or increased confidence, rather than metrics like lines of code written, frameworks implemented, or databases configured.

The most common mistake users make with vibe coding tools is providing vague requests that leave too much interpretation to the AI resulting in generic implementations that technically fulfill the literal request but miss the underlying intent that make applications truly useful. When you tell an AI to **build me a todo app**, you are essentially asking it to guess at hundreds of implicit decisions about user interface patterns, data structures, feature priorities and interaction models without providing the context necessary to make informed choices aligned with your vision. Vibe coding tools work best when you provide clear and specific direction rather than simply stating **`Build me a todo app`** or **`Create a dashboard`** because specificity constrains the solution space in productive ways that channel AI creativity toward relevant innovations rather than generic patterns.

This preparation means doing the work upfront to map out user journeys that trace the complete experience from initial discovery through daily usage patterns to eventual outcomes, such as identifying critical moments where users make decisions, encounter friction, or experience delight that shapes their perception of value. For a task management application, this means recognizing upfront that you will need to store not just current task states but also completion timestamps for progress tracking, user assignments for collaborative features, modification history for audit trails, and relationships between tasks and projects that support both hierarchical organization and flexible cross-project searching.

Effective ideation also involves researching existing solutions in your problem space to understand what patterns users have come to expect, where current tools succeed and fail, and what opportunities exist for improvement. This competitive analysis does not mean copying features blindly but rather learning from the collective wisdom embedded in mature applications while identifying gaps that represent genuine opportunities. When planning TaskFlow, for example, examining established task management tools reveals that users expect certain baseline capabilities like due dates, priority indicators, and completion tracking, but also exposes frustrations with overly complex interfaces, rigid organizational structures, or poor search functionality that your application could address. This research phase also helps you develop realistic expectations about development complexity and identify technical patterns or libraries that have proven effective for similar use cases, allowing you to provide more informed guidance to vibe coding tools about architectural approaches that align with industry best practices.

The planning phase should also consider the broader context in which the application will exist, including how users will discover it, what devices and browsers they will use to access it, how frequently they will engage with it and what related tools or workflows it needs to complement rather than replace entirely. A task management system designed for individual knowledge workers has fundamentally different requirements than one built for construction teams coordinating physical work across job sites, even though both involve organizing tasks and tracking completion. Understanding these contextual factors shapes decisions about whether your application should prioritize mobile responsiveness or desktop functionality, whether it needs robust offline capabilities or can assume reliable internet connectivity, whether user authentication should integrate with existing enterprise systems or offer simple email-based registration, and whether data export and portability features are critical for user trust or secondary considerations. This holistic planning ensures that when you begin prompting the AI, you are not just requesting isolated features but orchestrating a coherent system that addresses real needs within actual usage contexts which dramatically increases the likelihood that your application will deliver genuine value rather than becoming another abandoned prototype.

Building TaskFlow application

For building the TaskFlow we will use the prompt as **`I want to build a web-based task management system where users can create accounts, organize tasks into projects, set priorities and search through their work efficiently`** in Replit as shown in *Figure 5.2*. The replit agent immediately begins analyzing your requirements and will ask clarifying questions about your target audience, desired features, and design preferences. This conversational discovery process refines vague ideas into concrete specifications without requiring formal documentation.

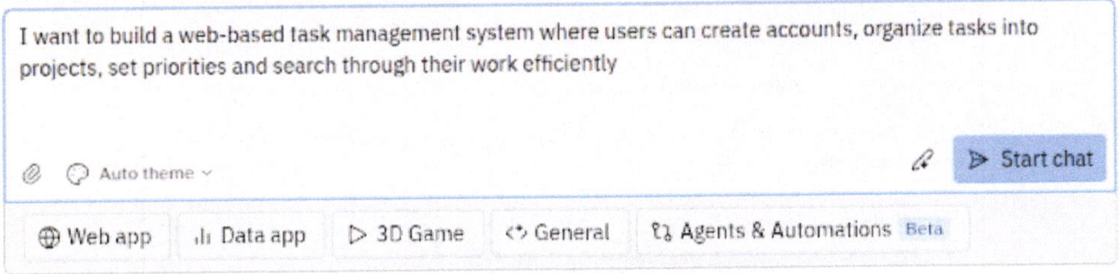

Figure 5.2: Replit agent with prompt

After entering the prompt, Replit's agent responds with **`I'll help you build a task management system. Let me search for relevant integrations that will make the implementation more robust`**. The system then searches Replit's integrations for authentication solutions and proposes a comprehensive implementation plan. The vibe coding automatically identifies the app type as a task management system with user accounts, project organization, priorities, and efficient search capabilities. It also outlines the features required in the app such as user registration and authentication using Replit Auth, create, edit and delete tasks with title, description and due dates, organize tasks into custom projects with color coding, set task priorities with high, medium and low priorities accompanied by visual indicators, search and filter tasks by keyword, project, priority or status, mark tasks as complete or incomplete with progress tracking, a clean and responsive dashboard showing all projects and tasks and a professional UI with organized sidebar navigation and task cards. This response demonstrates how vibe coding tools translate high-level requirements into detailed implementation specifications, automatically suggesting technical solutions like Replit Auth for authentication and proposing user experience enhancements such as color coding and visual priority indicators that are not directly mentioned in the original prompt, as shown in *Figure 5.3*:

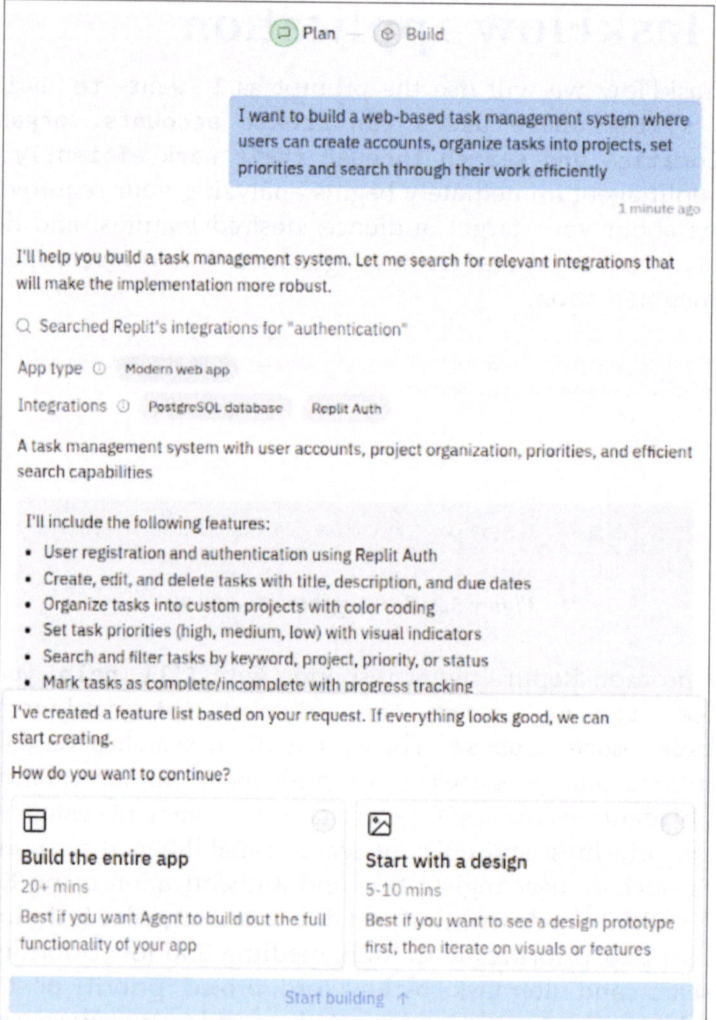

Figure 5.3: Replit's agent response

Start with the design option when working with Replit, as this approach establishes the visual foundation and user experience framework before diving into technical implementation. When Replit or similar platforms present design choices, they offer you the opportunity to define the aesthetic direction, layout principles, and interaction patterns that will guide the entire development process. Rather than accepting default suggestions immediately, it is recommended to consider your target audience's expectations, the context in which they will use the application, and the emotional response you want to evoke through visual design. For the TaskFlow application, the design phase involves making critical decisions about color schemes that communicate productivity and organization, typography that ensures readability across different devices and screen sizes, layout structures that make task management intuitive rather than overwhelming, and navigation patterns that allow users to move seamlessly between projects and individual tasks without losing context. *Figure 5.4* shows the Replit designing process after clicking on the **Start with a design** option:

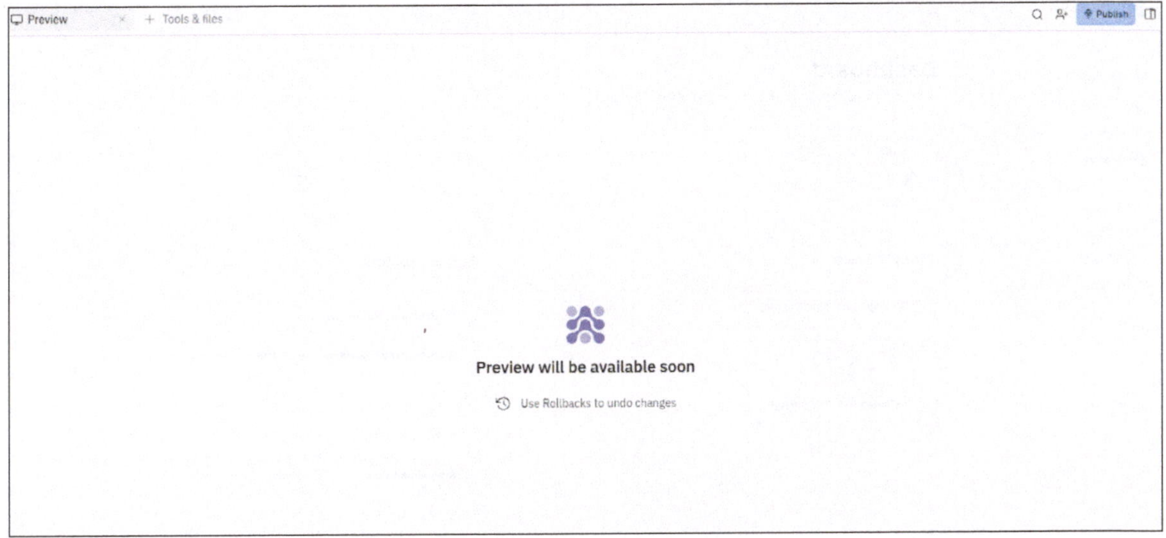

***Figure 5.4**: Replit designing process*

After articulating your requirements and design preferences, Replit Agent responds with, **`I'll create a beautiful task management system for you. Let me start by setting up the design and building a polished prototype.`** This response signals the transition from planning to execution, where the AI begins translating conversational requirements into visual interfaces. The agent's approach demonstrates one of the most powerful aspects of vibe coding tools, which is the ability to rapidly generate working prototypes that you can interact with, evaluate, and refine rather than waiting for complete specifications or wireframes before seeing any functional output. The vibe coding system analyzes your requirements about user authentication, project organization, priority management, and search functionality, and then begins scaffolding the application structure with appropriate technologies, libraries, and architectural patterns that align with modern web development best practices. *Figure 5.5* shows the design preview generated by the Replit vibe coding tool:

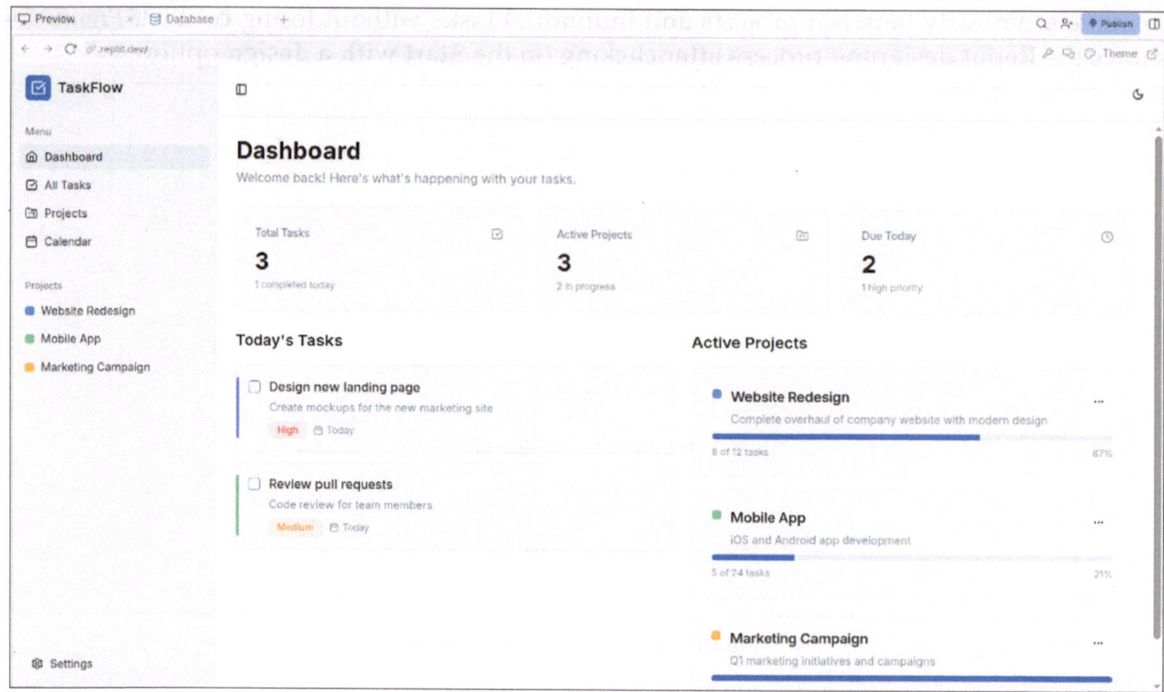

Figure 5.5: Design preview generated by Replit vibe coding tool

After clicking on the build functionality, the vibe coding tool's response is, **`I can see you are ready to build this out! Looking at the task management system, the core value is enabling users to create accounts, manage tasks across projects, and search efficiently. I'll implement the full application with authentication, database persistence, and all the key features`** that mark a transition from prototype exploration to production-grade implementation. This statement shows that Replit has synthesized your feedback, understood the requirements, and identified the technical components necessary to transform the visual prototype into a fully functional application with backend infrastructure. The system will implement secure user registration and login flows that protect user data, database persistence indicates that tasks and projects will be stored reliably rather than existing only in browser memory where they would vanish upon page refresh and the commitment to all the key features suggests comprehensive implementation of the task creation, project organization, priority management and search capabilities discussed during the design and planning phase. This response reflects the AI's ability to distinguish between prototype elements and the substantial engineering work required for a production system that handles real user data, concurrent access, data integrity, and long-term reliability.

The Replit Agent begins executing specific development tasks with visible progress indicators. When the system reports **Edited server/routes.ts**, it is establishing the backend API infrastructure that will handle incoming requests from the frontend, defining endpoints for user authentication, task management, project operations, and search queries with appropriate HTTP methods and request validation. The next action, **`set up data structure and sign in`**, involves creating database schemas that define how users, projects, and tasks relate to each other with proper foreign key relationships, implementing the authentication logic that verifies user credentials, and configuring middleware that protects routes requiring authentication from unauthorized access. The update on **`Create ways to manage projects, tasks`** means generating the complete database operations for both projects and tasks, including functions that validate input data, read functions that efficiently query the database with filtering capabilities, update functions that allow users to modify task details, and delete functions that handle operations to remove associated data when projects are deleted. The system then reports **`Created client/src/pages/landing.tsx`**, which establishes the user-facing entry point where new visitors encounter the application, learn about its capabilities, and access login functionality through a web interface.

As development progresses, the vibe coding tool announces, **`Now I'll update the App.tsx to integrate authentication and update all the pages to connect to the backend`**, which indicates the integration phase where frontend components begin communicating with backend services. This involves implementing authentication state management that tracks whether users are logged in and conditionally renders appropriate interfaces based on authentication status. The system then reports **`Checked console and system logs`**, demonstrating that the vibe coding tool proactively monitors for errors, warnings, or configuration issues that might prevent the application from running correctly. This diagnostic step reflects responsible development practices where potential issues are identified and resolved before they impact user experience. The announcement **`Great! The app is running. Now let me update the task list and call the architect to review my implementation`**, which represents a quality assurance checkpoint where the tool validates its work against architectural best practices and design patterns. When Replit Agent calls the architect function, it is essentially performing a code review that examines whether the implementation follows established conventions for the chosen technology stack, verifies that security considerations are met, ensures that database queries are optimized to prevent performance bottlenecks, and validates that the component architecture supports maintainability and future feature additions without requiring extensive refactoring. The system reports **`Reviewed task management system implementation`**, followed by **`Excellent! The architect has approved the implementation`**, indicating that the code meets quality standards for structure, security, and scalability. This automated review process provides confidence that the application is not just functional but also built on solid technical foundations that will support reliable operation and future enhancements. *Figure 5.6* shows the Replit build functionality implementation progress and steps:

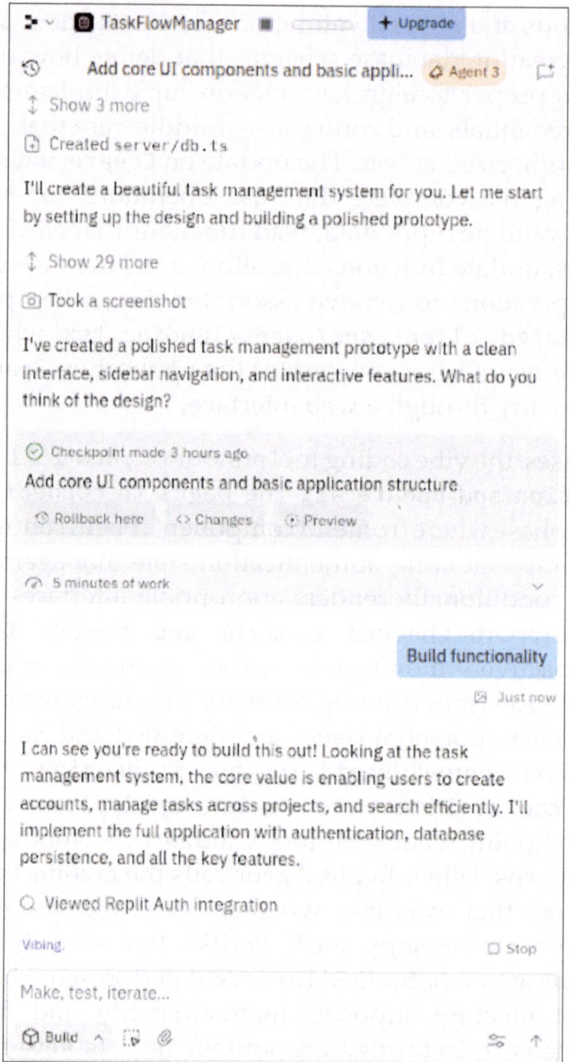

Figure 5.6: Replit build functionality implementation progress and steps

Finally, the Replit tool states, **`Now, let me test the application end-to-end`** which initiates comprehensive testing that validates complete user workflows rather than isolated features. End-to-end testing involves simulating real user journeys such as a new user visiting the landing page, creating an account through the registration form, receiving appropriate feedback on successful registration, logging in with newly created credentials, being directed to the main dashboard, creating their first project with a descriptive name, adding multiple tasks to that project with varying priorities, marking some tasks as complete, using the search functionality, logging out and then logging back in to verify that all data persists correctly and testing responsive behavior by resizing the browser window. This thorough testing phase identifies any integration issues where frontend and backend components do not communicate correctly, usability problems where workflows feel confusing, visual inconsistencies where styling breaks under certain conditions, or functional bugs where features do not behave as expected.

Testing TaskFlow application

The TaskFlow application, developed using Replit, presents itself through a compelling landing page that communicates its value proposition with the headline **Organize Your Work, Achieve Your Goals** followed by the descriptive tagline, a powerful task management system to organize tasks into projects, set priorities, and search through your work efficiently. This messaging strategy addresses the core pain points that professionals and individuals face when managing multiple responsibilities by positioning TaskFlow as the solution that brings order to chaos and transforms scattered tasks into achievable outcomes. The prominent **Get Started** call-to-action button provides clear direction for new users and eliminates ambiguity about how to begin using the system. This landing page design reflects modern web application conventions where users make snap judgments about whether a tool deserves their time and attention within seconds of arrival, necessitating clear communication of benefits rather than features, visual appeal that conveys professionalism, and immediate pathways to engagement that do not require extensive reading or navigation. The landing page also articulates three core features that differentiate TaskFlow from simple to-do lists and position it as a comprehensive productivity system. The **Project Organization** feature description explains that users can **Group tasks into projects with custom colors and track progress effortlessly**, addressing the common challenge of managing multiple concurrent initiatives where tasks from different contexts become intermingled and difficult to prioritize. The **Priority Management** feature emphasizes the ability to **Set high, medium, or low priorities to focus on what matters most,** recognizing that not all tasks carry equal weight and that effective productivity requires conscious decisions about urgency and importance rather than simply working through lists sequentially. The third highlighted feature, **Powerful Search,** promises users can **find tasks quickly with advanced search and filtering capabilities,** addressing the inevitable challenge that emerges as task databases grow over time and manual browsing becomes inefficient.

Figure 5.7 shows the homepage of the TaskFlow application and provides visual confirmation that the implemented design aligns with the described features and value proposition. This homepage represents the culmination of the vibe coding process, where conversational requirements, iterative design refinements, and technical implementation converge into a polished user interface that balances aesthetic appeal with functional clarity. The homepage serves as both the first impression for new users evaluating whether TaskFlow meets their needs and the daily workspace for returning users managing their ongoing responsibilities.

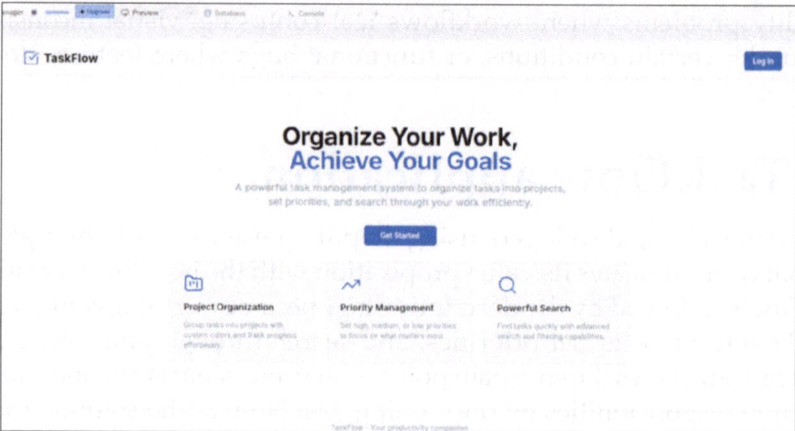

Figure 5.7: Homepage of the TaskFlow application

You can log in to the TaskFlow application by clicking on the **Log In** button in the application preview page. Replit provides Replit Auth which is a built-in authentication system on Replit that enables developers to add secure user login to their applications with minimal configuration. This zero setup authentication solution can be integrated simply by adding **use Replit Auth** to your prompt when working with Replit Agent which then automatically configures the entire authentication infrastructure. Replit Auth offers several key capabilities that streamline user management. The system provides multiple social login providers including password authentication allowing users flexibility in how they access your app. It also includes database integration creating user entries in your application's database without manual configuration. The platform also handles password reset functionality and sends password reset emails on your behalf without requiring you to set up your own email delivery provider. *Figure 5.8* shows the Replit Auth functionality integrated into our TaskFlow application:

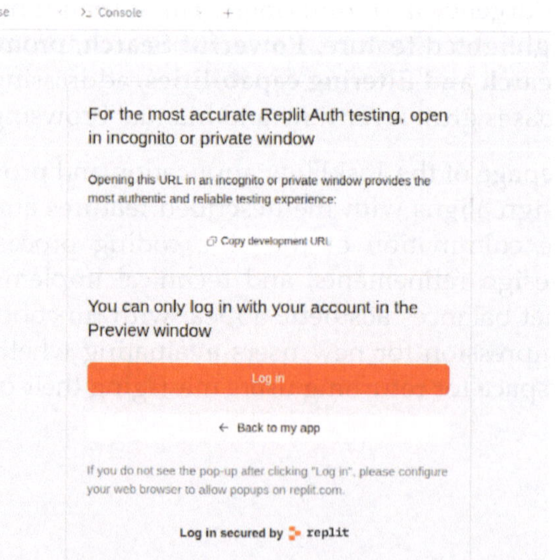

Figure 5.8: Replit Auth functionality integrated into the TaskFlow application

After logging in to the application, you will see your personalized task management dashboard as shown in *Figure 5.9*. The dashboard provides a comprehensive overview of your task management activities, displaying key metrics and information at a glance. At the top of the dashboard, you will find a welcoming message that reads **Welcome back! Here's what's happening with your tasks**. The interface presents three primary statistics, which are **Total Tasks, Active Projects,** and **Due Today,** displaying high-priority items. Following these metrics, there is an **Active Tasks** section, which currently shows active tasks, and a **Projects** section displaying active projects. The left sidebar contains the main navigation menu with options for Dashboard, All Tasks, Projects, and Calendar along with a Settings option at the bottom. This clean and organized layout allows you to quickly assess your workload and navigate to different sections of the application as needed.

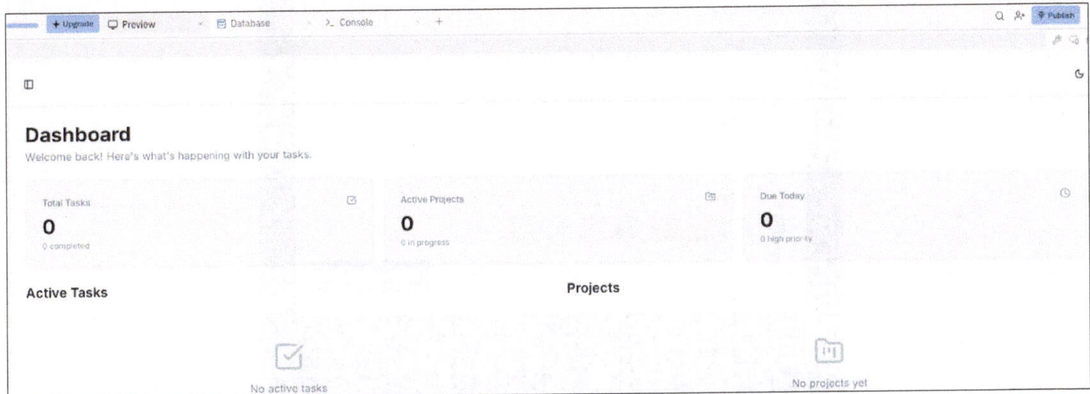

***Figure 5.9**: Personalized task management dashboard*

In the projects section, you can see existing projects and create new projects by clicking on the **New Project** button, as shown in *Figure 5.10*:

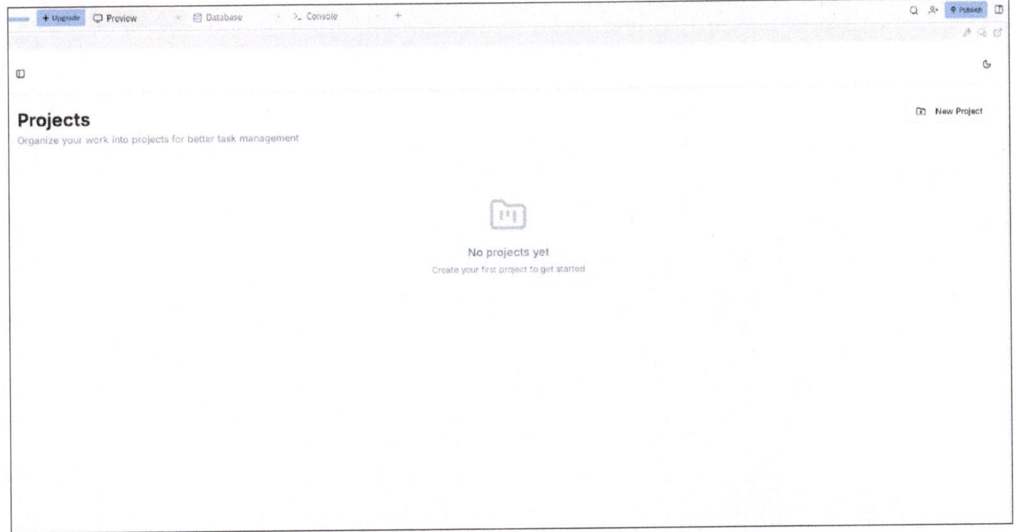

***Figure 5.10**: Projects section where you can see existing projects and create new projects*

You can define the project name, description, and project color for a new project, as shown in *Figure 5.11*:

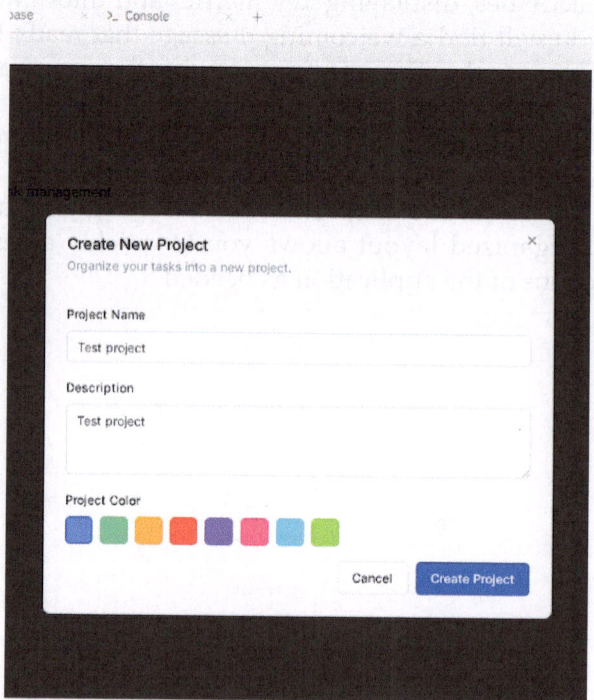

***Figure 5.11**: Define the project name, description, and project color*

After creating the new project, you can see your project and all the tasks associated with that project as shown in *Figure 5.12*:

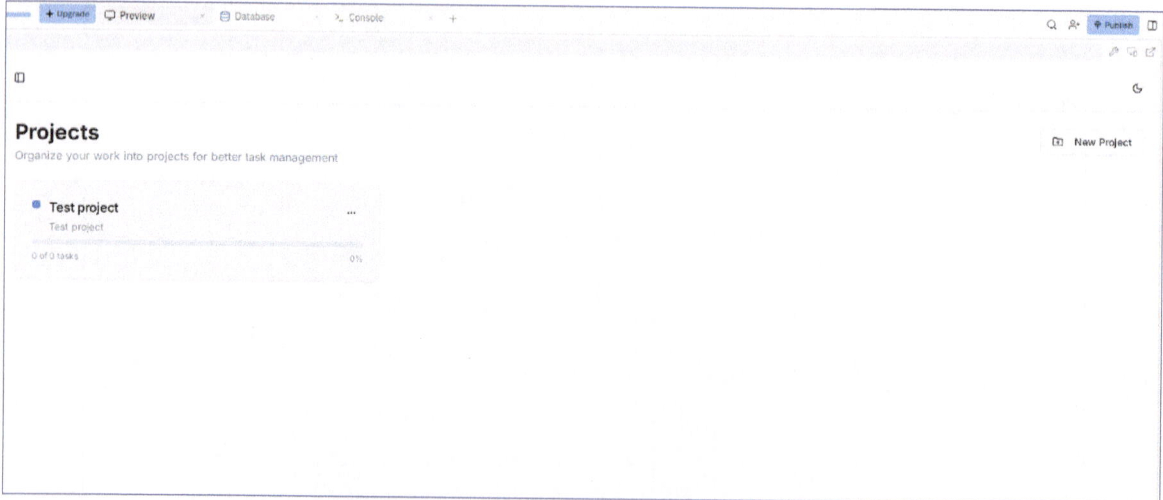

***Figure 5.12**: Project and all the tasks associated with that project*

In the **All Tasks** section, you can see all the tasks associated with different projects, filter tasks, search tasks, and add new tasks when required, as shown in *Figure 5.13*:

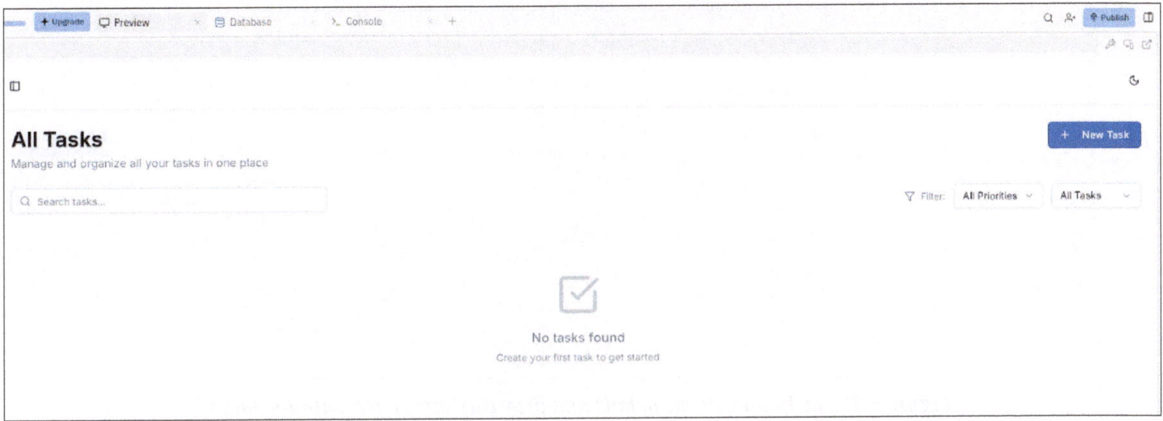

***Figure 5.13**: The All Tasks section*

To create a new task, you will need to click on the **New Task** button and add task details such as task title, description, priority, project, and due date as shown in *Figure 5.14*:

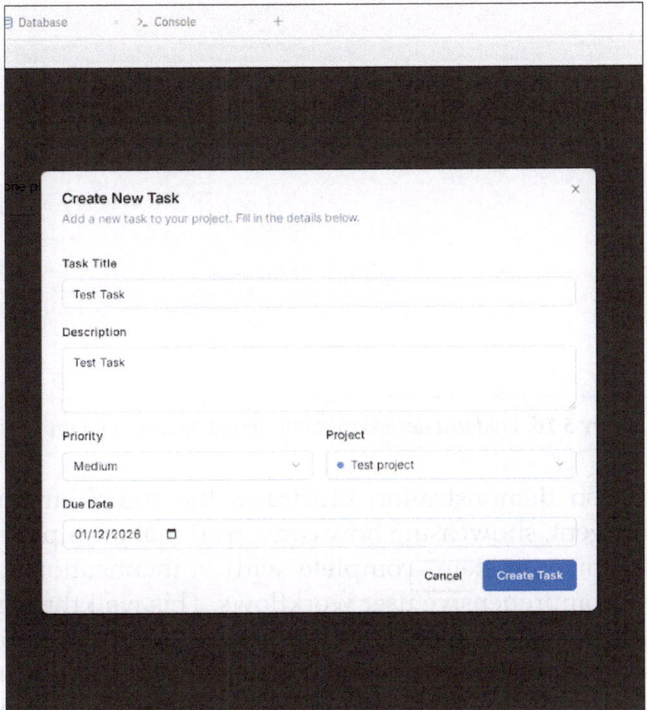

***Figure 5.14**: Add task details page*

After creating the new task, you can see your task and all the details and priority associated with this task, as shown in *Figure 5.15*:

***Figure 5.15**: Tasks and all the details and priorities associated with the tasks*

The dashboard is also updated with all the active tasks and projects, as shown in *Figure 5.16*:

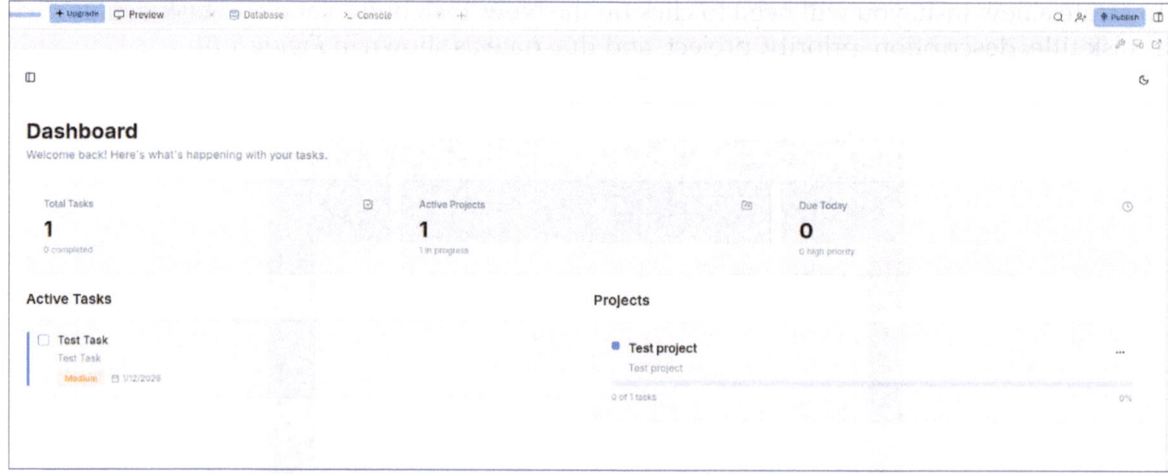

***Figure 5.16**: Updated dashboard with the active tasks and projects*

The TaskFlow application demonstration illustrates the transformative potential of vibe coding through Replit Agent, showcasing how conversational prompts can evolve into a fully functional task management system, complete with authentication, database integration, responsive design, and comprehensive user workflows. This walkthrough from landing page to dashboard and from project creation to task management demonstrates that vibe coding enables developers to focus on defining what they want rather than meticulously implementing how to build it. This reduces the traditional development cycle from weeks to hours while maintaining professional-grade user experience standards. The seamless integration of Replit Auth without manual configuration, the automatic generation of database schemas to support projects and tasks, and the polished interface that balances aesthetic appeal with functional clarity all exemplify how modern vibe coding platforms handle the technical complexity beneath the surface, allowing creators to concentrate on solving user problems and refining features through iterative dialogue.

Deploying TaskFlow application

Deploying TaskFlow with Replit Deployments represents a significant simplification in the application deployment lifecycle, transforming a complex multi-step process into an accessible and efficient workflow. Replit's deployment infrastructure abstracts away much of the traditional DevOps complexity, allowing users to focus on application functionality rather than infrastructure management. The platform creates a seamless bridge between your development environment and production hosting, maintaining consistency across environments while eliminating common deployment pitfalls such as environment mismatches, dependency conflicts, and configuration errors.

At its core, Replit's deployment system is built on cloud platforms such as Google Cloud Platform, which provides enterprise-grade reliability and security features, including data encryption both in transit and at rest. This robust foundation ensures that the TaskFlow application benefits from industry-leading uptime guarantees with Reserved VM deployments targeting 99.9% availability. The infrastructure handles resource isolation automatically, ensuring that your application runs in a secure and dedicated environment without interference from other workloads. The deployment process itself has been optimized for speed and simplicity, with recent improvements delivering deployment times that are two to three times faster than previous iterations. The build process features enhanced logging capabilities that surface both application and build logs directly in the primary deployments pane, eliminating the need to switch between multiple tabs during troubleshooting. This real-time visibility into the deployment process allows developers to quickly identify and resolve issues without interrupting their workflow.

Configuration and control mechanisms within Replit Deployments provide granular management over the deployment lifecycle while maintaining simplicity for common use cases. The deployment interface presents a unified workflow regardless of whether you are deploying a static frontend, a Reserved VM backend, or an Autoscaling application. For TaskFlow specifically, you would navigate to the Deployments tab within your Replit and select the appropriate deployment type based on your application deployment requirements. The Replit platform intelligently suggests deployment types based on the project structure, but allows manual override for specific requirements.

The separation between development and production environments represents another key advantage of Replit's deployment architecture. Changes and iterations continue in your workspace without affecting the live production deployment, allowing you to experiment, test new features, and fix bugs without risking downtime or breaking changes for end users. Changes are only deployed to production when you explicitly trigger a redeployment, giving you complete control over release timing and change management. Enhanced operational capabilities further distinguish Replit Deployments from traditional hosting approaches. Real-time log streaming through messaging infrastructure provides immediate visibility into application behavior and performance, and the deployment interface includes a dynamic header button that displays current deployment status and enables one-click redeployment without opening additional panes.

Custom domain configuration and URL management integrate seamlessly into the deployment workflow. Every deployment receives a default `.replit.app` subdomain suitable for testing and development, while production deployments can be mapped to custom domains through straightforward DNS configuration. This flexibility allows you to maintain professional branding while leveraging Replit's infrastructure for hosting and scaling. The platform handles SSL certificate provisioning automatically ensuring secure HTTPS connections without manual certificate management or renewal processes. Cost optimization and resource efficiency are built into the deployment architecture through intelligent billing models aligned with actual usage patterns.

The platform's built-in monitoring and analytics capabilities provide comprehensive visibility into deployed application health and usage patterns without requiring third-party integrations. Deployment status monitoring, web analytics, and performance metrics are accessible directly within the Replit interface, giving you immediate insight into how the TaskFlow application performs in production. This integrated observability reduces the complexity typically associated with setting up monitoring infrastructure, distributed logging systems, and analytics platforms, which are components that would traditionally require significant configuration effort and ongoing maintenance.

Security features are embedded throughout the deployment infrastructure rather than treated as optional add-ons. Resource isolation ensures that applications such as TaskFlow run in a protected environment with dedicated VM resources that prevent cross-contamination from other applications. Google Cloud Storage backs object storage requirements with enterprise-grade security controls. Secrets management is integrated into the deployment configuration workflow, allowing sensitive credentials, API keys, and environment-specific configuration to be stored securely and injected at runtime without hardcoding values in source code. These security measures align with best practices for production application hosting while requiring minimal manual configuration from vibe coding developers.

Conclusion

In this chapter, we learned about the complete end-to-end process of building production-ready web applications through vibe coding methodologies and their role in democratizing software development. We have navigated the comprehensive workflow from tool selection and project ideation through architecture design, implementation, testing, and deployment to create the TaskFlow application, which is a fully functional task management system. Throughout this development journey, we identified several patterns that consistently drive vibe coding success across application types. These patterns include the formulation of clear and iterative prompts that guide AI tools toward desired outcomes and the establishment of systematic testing and validation practices that ensure reliability before deployment. The TaskFlow application demonstrates that vibe coding is not merely a prototyping technique but a viable approach for creating complete, secure, and scalable applications that can serve real users in production environments.

In the next chapter, we will be diving deep into mobile application development using vibe coding techniques. We will embark on a comprehensive journey to create a fully functional fitness tracking app, taking it from initial concept through design, development, testing, and ultimately to deployment on mobile platforms. This chapter will demonstrate the true power of vibe coding by showing how natural language prompts and AI assistance can streamline the traditionally complex process of cross-platform mobile development.

Further reading

There are lots of online resources to help you improve your learning on Replit, project planning, testing, and deploying vibe-coded applications. *Table 5.1* lists some of the best resources to further improve your understanding of Replit, project planning, testing, and deploying vibe-coded applications.

Resource name	Link
What is Replit AI?: The AI-Powered Development Platform	**https://medium.com/@tahirbalarabe2/what-is-replit-ai-the-ai-powered-development-platform-46997a5124e5**
Vibe coding 101: from idea to published app	**https://docs.replit.com/tutorials/vibe-coding-101**
Complete Vibe Coding Tutorial: Build a Full Stack App in 30 Min with AI | Matt Palmer	**https://creatoreconomy.so/p/complete-ai-vibe-coding-tutorial-build-full-stack-app-replit-matt-palmer**
Vibe coding tutorial with Replit and GitHub Copilot	**https://www.theserverside.com/tutorial/Vibe-coding-tutorial-with-Replit-and-GitHub-Copilot**
Vibe Coding with Replit	**https://www.datacamp.com/courses/vibe-coding-with-replit**
Efficient prompting with Replit AI	**https://docs.replit.com/tutorials/effective-prompting**
Vibe Coding with Replit AI – Build Real Apps Without Coding	**https://www.udemy.com/course/vibe-coding-with-replit-ai-build-real-apps-without-coding-w/?couponCode=25BBPMXNVD35V1**

Resource name	Link
Lovable, Bolt.new, or Replit ? Vibe coding Tools Review for Beginners in 2025	**https://momen.app/blogs/vibe-coding-tools-review-replit-lovable-boltnew-2025/**
Replit: The Safest Place for Vibe Coding	**https://blog.replit.com/safe-vibe-coding**
From Zero to Replit Fluent: How 9 Apps and 500,000 Users Taught Me to How to 'Vibe' Apps Into Production	**https://www.saastr.com/from-zero-to-replit-fluent-how-9-apps-and-500000-users-taught-me-to-how-to-vibe-apps-into-production/**
What is Replit? Everything you should know	**https://www.prismetric.com/what-is-replit/**
Replit Agent: A Guide With Practical Examples	**https://www.datacamp.com/tutorial/replit-agent-ai-code-editor**
What is Ideation – and How to Prepare for Ideation Sessions	**https://www.interaction-design.org/literature/article/what-is-ideation-and-how-to-prepare-for-ideation-sessions**
What is project planning? Definition, stages, process and examples	**https://plane.so/blog/what-is-project-planning**
Product development life cycle: The 7 stages explained	**https://www.atlassian.com/agile/product-management/product-development**
The Complete Guide to Product Ideation and Discovery: Crafting User-Centric Excellence	**https://www.linkedin.com/pulse/complete-guide-product-ideation-discovery-crafting-user-centric/**
Vibe Coding for Noobs: Product Managers Roadmap to AI coding.	**https://medium.com/@pmclub/vibe-coding-for-noobs-product-managers-roadmap-to-ai-coding-cd90a077ef81**
The Vibe Coding Imperative for Product Managers	**https://cacm.acm.org/blogcacm/the-vibe-coding-imperative-for-product-managers/**
How I Built A Task Management Tool For Almost Nothing	**https://www.techdirt.com/2025/06/03/how-i-built-a-task-management-tool-for-almost-nothing/**
Vibe coding a task manager	**https://joshuawold.com/vibe-coding-a-task-manager/**
Vibe coding examples: Non-developers share their real, working vibe coding projects	**https://zapier.com/blog/vibe-coding-examples/**

Resource name	Link
What are Vibe Coding and Vibe Testing?	**https://testrigor.com/blog/what-are-vibe-coding-and-vibe-testing/**
How Do I Test and Debug Apps Built with Vibe Coding?	**https://thisisglance.com/learning-centre/how-do-i-test-and-debug-apps-built-with-vibe-coding**
How to secure AI-coded (vibe-coded) applications	**https://dev.to/zvone187/how-to-secure-ai-coded-vibe-coded-applications-18ge**
The Importance of Testing Applications Created with AI-Assisted Vibe Coding	**https://www.softwaretestingbureau.com/en/testing-vibe-coding-apps/**
Share your Replit Apps with the world in just a few clicks.	**https://docs.replit.com/category/replit-deployments**
Replit Deployments - the fastest way from idea → production	**https://blog.replit.com/deployments-launch**
How to Use Replit and Deploy Your App: A Beginner's Tutorial with Replit Agent	**https://learn.thedesignsystem.guide/p/complete-guide-to-building-and-deploying**
Complete Guide to Building and Deploying Your First App with Replit	**https://www.deployhq.com/guides/replit**
Using Replit with Node.js to build and deploy apps	**https://blog.logrocket.com/using-replit-node-js-build-deploy-apps/**
Building with AI + Replit: how to rapidly build and deploy AI-powered apps	**https://catalog.bensbites.com/blog/building-with-ai-replit-how-to-rapidly-build-and-deploy-ai-powered-apps**
Replit AI: Can it build production-ready apps from a prompt?	**https://www.dronahq.com/replit-ai-review/**

Table 5.1: *Replit, project planning, testing and deploying vibe-coded applications*

Questions

1. What are the advantages of using Replit vibe coding platform?
2. What is Replit Agent?
3. How do Replit's AI capabilities help with building web applications?
4. Why is project ideation and planning?
5. What are the benefits of project planning?
6. What is the most common mistake users make with vibe coding tools?
7. Why is preparation work required for building vibe codified applications?
8. What does effective ideation involve?
9. What are the things that the planning phase should consider?
10. How can you build a TaskFlow application on Replit?
11. Why is start with the design option recommended for building web applications?
12. When should you start the build functionality function of Replit?
13. What are the steps taken by Replit for development tasks?
14. How can you test the TaskFlow application?
15. What are the advantages of the vibe-coded TaskFlow application?
16. What are the advantages of deploying an application using Replit?
17. What are the different types of configuration and control mechanisms within Replit?
18. What are the key advantages of Replit's deployment architecture?
19. How are security features embedded throughout the deployment infrastructure in Replit?
20. What are the Replit platform's built-in monitoring and analytics capabilities?

Chapter 6
Building Mobile Applications with Vibe Coding

Introduction

In this chapter, we will build a complete mobile application from scratch using prompts and AI assistance with no manual coding. We will create a FitTrack application which is a comprehensive fitness tracking system that demonstrates the entire vibe coding workflow from initial concept to live deployment with native mobile conversion. This production ready application features user authentication, workout tracking for progressive overload monitoring, exercise library management and a responsive design that works seamlessly on mobile devices. You will learn how to translate fitness tracking application ideas into actionable specifications during project planning, develop both backend database logic and frontend interfaces through conversational prompts, ensure application security through automated vulnerability scanning and finally explore multiple options to make your application live for real users through Lovable Cloud hosting and native mobile deployment via Capacitor.

Structure

In this chapter, we will cover the following sections:

- Selecting the vibe coding tool
- Project ideation and planning
- Creating FitTrack application
- Enhancing FitTrack application
- Deploying FitTrack application

Objectives

This chapter will provide a comprehensive, hands-on guide to building complete mobile applications through vibe coding from initial concept to production deployment and native mobile conversion. It will equip you with the practical skills and strategic techniques needed to effectively communicate with Lovable's vibe coding platform at every stage of the development lifecycle.

By the end of this chapter, you will understand the complete vibe coding development process through the construction of the FitTrack application, mastering how to orchestrate AI assistance for planning, architecture design, implementation, visual customization, security scanning, testing, and deployment while navigating real-world challenges such as user authentication and responsive design optimization that arise in production mobile applications. You will also learn how to extend your web application to native mobile platforms using Capacitor, enabling access to device-specific features like camera, notifications, and offline capabilities while maintaining a single codebase.

Selecting the vibe coding tool

Mobile applications have become essential tools in our daily lives, but their development has traditionally required specialized skills in platform-specific languages and frameworks. Vibe coding transforms this landscape by enabling users to create sophisticated mobile applications through natural language descriptions and AI-powered assistance. Mobile vibe coding extends the principles of AI-assisted development to the unique challenges of mobile application development. Unlike traditional mobile development that requires separate codebases for iOS and Android, vibe coding platforms can generate cross-platform solutions from a single set of natural language instructions.

In this chapter, we will be using Lovable (**https://lovable.dev/**), which is one of the popular vibe coding platforms that stands out as an excellent choice for fitness mobile application development through vibe coding. Lovable has gained significant popularity by offering a conversational approach to building full-stack applications, where developers can describe their vision in natural language and watch as the AI transforms their ideas into functional code. The platform generates production-ready React frontends, Node.js backends, and database schemas from prompts, which can then be adapted into mobile-optimized web apps or wrapped as native apps for iOS and Android using tools like Capacitor (**https://capacitorjs.com/**). *Figure 6.1* shows the Lovable homepage, where you can start describing your requirements to build applications using prompts:

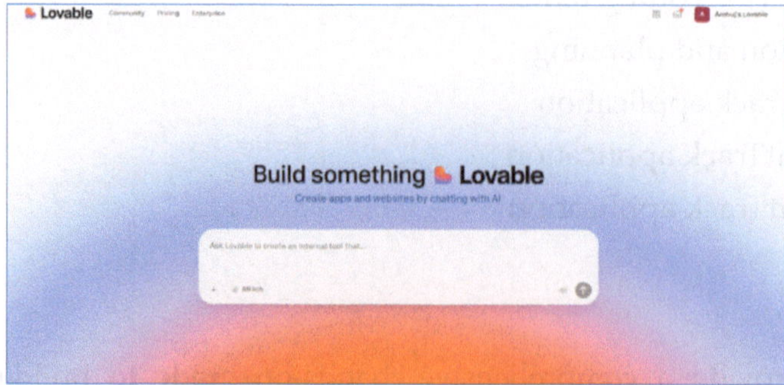

***Figure 6.1**: Lovable homepage where you can start describing your requirements to build applications*

Lovable offers distinct modes for interacting with the AI to facilitate different stages of the development lifecycle. Agent mode allows the AI to operate autonomously, enabling it to plan and execute complex development tasks independently. With agent mode, Lovable can interpret requests, explore the codebase, read and refactor code, proactively debug issues by inspecting logs, and search the web for documentation. In contrast, chat mode is a conversational interface where the AI acts as an interactive assistant without directly modifying the code. This mode is ideal for planning projects, asking questions, and debugging with the AI's guidance. The AI can reason through multi-step problems and can switch to Agent Mode to implement the necessary code changes if the plan is approved.

For mobile-oriented projects, the vibe coding workflow starts with prompting the AI to build a responsive app that targets phone form factors, navigation patterns, and touch interactions from the outset. Lovable's agents can wire up React UI components, backend APIs, authentication, databases, and sync the codebase to GitHub so that users can refine layouts, breakpoints, and interaction patterns as required. The prompts for mobile applications should call out mobile requirements such as single-handed use, bottom navigation, and offline-friendly flows. Lovable Cloud provides managed infrastructure for auth, storage, and serverless functions, which is particularly useful for mobile apps that need secure APIs, image uploads, and background processes without extra development work.

Lovable offers several compelling advantages for building mobile applications by turning our requirements into a full-stack codebase that we can iterate on rapidly while still owning and controlling the underlying source. Lovable's AI coding and agent style workflows help wire up CRUD operations, relationships between users, workouts, and goals, as well as common patterns like role-based access, which eliminates the manual effort needed for each new feature. Lovable is built to support both individual creators and collaborative teams. Its workspace feature provides a shared environment where team members can co-design, review, and iterate on projects in real-time. This facilitates smoother communication and faster feedback cycles, making it suitable for startups and agile teams. In the next section, we will look at the process of project ideation and planning for the development of mobile applications and cross-platform solutions using vibe coding tools.

Project ideation and planning

Developing a fitness tracking application on a vibe coding platform like Lovable requires a distinct approach that blends traditional product management with modern AI prompt engineering strategies. Understanding user needs forms the foundation of any successful application, and this initial phase requires deep research into your target audience's goals, pain points, and behavior patterns. Before approaching any development work on Lovable, you must clearly define whether your users are casual fitness enthusiasts, professional athletes, or individuals seeking health management solutions. Conducting thorough market research to analyze existing fitness applications, identifying gaps in functionality, and unique value propositions will differentiate your solution from existing competitors. Understanding user demographics, preferences, and fitness needs will allow you to create detailed user personas that will guide every subsequent decision in your development process.

Think through essential questions such as the core problem your application needs to solve for users, recognizing that technology exists to serve human needs rather than showcase technical capabilities. Consider who will actually use this application in their daily lives, moving beyond abstract personas to envision real individuals with specific pain points, like the busy parent squeezing in 20-minute home workouts or the powerlifter tracking complex progressive overload cycles. Define what success looks like from the end user's perspective rather than from a technical standpoint, focusing on outcomes like improved consistency, measurable strength gains, weight management, or increased motivation rather than metrics like database schema complexity or UI component libraries used.

The most common mistake users make with vibe coding tools like Lovable is providing vague requests that leave too much interpretation to the AI, resulting in generic implementations that technically fulfill the literal request but miss the underlying intent that makes applications truly useful. When you tell Lovable to **`Build me a fitness tracker`**, you are essentially asking it to guess at hundreds of implicit decisions about input methods, data visualization, exercise libraries, and gamification elements without providing the context necessary to make informed choices aligned with your vision. Vibe coding tools work best when you provide clear and specific direction rather than simply stating something like **`Create a workout app`** because specificity constrains the solution space in productive ways that channel AI creativity toward relevant innovations rather than generic templates.

This preparation means doing the work upfront to map out user journeys that trace the complete experience from initial onboarding through daily gym usage to eventual outcomes such as identifying critical moments where users feel pride in a new personal record or frustration when modifying a routine mid-workout. This also involves researching existing solutions in your problem space to understand what patterns users have come to expect and what opportunities exist for improvement. This competitive analysis does not mean copying features blindly but rather learning from the collective wisdom embedded in mature applications while identifying gaps that represent genuine opportunities.

The planning phase should also consider the broader context in which the application will exist, including how users will discover it, the physical environment where they will use it (such as a crowded gym or outdoors), and what related tools it needs to complement. A fitness system designed for casual walkers has fundamentally different requirements than one built for competitive athletes, even though both involve tracking physical activity. Understanding these contextual factors shapes decisions about whether your application should prioritize large and thumb-friendly buttons for sweaty hands, whether it needs robust offline capabilities for gyms with poor signal, and whether data export is critical for users who want to own their training logs. This holistic planning ensures that when you begin prompting Lovable, you are not just requesting isolated features but orchestrating a coherent system that addresses real needs within actual usage contexts, which dramatically increases the likelihood that your application will deliver genuine value rather than becoming another abandoned prototype.

In the next section, we will look at the development of mobile applications using prompts on Lovable.

Creating FitTrack application

For building FitTrack, which is our fitness tracking mobile application, we will use the prompt, **`I want to build a mobile-first fitness tracking application named FitTrack where users can log workout sessions, create custom exercise routines, track progressive overload stats like weight and reps, and visualize strength gains with charts`**, in Lovable, as shown in *Figure 6.2*. Lovable immediately interprets these requirements and generates a fully functional application, often inferring necessary features like bottom navigation bars, exercise databases, and input forms. This rapid visualization process transforms vague ideas into a live application in seconds, allowing you to critique and refine the actual user experience through the conversational sidebar, turning the development process into a real-time dialogue where you iterate on a working product rather than static specifications.

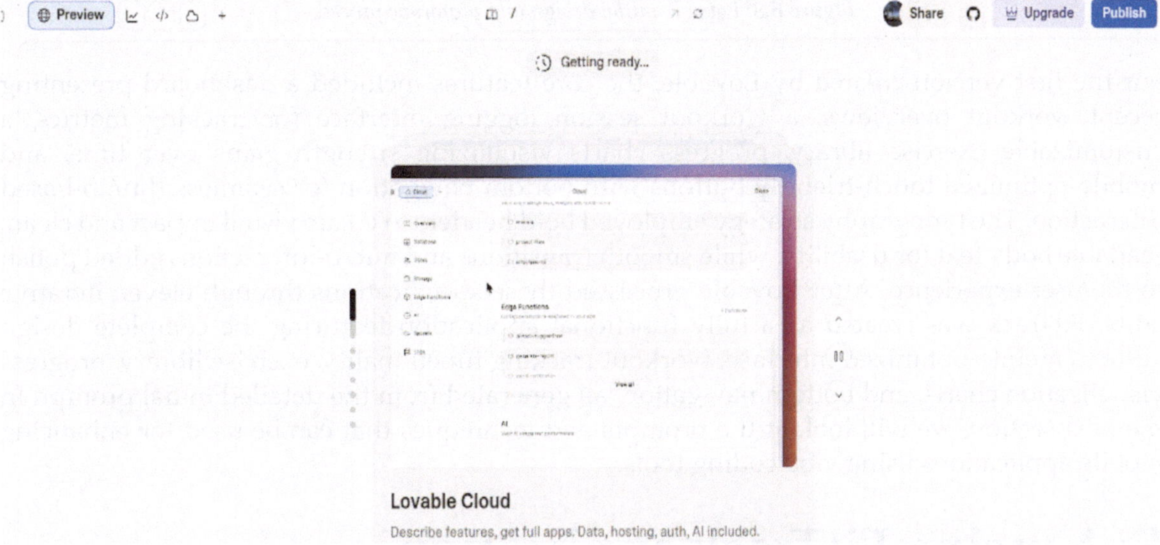

Figure 6.2: Lovable vibe coding applications based on the user requirements

The Lovable vibe coding tool designed the FitTrack application as a mobile-first experience, emphasizing clean interfaces, data-focused displays, and motivational design elements. The initial prompt specified comprehensive requirements, including workout logging capabilities, custom routine creation, progressive overload tracking, and strength visualization charts, all optimized for mobile usage with bottom navigation. The design system centered on a vibrant teal primary color to evoke athletic freshness, complemented by orange accents for motivation and green indicators for achievements, while incorporating bold hero gradients for visual impact and subtle card depth for hierarchy. *Figure 6.3* shows the Lovable initial design and prototype process after working on the user requirements:

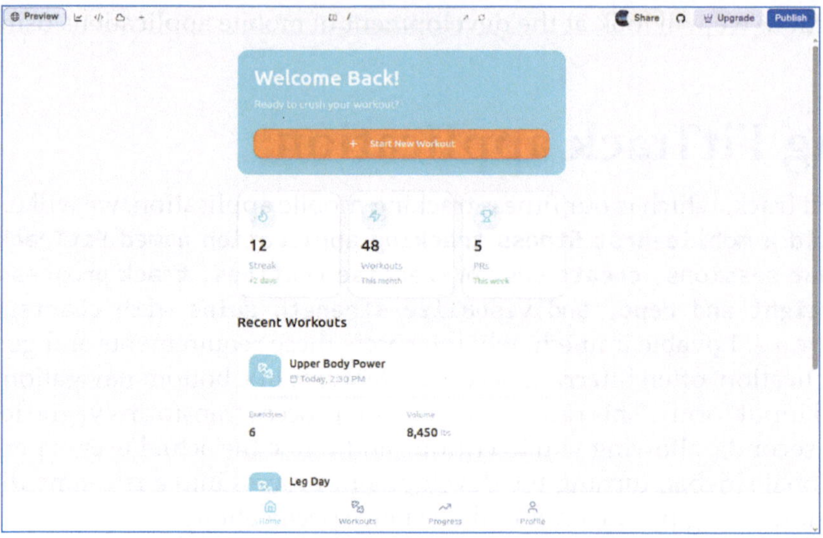

***Figure 6.3**: Lovable initial design and prototype process*

For the first version created by Lovable, the core features included a dashboard presenting recent workout overviews, a workout session logging interface for tracking metrics, a customizable exercise library, progress charts visualizing strength gains over time, and mobile-optimized touch-friendly buttons with bottom navigation for seamless thumb-based interaction. The typography strategy employed bold headers to create visual impact and clean, readable body text for usability, while smooth transitions and micro-interactions added polish to the user experience. After Lovable processed these specifications through eleven iterative edits, FitTrack was created as a fully functional application featuring the complete design system, mobile-optimized interface, workout tracking functionality, exercise library, progress visualization charts, and bottom navigation, all generated from the detailed initial prompt. In the next section, we will look at the prompts and techniques that can be used for enhancing mobile applications using vibe coding tools.

Enhancing FitTrack application

Lovable offers multiple paths for enhancement where users can refine the visual design, strategically plan advanced functionality, and integrate persistent backend systems to transform FitTrack from a prototype into a production-ready application. For design refinement, users can iterate on the color palette by providing specific prompts, such as, **`Refine the primary teal color to be more vibrant and energetic blue. Adjust the orange accent buttons to have a subtle gradient from #FF6B35 to #FF8C42. Add a dark-to-light gradient overlay on the dashboard hero section that transitions to transparent for better depth perception`**. When Lovable processes these refinement requests, the system interprets the design intent and immediately implements the changes, updating the primary color scheme to vibrant blue throughout the application interface, applying the specified orange gradient to all accent buttons for consistent visual language, and enhancing the hero section with the depth overlay that adds dimensional sophistication to the dashboard, as shown in the following figure:

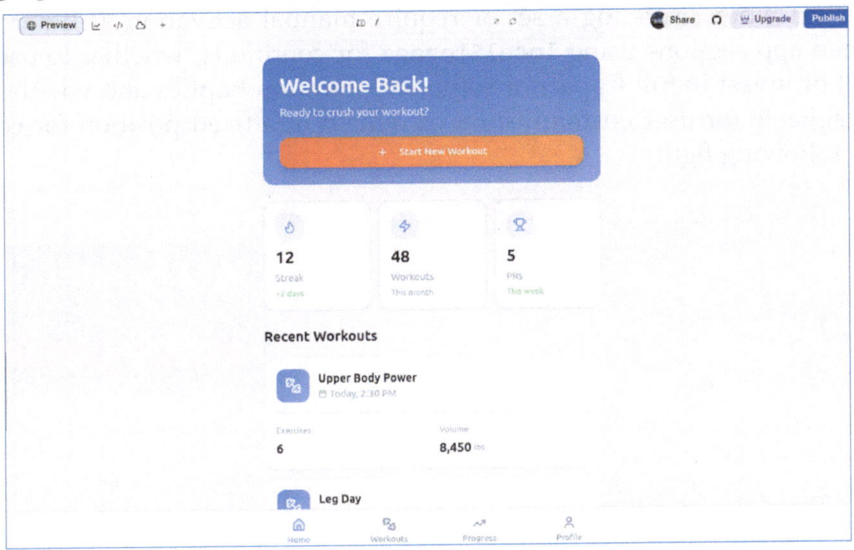

Figure 6.4: Enhancing applications on Lovable

You can also add new features through Lovable's chat mode, such as a workout timer feature with a prompt, like **`I want to plan a rest timer feature for between sets. Users should see a countdown (default 90 seconds and customizable 30-300s), receive haptic feedback when time expires, and have quick +15s/-15s adjustment buttons. The timer should persist across navigation and show as a floating widget during active workouts.`** Lovable's chat mode responds by discussing the architectural approach before implementation and proposes a global **`RestTimerContext`** for state management that tracks the current countdown time, stores default and custom duration preferences within the 30-300 second range, monitors timer active state, and maintains awareness of the overall workout session status. The component structure includes a floating **`RestTimerWidget`** displaying a circular progress indicator with countdown visualization, the +15s/-15s quick adjustment buttons for intuitive time modifications and start/pause/reset controls that remain visible across all navigation tabs during active workout sessions plus a **`RestTimerSettings`** configuration panel where users set their default rest duration through a slider interface and configure options for auto starting the timer after completing a set along with sound and haptic preferences.

For haptic feedback implementation, Lovable presents two technical options, namely, the Vibration API, which works immediately in mobile browsers with simple pattern vibration and requires no additional setup, or a full Capacitor (**https://capacitorjs.com/**) integration that provides richer native haptic feedback but requires native app configuration with the Vibration API recommended for simpler immediate functionality. The floating widget behavior positions it fixed at the bottom right of the screen with optional draggable functionality and makes it dismissible while automatically re-showing whenever the timer is running. Before implementing the feature, Lovable asks critical clarifying questions such as whether the timer should auto-start when users log a set or require manual activation, if timer state should persist between app sessions using **`localStorage`** for continuity, whether to use the simpler Vibration API or invest in full Capacitor setup for premium haptics and whether the widget should be draggable for user customization or remain in a fixed position for consistency as shown in the following figure:

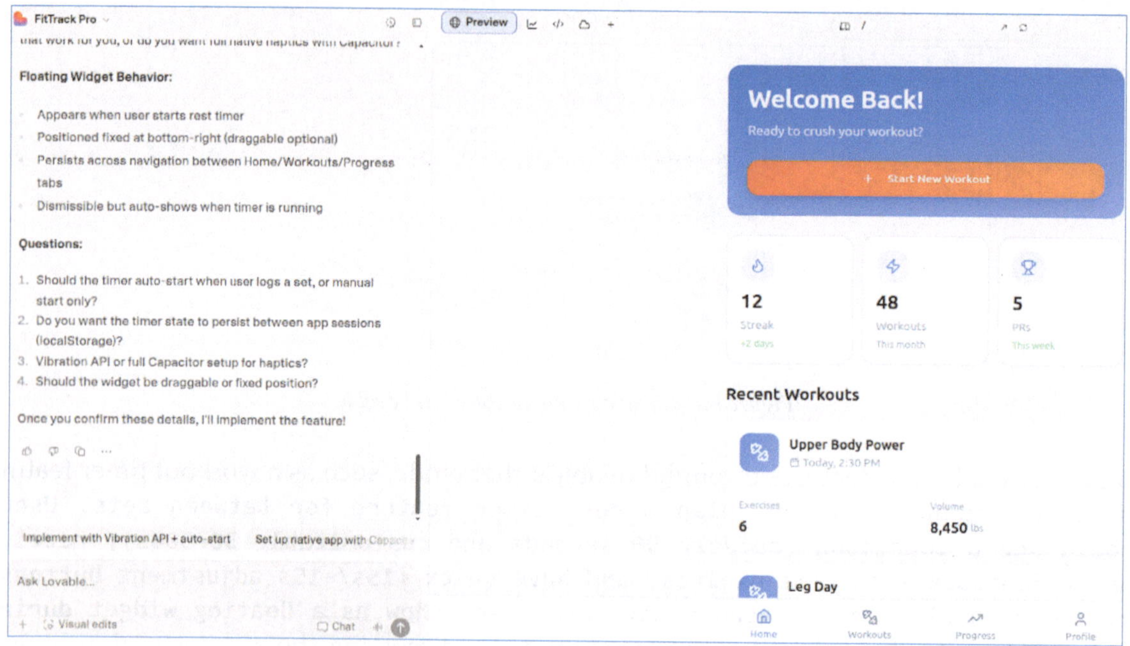

Figure 6.5: Implementing haptic feedback using Lovable

For now, we will use the Vibration API and reply to the questions with the follow-on prompt as, **`Use Vibration API for haptic feedback and implement the rest timer with auto-start after completing sets. Timer state should persist in localStorage.`** Lovable acknowledges these requirements and proceeds with implementation, leveraging the browser-based Vibration API, which triggers tactile feedback through JavaScript's **`navigator.vibrate()`** method, which is a widely supported approach in modern mobile browsers like Chrome and Firefox that provides haptic sensations without requiring native app permissions. Through iterative edits, Lovable successfully implements the complete rest timer feature with integrated Vibration API haptics that trigger when the countdown expires, auto-start functionality that launches the timer immediately when users tap the workout completion button, **`localStorage`** persistence that saves timer preferences and a floating widget displaying the circular countdown visualization with +15s/-15s quick adjustment controls that remain accessible during active workouts as shown in the following figure:

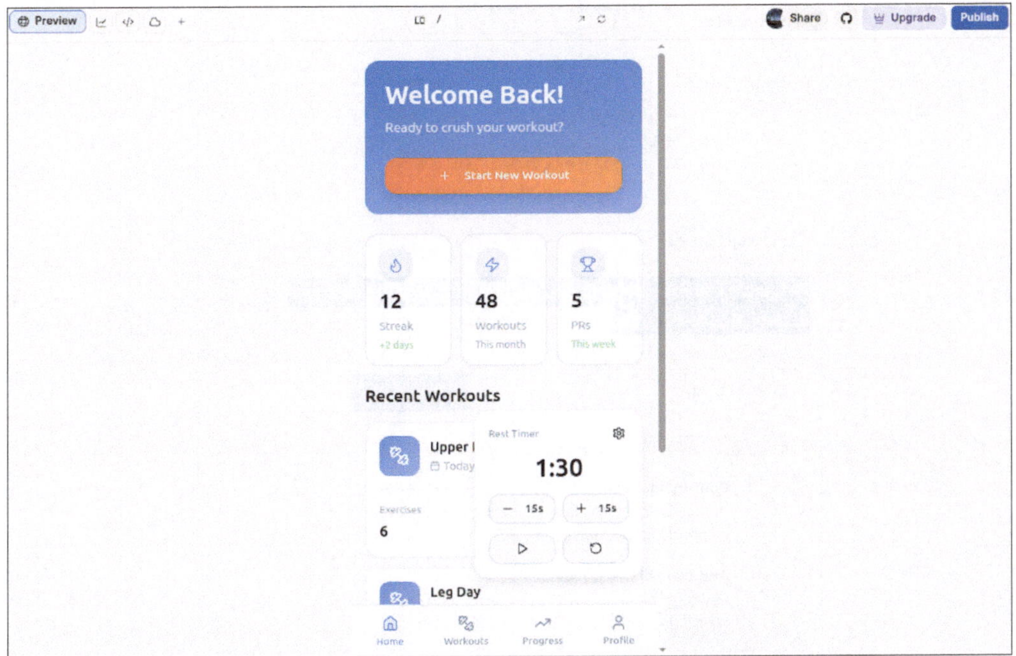

Figure 6.6: Timer with Vibration API for haptic feedback

We can ask Lovable to integrate backend capabilities in our application through a prompt such as **`Integrate Lovable Cloud authentication and backend database for persistent storage`**. For backend development, Lovable features a comprehensive cloud infrastructure called *Lovable Cloud* that provides database, storage, authentication, and backend logic functionality, which are all ready to use out of the box without complex configuration. Lovable Cloud operates as a built-in backend solution that eliminates the need for external server setup by hosting data on secure servers, allowing applications like FitTrack to transition from a frontend-only prototype storing temporary data in local storage to a production-ready application with persistent multi-device synchronization and user account management. The integration process follows a streamlined workflow where Lovable asks users when features require backend functionality, offering options such as allowing the integration for the current project, which creates and connects a cloud project with all necessary backend features or denying the integration temporarily while preserving the option to enable it later as shown in the following figure:

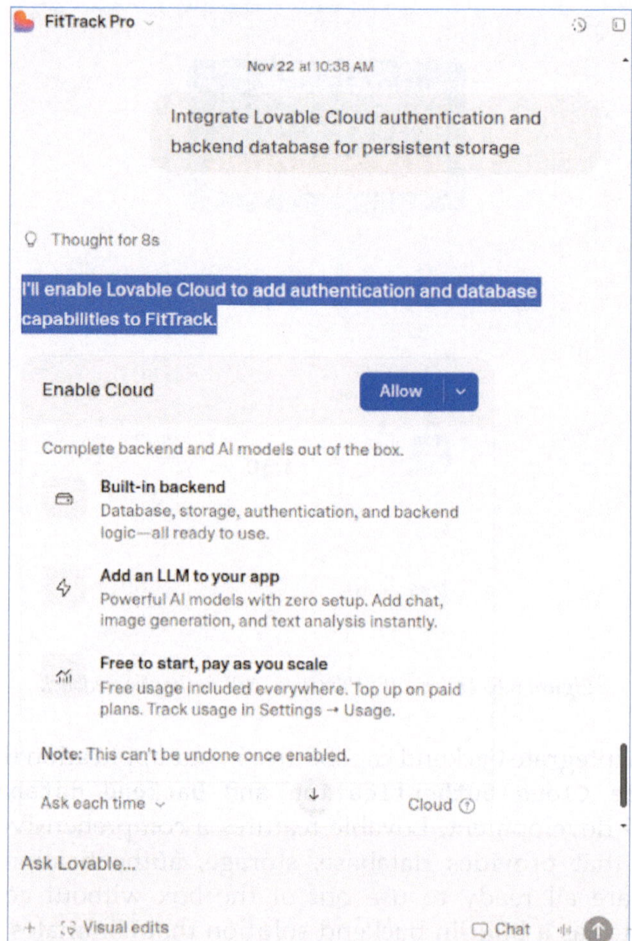

***Figure 6.7**: Integrating backend capabilities using Lovable*

We need to enable *Lovable Cloud* for FitTrack which provides a comprehensive backend infrastructure that includes authentication for creating and managing user logins, a PostgreSQL database for storing workouts, exercises and progress data persistently across devices, backend functions for running server-side code to handle complex operations and file storage capabilities for managing user profile images and workout media such as progress photos or form check videos. Upon approval of Lovable Cloud functionality, the tool implements a complete authentication system featuring email/password login functionality while simultaneously creating the database schema with tables for storing workout sessions, exercise logs, user profiles, and custom exercises, all protected by row-level security policies that ensure users can only access their own fitness data. *Figure 6.8* shows the cloud configuration options available in Lovable:

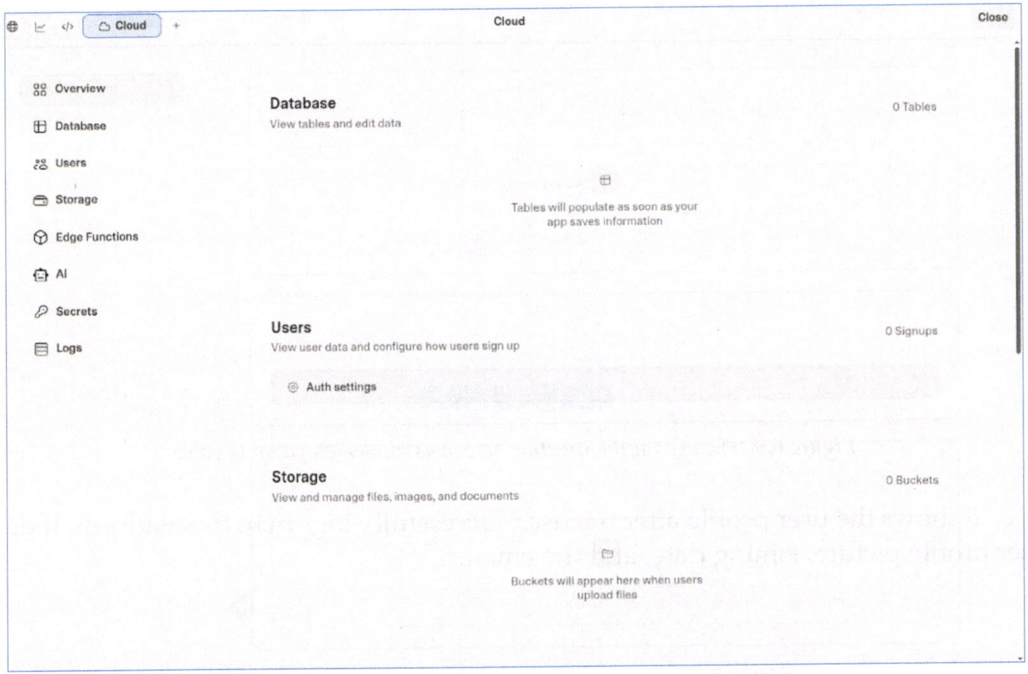

Figure 6.8*: Cloud configuration options available in Lovable*

Lovable implements comprehensive authentication and database infrastructure through a multi-step process that begins with creating a PostgreSQL schema featuring four core tables. The profiles table stores user information like email, full name, and avatar **`url`** with automatic timestamp tracking. The exercises table maintains a user's custom exercise library with muscle group categorization and unique name constraints. The workouts table records workout sessions with date, name, and optional notes, and the **`workout_sets`** table captures detailed performance metrics, including set number, reps, and weight as decimal values linked to both workouts and exercises through foreign key relationships. Every table implements row-level security policies, ensuring users can only view, create, update, and delete their own data through ID verification. The system includes automated triggers and functions such as **"`handle_new_user`"** which automatically creates a profile record whenever a new user signs up by reading email and full name from authentication metadata, and **"`handle_updated_at`"** which maintains accurate timestamps on profiles whenever modifications occur. After configuring the database schema and addressing security requirements, Lovable deploys authentication components that create signup/login pages with email/password functionality, integrates auto-confirm email settings for streamlined onboarding and connect all workout tracking features to the persistent backend transforming FitTrack from a local storage based prototype into a production ready application where users can securely create accounts, log workouts that sync across devices and maintain their complete fitness history with enterprise grade security protecting their personal training data. *Figure 6.9* shows the user authentication screen as implemented by Lovable:

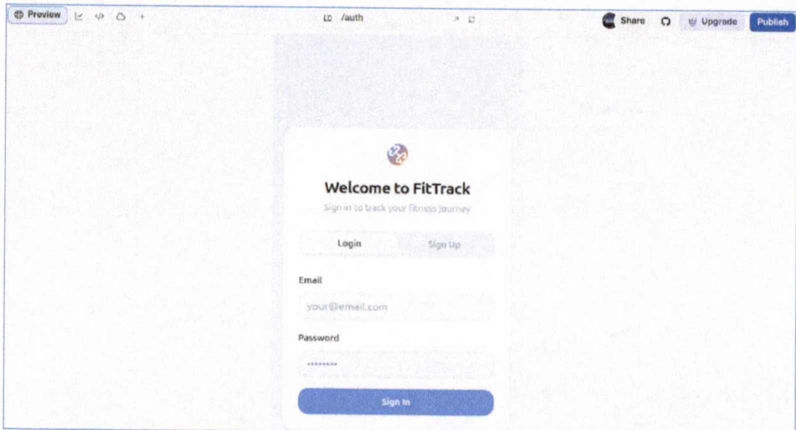

Figure 6.9: The user authentication screen as implemented by Lovable

Figure 6.10 shows the user profile after the user successfully logs in to the platform. It displays the user profile picture, joining date, and the email:

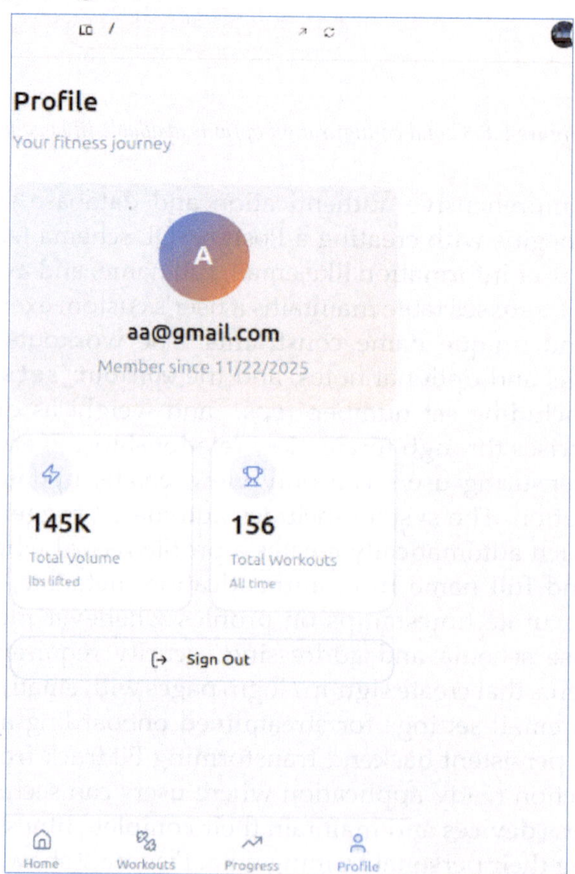

Figure 6.10: The user profile after the user successfully logs in on the platform

Lovable also has a code section (also called code mode) that provides direct access to view and edit the project's raw source code within the Lovable editor, bridging the gap between AI-generated applications and traditional development workflows. This feature allows developers to inspect and modify the human-readable codebase that is generated by Lovable. The code editor enables users to make precise changes supporting advanced customizations, debugging, and integration of custom logic. The code can seamlessly integrate with GitHub, allowing developers to export projects to their repositories for version control, collaborative development, and deployment through external services like Vercel. The code mode is available via the code icon shown in the following figure:

```
import { Toaster } from "@/components/ui/toaster";
import { Toaster as Sonner } from "@/components/ui/sonner";
import { TooltipProvider } from "@/components/ui/tooltip";
import { QueryClient, QueryClientProvider } from "@tanstack/react-query";
import { BrowserRouter, Routes, Route } from "react-router-dom";
import { AuthProvider } from "./contexts/AuthContext";
import Index from "./pages/Index";
import Auth from "./pages/Auth";
import NotFound from "./pages/NotFound";

const queryClient = new QueryClient();

const App = () => (
  <QueryClientProvider client={queryClient}>
    <AuthProvider>
      <TooltipProvider>
        <Toaster />
        <Sonner />
        <BrowserRouter>
          <Routes>
            <Route path="/" element={<Index />} />
            <Route path="/auth" element={<Auth />} />
            {/* ADD ALL CUSTOM ROUTES ABOVE THE CATCH-ALL "*" ROUTE */}
            <Route path="*" element={<NotFound />} />
          </Routes>
        </BrowserRouter>
      </TooltipProvider>
    </AuthProvider>
  </QueryClientProvider>
);

export default App;
```

Figure 6.11: *Code mode on Lovable*

Lovable provides a visual edits section, which is a Figma-like editing experience that allows developers to modify UI elements directly on the page without writing prompts or consuming AI credits, as shown in the following figure:

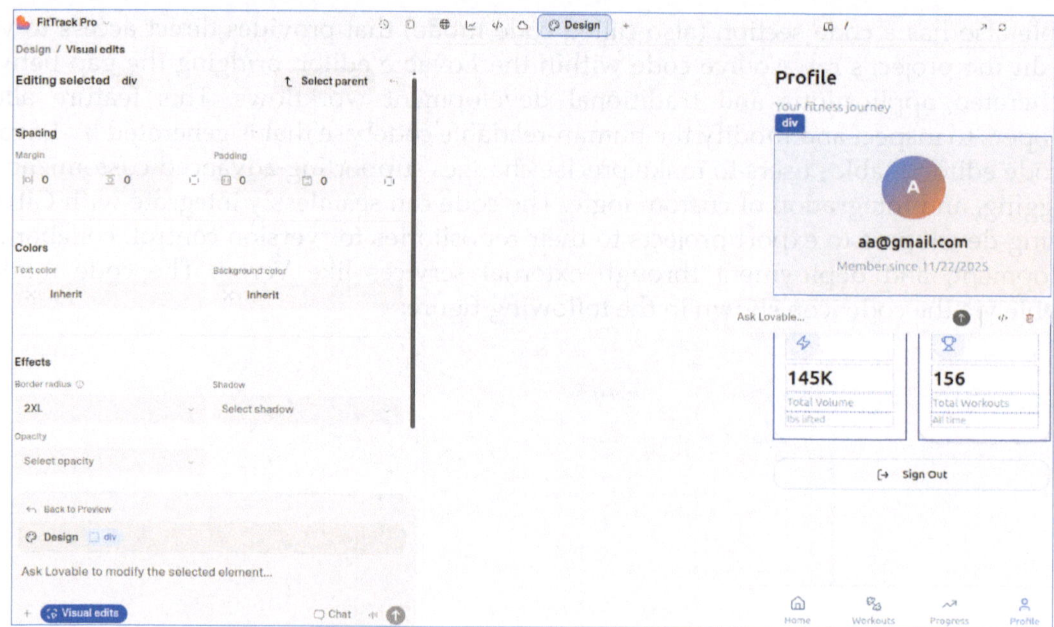

Figure 6.12: Visual edits section on Lovable

The visual edits feature enables users to select any component and instantly adjust its properties, including text content, colors, fonts, sizing, margins, padding, borders, and transparency through an intuitive sidebar interface. Visual edits supports advanced capabilities such as multi-selecting elements for batch modifications, precise layout controls for alignment and positioning, enhanced text formatting with line breaks and inline styling, and image replacement via uploads or URLs. Changes made through visual edits are applied instantly to the live preview and can be saved without additional AI processing, making it ideal for rapid prototyping and fine-tuning design details. In the next section, we will look at the development of mobile applications and cross-platform solutions using vibe coding tools.

Deploying FitTrack application

Lovable provides a security scan feature, which is an AI-powered security analysis tool that automatically examines your application for potential vulnerabilities before publishing. When you attempt to publish a Lovable app connected to a backend, the platform runs a comprehensive scan that checks for common security issues, including **Row Level Security** (**RLS**) policy configurations, exposed secrets, SQL injection risks, **cross-site scripting** (**XSS**) vulnerabilities, authentication flow weaknesses, and input sanitization problems. The scan integrates directly into the publishing workflow, displaying warnings in the publish dialog and requiring confirmation if serious issues are detected. Additionally, users can request on-demand security reviews at any time by asking in Lovable chat to **scan security**, which triggers a detailed analysis of the entire codebase with specific recommendations for remediation, as shown in the following figure:

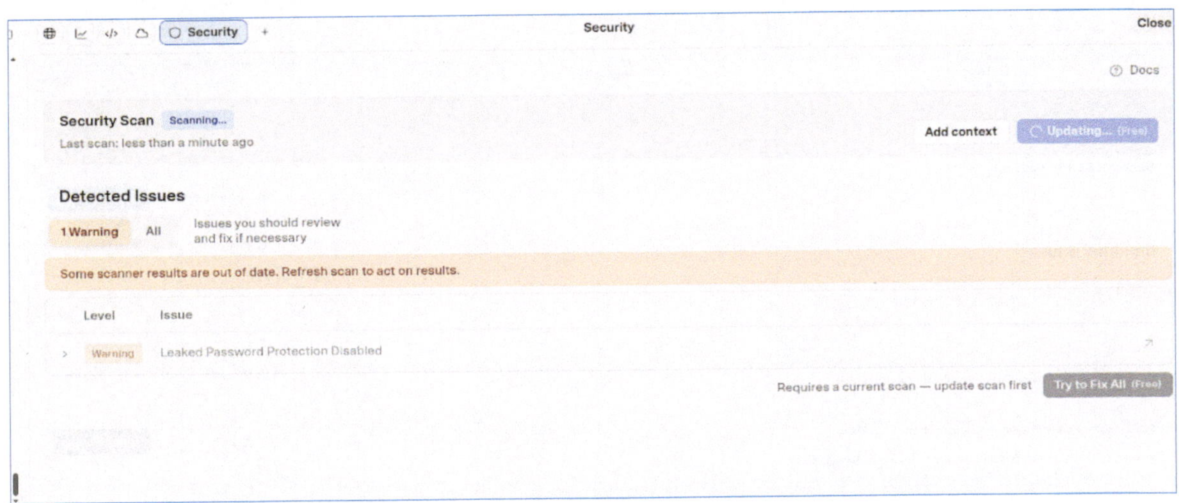

***Figure 6.13**: Lovable's scan security feature that triggers a detailed security analysis*

The security review on FitTrack confirms that the application demonstrates excellent security practices across authentication, database protection, input validation, and code implementation through properly configured authentication with secure session handling, correctly configured email redirect URLs, and automatic unauthenticated user redirection. The database implementation has RLS enabled on all four tables, where RLS policies correctly scope access to the user ID, which ensures users can only interact with their own data. Input validation follows security best practices through schemas validating all authentication inputs with email format verification, password minimum length requirements, full name maximum length constraints of 100 characters, and functions preventing whitespace issues. Minor observations by security review include the profiles table intentionally lacking INSERT or DELETE policies because profiles are created automatically via database triggers during signup, representing correct architectural design. The review confirms that no critical vulnerabilities exist with properly implemented authentication, appropriate security policies protecting all database tables, and input validation securing user authentication flows. There is a security review warning about leaked password protection that represents an informational notice about activating the password **Have I Been Pwned** (**HIBP**) check in Lovable cloud settings, rather than a code vulnerability. For future development, recommendations include validating all user inputs for workout logging functionality before database operations, adding reasonable length limits to text fields like exercise names and workout notes, preventing abuse, considering rate limiting for production-sensitive endpoints, enabling multi-factor authentication for additional security layers, and monitoring authentication events and database queries to detect suspicious behavior, as shown in the following figure:

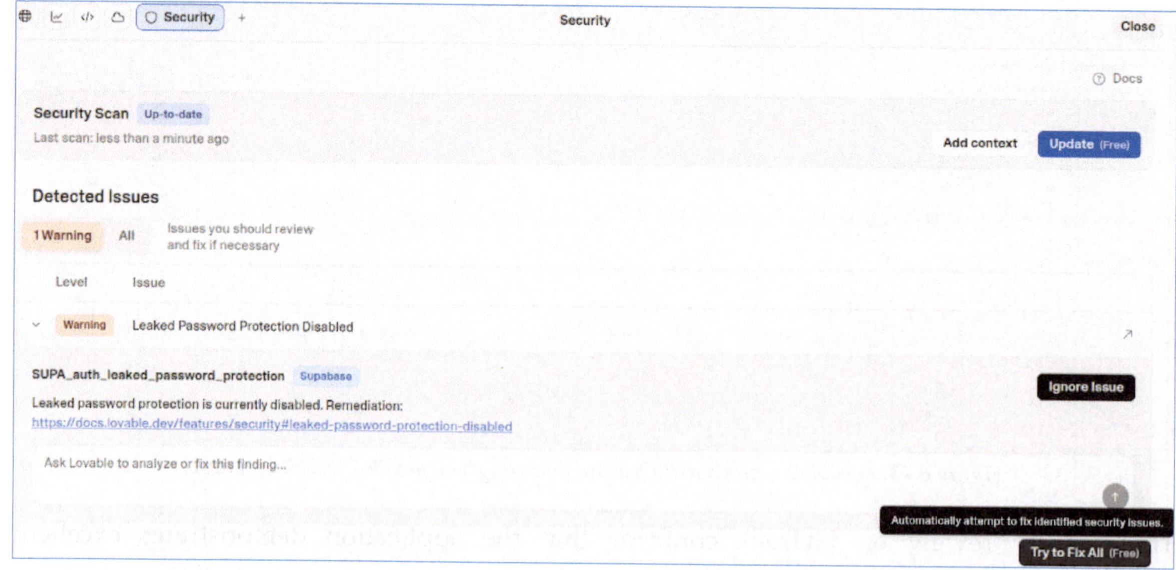

Figure 6.14: Fixing security scan issues on Lovable

To enhance authentication security and fix the warning in your Lovable project, navigate to the **Cloud** tab and access the Authentication settings section. Within these settings, you can enable Leaked Password Protection, which is a critical security feature that leverages the HIBP database to reject passwords that have been exposed in known data breaches or are easy to guess, as shown in *Figure 6.15*. This hosting and infrastructure level configuration acts as a frontline defense by automatically checking user passwords against millions of compromised credentials before allowing account creation or password changes.

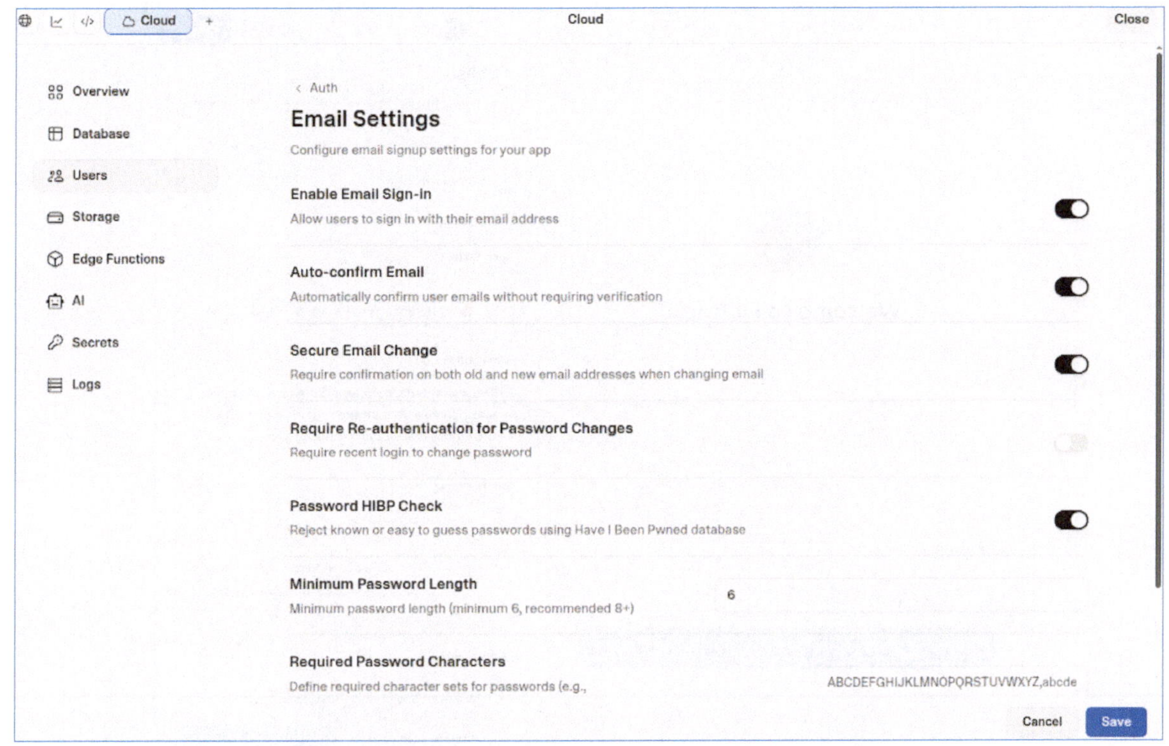

***Figure 6.15**: Enhancing authentication security on Lovable*

Lovable provides a **Publish** feature that allows you to deploy your project and make it live on the web with a single click, and it automatically generates a public URL at `[project-name].lovable.app`. Before publishing, you can configure essential website metadata, including a custom icon, title (such as FitTrack - Your Personal Fitness Companion), and a detailed description that appears in search results and social media shares to optimize discoverability, as shown in *Figure 6.16*. Once published, your app is instantly accessible at the generated URL (like **https://fitrack-progress-hub.lovable.app**), allowing users worldwide to access your application without additional deployment steps. Paid plans offer custom domain support, while business and enterprise tiers provide granular access controls to restrict visibility to workspace members, making it suitable for internal tools and sensitive projects.

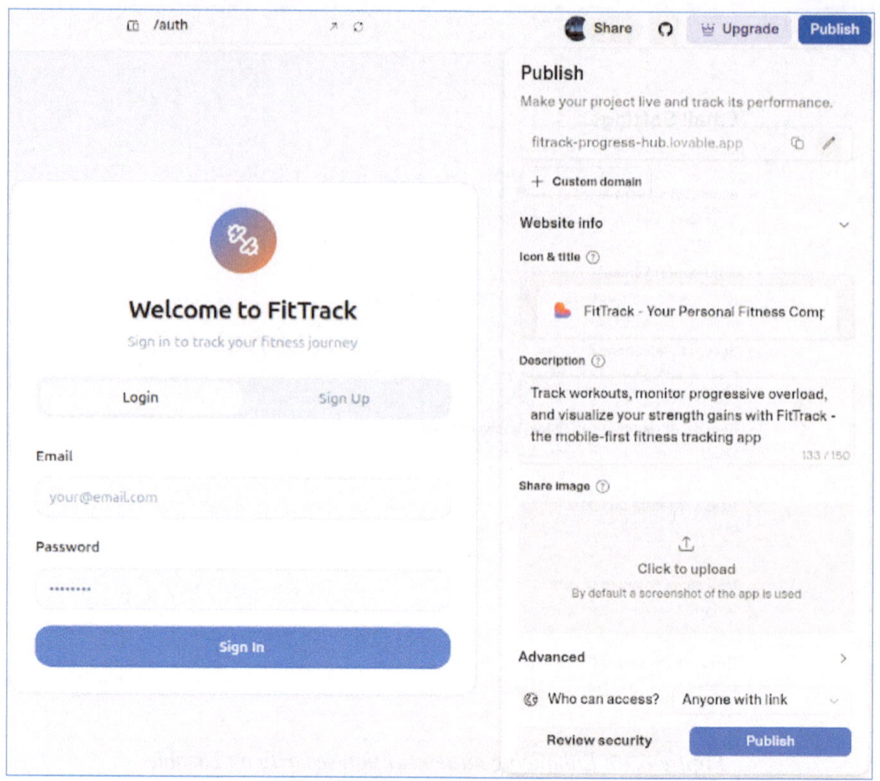

Figure 6.16: Lovable's Publish feature that allows you to deploy your project on the web

To deploy our application, we can use native Capacitor (**https://capacitorjs.com/**), which is a modern and open-source native runtime developed by the Ionic team that makes it easy to convert web apps into fully native mobile applications for iOS and Android. By acting as a bridge between your web code and native device features, Capacitor allows you to use familiar web technologies such as JavaScript, HTML, and CSS while still gaining seamless access to native APIs such as camera, geolocation, notifications, file system, haptics, accelerometer, and more. This makes it ideal for projects like FitTrack, where cross-platform mobile access and hardware integration are essential.

To convert your FitTrack web app into a native mobile application, begin by prompting Lovable's chat mode with instructions such as, **`Convert to native runtime in mobile using Capacitor`** to receive step-by-step guidance on configuring Capacitor within your project, as illustrated in *Figure 6.17*. Lovable will automatically generate the necessary configuration files setting up Capacitor's cross-platform runtime to bridge your web code with native mobile functionality. The conversion workflow starts by exporting your project to GitHub using the GitHub button in Lovable's interface, then cloning the repository locally and installing required dependencies with **`npm install`**. This ensures your development environment is properly configured with Capacitor's CLI and core libraries. You can add the target mobile platforms by running **`npx cap add ios`** for iOS development (requires macOS with Xcode installed) or **`npx cap add android`** for Android development (requires Android Studio). After platform setup, build your web application using **`npm run build`** to generate optimized production assets. To launch your app on a physical device or emulator, execute **`npx cap run android`** for Android or **`npx cap run ios`** for iOS, which automatically compiles the native application and deploys it to your connected device.

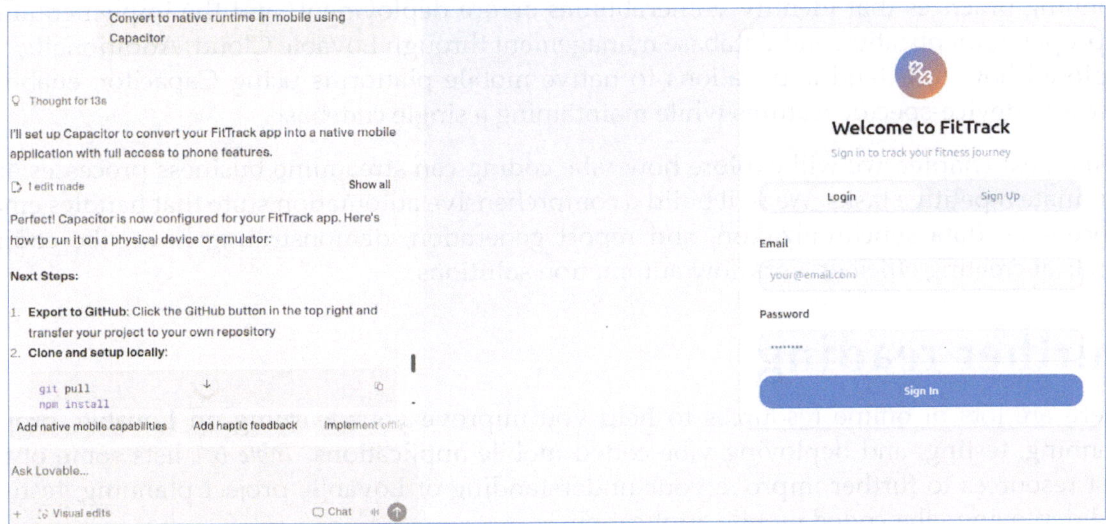

Figure 6.17: Converting application to native runtime in mobile using Capacitor

Lovable's platform, combined with Capacitor's native runtime capabilities, represents a paradigm shift in how modern mobile applications are developed and deployed. By leveraging Lovable's AI-powered development environment with features like **Visual edits** for hands-on UI customization, **Code mode** for direct source access, and automated security scans for vulnerability detection, users can rapidly prototype and iterate on mobile applications while maintaining enterprise-grade quality standards. The seamless integration with Lovable Cloud's authentication system, including advanced protections, ensures that security is built into the foundation rather than added on as an afterthought. The combination of Lovable's vibe coding platform and Capacitor's native runtime creates a development pathway that reduces technical complexity, accelerates time-to-market, and enables iterative improvements. As mobile development continues to evolve, platforms that bridge web and native technologies while preserving developer productivity will remain essential tools for shipping high-quality applications efficiently.

Conclusion

In this chapter, we learned about the complete end-to-end process of building production-ready mobile applications through vibe coding methodologies and their role in democratizing software development. We navigated the comprehensive workflow from tool selection and project ideation through architecture design, implementation, visual customization, security scanning, testing, and deployment to create the FitTrack application, which is a fully functional fitness tracking system. Throughout this development journey, we identified several patterns that consistently drive vibe coding success across application types. These patterns include the formulation of clear and iterative prompts that guide AI tools toward desired outcomes, the use of visual edits for hands-on UI refinement, the establishment of systematic security scanning practices that identify vulnerabilities before deployment, and the implementation of proper authentication and database management through Lovable Cloud. Additionally, we explored how to extend applications to native mobile platforms using Capacitor, enabling access to device-specific features while maintaining a single codebase.

In the next chapter, we will explore how vibe coding can streamline business processes and eliminate repetitive tasks. We will build a comprehensive automation suite that handles email processing, data synchronization, and report generation, demonstrating how vibe coding excels at creating efficient workflow automation solutions.

Further reading

There are lots of online resources to help you improve your learning on Lovable, project planning, testing, and deploying vibe-coded mobile applications. *Table 6.1* lists some of the best resources to further improve your understanding of Lovable, project planning, testing, and deploying vibe-coded mobile applications.

Resource name	Link
Vibe Coding: The Future of Software Development or Just a Trend?	**https://lovable.dev/blog/what-is-vibe-coding**
Vibe Coding on Lovable AI for Absolute Beginners (Frontend, Backend, Prompting - all of it)	**https://lovable.dev/video/vibe-coding-on-lovable-ai-for-absolute-beginners-frontend-backend-prompting-all-of-it**
Lovable AI: Complete Guide for Vibe Coding	**https://www.udemy.com/course/lovable-ai-complete-guide-for-vibe-coding/**
Vibe Coding with Lovable, Cursor, Windsurf, and Claude Code (4 Amazing Tools)	**https://www.nocode.mba/articles/vibe-coding-4-tools**
Honest review of Lovable from an AI engineer	**https://medium.com/firebird-technologies/honest-review-of-lovable-from-an-ai-engineer-38e49f7069fb**
Lovable AI: A Guide With Demo Project	**https://www.datacamp.com/tutorial/lovable-ai**
I tried the Lovable no-code app development platform, an found how it uses AI to not just create, but also extend, and debug fully responsive, feature-rich web apps.	**https://www.techradar.com/pro/software-services/lovable-review**

Resource name	Link
5 Steps to Take Your Mobile App Project from Idea to Reality	**https://thunkable.com/blog/prepare-for-takeoff-5-steps-for-planning-your-mobile-app-project**
Mobile App Development Process – Step 1 Ideation & Product Discovery	**https://mobisoftinfotech.com/resources/blog/mobile-app-development-process-product-discovery**
Mobile App Development: From Ideation to Polished Product	**https://brightmarbles.io/blog/mobile-app-development-from-ideation-to-polished-product/**
Major Steps In Planning For A Mobile App	**https://www.telliant.com/major-steps-in-planning-for-a-mobile-app/**
Mobile App Development Plan: Concept, Audiences, Design, Wireframing	**https://www.appventurez.com/blog/mobile-app-development-planning**
I Built an IOS App in 3 Days with Literally No Prior Swift Knowledge	**https://towardsdatascience.com/i-built-an-ios-app-in-3-days-with-literally-no-prior-swift-knowledge/**
How to build a web app using vibe coding and natural language prompts	**https://graphite.com/guides/vibe-coding-web-app**
Vibe Coding Your First Mobile App in 2025	**https://addjam.com/blog/2025-05-06/vibe-coding-your-first-mobile-app-in-2025/**
Transform Your Lovable.dev Next.js App into Native Mobile Apps with Capacitor	**https://capgo.app/blog/transform-lovable-dev-app-to-mobile-with-capacitor/**
Publish your app on Lovable	**https://docs.lovable.dev/features/publish**
Modes - Lovable	**https://docs.lovable.dev/features/modes**
How Capacitor Works	**https://capacitorjs.jp/blog/how-capacitor-works**
Capacitor: Everything You've Ever Wanted to Know	**https://ionic.io/blog/capacitor-everything-youve-ever-wanted-to-know**
Passing the Security Vibe Check: The Dangers of Vibe Coding	**https://www.databricks.com/blog/passing-security-vibe-check-dangers-vibe-coding**
Lovable is where vibe coding meets security	**https://lovable.dev/blog/lovable-security**
Vibe Coding Full-Stack: Build a Fitness App from Scratch	**https://www.udemy.com/course/live-vibe-coding-fullstack-build-a-fitness-app-test-fix/?couponCode=CP251118BG1**
Versioning, Dev Mode & Lovable Livestream with Clerk	**https://lovable.dev/blog/versioning-dev-mode**

Table 6.1: *Lovable, project planning, testing, and deploying vibe-coded mobile applications*

Questions

1. What are the advantages of using the Lovable vibe coding platform?
2. What is the Lovable Agent?
3. How is Lovable Chat mode different from an agent?
4. Why is Lovable one of the most popular vibe coding tools?
5. How is Capacitor used to build native apps?
6. What are the advantages offered by Lovable for building mobile applications?
7. How can teams use Lovable for collaboration?
8. What is the common mistake users make with vibe coding tools like Lovable?
9. How can you iterate on features in Lovable?
10. What is the Vibration API?
11. What are the backend capabilities offered by Lovable?
12. How can you manage databases in Lovable?
13. What are the different authentication methods available in Lovable?
14. What are the advantages of using code mode in Lovable?
15. Why does Lovable offer a visual edits feature?
16. How can you publish applications?
17. Why is a security scan important for vibe-coded applications?
18. How can you fix the security vulnerabilities identified?
19. What are the advantages of using Capacitor's native runtime capabilities?
20. What are the advantages of building mobile applications using Lovable and Capacitor?

Join our Discord space

Join our Discord workspace for latest updates, offers, tech happenings around the world, new releases, and sessions with the authors:

https://discord.bpbonline.com

Chapter 7
Automating Tasks and Workflows with Vibe Coding

Introduction

In this chapter, we will build a complete business automation suite from scratch using prompts and AI assistance with no manual coding. We will create AutoFlow Enterprise Suite, which is a comprehensive automation platform that demonstrates the entire vibe coding workflow from initial concept to live deployment with intelligent workflow orchestration. This production-ready application features email processing with AI-powered categorization, bidirectional data synchronization across multiple systems, automated report generation with visual analytics, and a responsive dashboard that works seamlessly across devices. You will learn how to translate business automation requirements into actionable specifications during project planning, develop both backend integration logic and frontend interfaces through conversational prompts with Google AI Studio, enhance applications iteratively using visual annotation tools for rapid refinement, and finally deploy your automation suite to production through Google Cloud Run. The chapter also explores n8n as a specialized workflow automation platform, demonstrating how AI-powered workflow builders can complement vibe-coded applications by orchestrating complex backend processes, integrating over 800 pre-built services, and handling sophisticated business logic that extends beyond traditional application interfaces.

Structure

In this chapter, we will cover the following sections:

- Vibe coding for automation
- Selecting the vibe coding tool
- Building automation workflow
- Enhancing automation workflow
- Deploying automation workflow
- Using AI workflow builder n8n for automation

Objectives

This chapter will provide a comprehensive, hands-on guide to building business automation systems through vibe coding from initial concept to production deployment. It will equip you with the practical skills and strategic techniques needed to effectively communicate with AI coding tools at every stage of the automation development lifecycle, transforming high-level business process requirements into functional workflow solutions.

By the end of this chapter, you will understand the complete vibe coding development process through the construction of AutoFlow Enterprise Suite, mastering how to orchestrate AI assistance for requirements specification, module design, implementation, iterative enhancement, and cloud deployment while navigating real-world challenges such as API integration, data synchronization, security configuration, and visual refinement that arise in production automation platforms. You will also gain expertise in selecting the appropriate automation tool for different scenarios, understanding when to use application-focused vibe coding platforms like Google AI Studio for rapid prototyping of user-facing dashboards versus specialized workflow orchestration tools like n8n for complex backend process automation, API orchestration, and enterprise system integration that requires deep connectivity across multiple data sources and business applications.

Vibe coding for automation

Business automation represents one of the most tangible ways organizations can reclaim employee time and reduce operational costs. Employees spend hours manually processing emails, copying data between systems, and compiling reports that could be automated. These repetitive tasks drain productivity and prevent teams from focusing on strategic work that actually moves the business forward. The challenge has always been that building custom automation solutions requires significant development resources, making it impractical for many organizations to automate processes that would benefit most from it.

Vibe coding transforms business automation from a months-long development project into an afternoon conversation with the vibe coding tool. Building this automation suite through vibe coding demonstrates a fundamentally different development workflow than traditional programming. We start by describing the complete vision in natural language. The AI then generates the initial application structure, creating the dashboard, navigation, and basic module layouts. We can then iterate on each component, refining the user interface, adding specific features, and connecting the pieces into a cohesive system. This conversational development process keeps you focused on what the automation should accomplish rather than how to implement technical details.

The ROI from automation initiatives built with vibe coding can be substantial and rapid. Companies implementing business process automation can achieve an average ROI of 240%, typically recouping their investment within six to nine months. Successful vibe coding for automation follows a structured approach of implementing features end-to-end in manageable and incremental slices. Rather than building entire systems at once, you can add complexity gradually, starting with a basic workflow, then layering on additional features, integrations, and business logic as required. This vertical slicing methodology allows you to validate each automation component before moving forward, ensuring that the foundation remains solid as you expand capabilities.

Vibe coding democratizes automation by making it accessible to non-developers who understand business processes but lack programming expertise. Marketing professionals, operations managers, and other domain experts can now build functional automation tools by describing workflows in plain language. This accessibility removes technical barriers that previously prevented organizations from automating processes where the cost of traditional development outweighed the benefits. The result is that automation can now be applied to smaller-scale department-specific workflows that were never economically viable before.

Business automation built through vibe coding typically addresses repetitive administrative tasks that consume significant employee time. Email processing automation workflows can automatically categorize, respond to, and route messages based on content and urgency. Data synchronization automation tools eliminate manual copying between CRM systems, spreadsheets, and databases. Report generation automation pulls data from multiple sources, formats it consistently, and distributes it on schedule. Task management automation systems can track project status, send reminders, and escalate issues without human intervention.

Modern vibe coding platforms excel at connecting disparate business systems through natural language instructions. You can describe integration requirements such as **`Pull customer data from Salesforce, check inventory in our ERP system, and update the order status in our database`**, and the AI generates the necessary API calls, data transformations, and error handling. This orchestration capability makes it practical to automate workflows that span multiple applications, which is something that previously required extensive custom development work.

While vibe coding dramatically accelerates automation development, outputs require careful review to ensure security and maintainability. AI-generated workflows may introduce brittle configurations, hardcoded values, or inadequate error handling if not properly validated. The speed advantage of vibe coding should not eliminate thoughtful testing and review processes. Organizations implementing vibe-coded automation need to establish guidelines for reviewing AI-generated solutions, particularly around data security, credential management, and exception handling.

Companies successfully using vibe coding for automation often follow a hybrid approach that involves prototyping rapidly with AI assistance, then refining in traditional development environments before production deployment. This pattern allows teams to leverage the speed of vibe coding while maintaining code quality standards for mission-critical systems. Some organizations use vibe coding platforms for initial feature prototyping, then move to more traditional IDEs for fine-tuning and hardening before shipping to production. This workflow delivers the benefits of both rapid iteration and production reliability. In the next section, we will look at using Google AI Studio for building automation workflows.

Selecting the vibe coding tool

In this chapter, we will be using Google AI Studio (**https://aistudio.google.com/apps**), which is one of the popular vibe coding platforms that stands out as an excellent choice for building automation systems through vibe coding. Google AI Studio positions itself as a compelling alternative to established tools like Lovable and Replit with the tagline **From Prompt to Product**, capturing its core value proposition. The platform eliminates traditional barriers like API key management and complex service integration, allowing developers and non-coders alike to build AI-powered applications in minutes.

The platform's strength lies in its seamless integration with Google's ecosystem, automatically connecting your app to powerful services like Veo for video generation, Nano Banana for image editing, and Google Search for information retrieval. When you describe an application concept, Google AI Studio interprets the required capabilities and wires up the appropriate Gemini models and APIs behind the scenes. Google AI Studio also has an annotation mode, which is a visual interface that revolutionizes how you refine applications. Instead of writing detailed change descriptions or editing code directly, you can simply highlight interface elements and describe modifications in natural language with commands like `Make this button blue or animate the image in here from the left`, and immediately update your application. This approach maintains creative flow and reduces the friction between concept and implementation, making the development process feel more like a conversation with an intelligent design partner.

One of Google AI Studio's most compelling advantages is its free access model with reasonable usage limits. Unlike other vibe coding tools, Google AI Studio allows you to build applications without an initial investment. The platform offers the option to add your own API key if you exhaust the free quota, automatically switching back to the free tier when it renews. This flexibility makes it particularly attractive for experimentation, prototyping, and learning without financial commitment. The platform excels in scenarios requiring deep integration with Google services, making it ideal for applications involving image generation, editing, video creation, or search functionality. *Figure 7.1* shows the Google AI Studio homepage, where you can start describing your requirements to build applications using prompts.

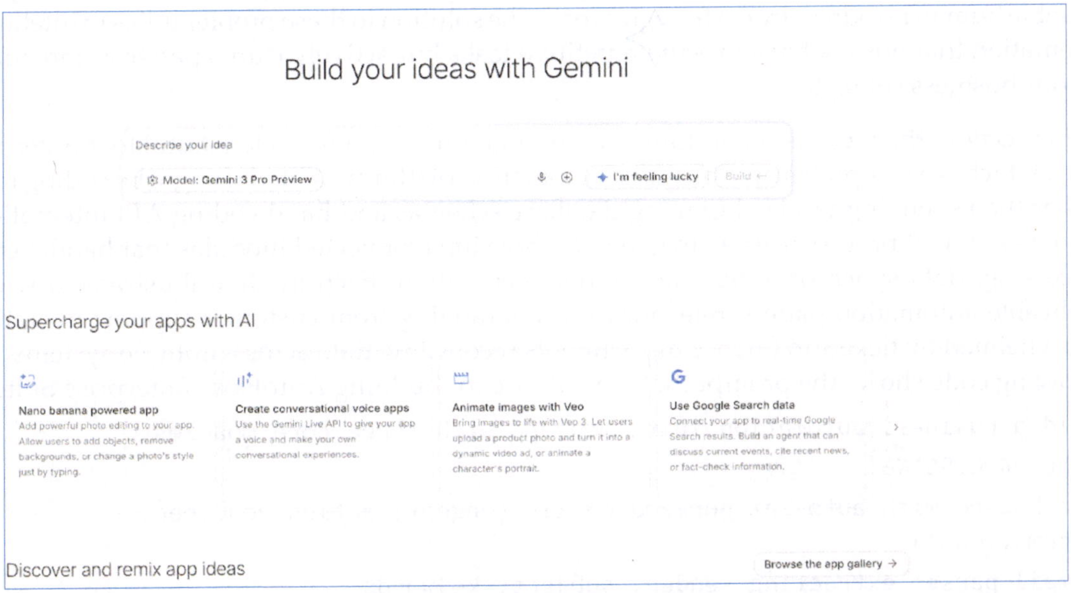

***Figure 7.1**: Google AI Studio homepage, where you can start describing your requirements to build applications*

Google AI Studio further provides code access and editing capabilities, which allow you to transition from prompt-based development to traditional coding when needed. The platform includes **Get code** functionality that exports your work for further development outside the studio environment. This hybrid approach supports both the initial rapid prototyping phase and subsequent refinement, making it suitable for developers who want to start with vibe coding but maintain control over the final implementation. The platform also supports various prompt types, including chat prompts, real-time streaming, and video generation with adjustable model parameters and safety settings.

Google AI Studio provides comprehensive quickstart documentation and tutorial playlists to accelerate onboarding. The learning curve is intentionally minimal, and you can start building by simply describing your application idea in natural language. The platform's design philosophy prioritizes immediate productivity over configuration complexity, allowing you to experiment with different prompts and models through intuitive interfaces before deepening your understanding of the underlying systems. This approach makes Google AI Studio particularly accessible for those new to vibe coding while still offering depth for experienced developers exploring AI-powered application patterns. In the next section, we will look at using Google AI Studio for building the AutoFlow Enterprise Suite.

Building automation workflow

Modern businesses generate thousands of data points, such as daily emails flooding inboxes, information flows between disconnected systems, and stakeholders demand timely reports. Managing these workflows manually creates bottlenecks, increases error rates, and diverts valuable human resources from strategic work. The solution to these problems lies in intelligent automation that does not just execute repetitive tasks but actively learns patterns and adapts to your business context.

In this section, the focus is on building an automation workflow called AutoFlow Enterprise Suite, which is a comprehensive business automation platform created using vibe coding tools. Rather than spending weeks designing database schemas and hand-coding API integrations, the development process uses AI to generate three interconnected modules that handle email processing, data synchronization, and report generation. Each module illustrates a widely applicable automation pattern relevant to teams ranging from customer support operations overwhelmed by tickets to finance departments reconciling data across multiple systems. The following code shows the prompt that we will use for building AutoFlow Enterprise Suite:

```
Build a business automation suite web app with three core modules:
EMAIL PROCESSING:
- Dashboard with auto-categorized emails (urgent, action required,
informational)
- Email parser extracting sender, subject, keywords
- Custom automation rules (if/then logic)
- Auto-response templates
- Team routing based on rules
DATA SYNC:
- Connect multiple data sources (APIs, databases, CSV)
- Field mapping between systems
- Bidirectional sync with conflict resolution
- Scheduling options (real-time, scheduled, manual)
- Sync history log
REPORT GENERATION:
- Visual report builder with charts and tables
- Multi-source data aggregation
- Automated scheduling and distribution
- Export formats (PDF, Excel, email)
- Report templates
```

This prompt follows best practices for vibe coding by being explicit about desired features while staying technology agnostic, allowing the AI to choose optimal implementation details. It organizes requirements into logical modules with clear functional specifications rather than prescribing specific frameworks, programming languages, or database technologies. *Figure 7.2* illustrates Google AI Studio processing this prompt and initiating the development workflow as the AI model begins generating the application's files and demonstrating the platform's automated code creation capabilities.

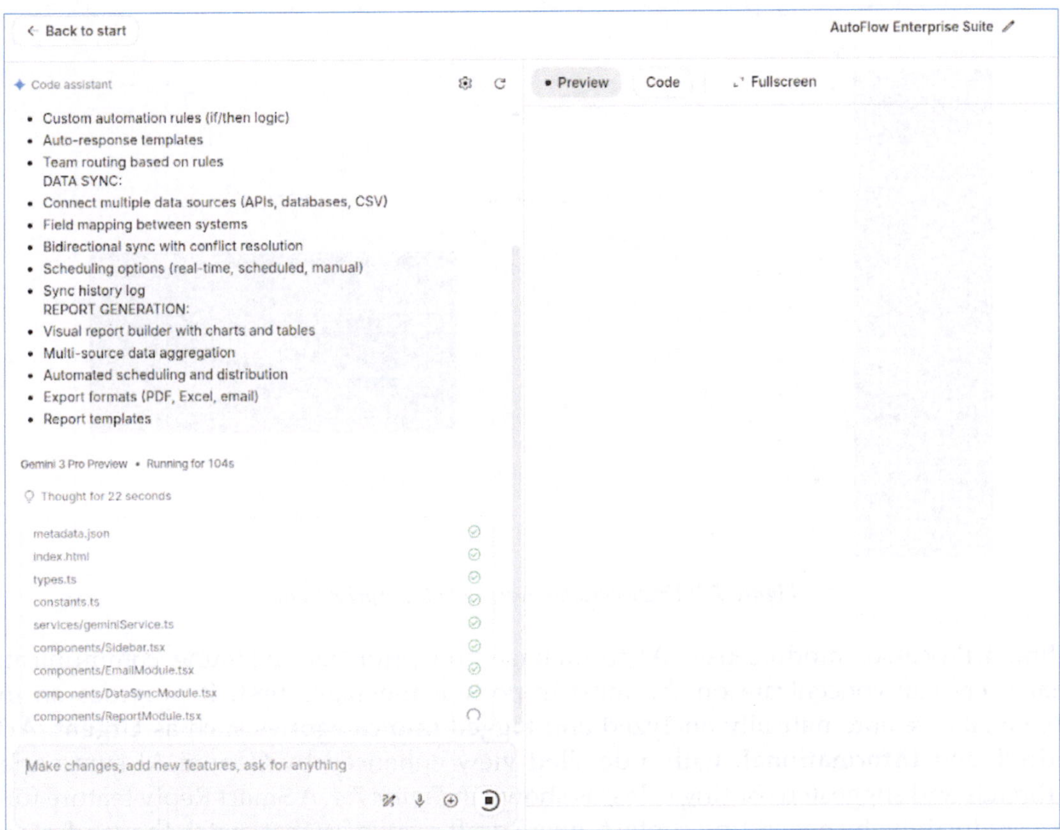

***Figure 7.2:** Google AI Studio processing prompt and initiating the development workflow*

The Google AI Studio vibe coding tool creates the complete application from this single structured prompt, automatically generating the user interface, data models, API integrations, and automation logic for all three modules in a single end-to-end workflow. It not only creates the core screens such as the **Dashboard**, **Email Processor**, **Data Sync**, and **Reports & Analytics**, but also wires them together with the necessary navigation, state management, and background jobs so the workflow is immediately usable with minimal manual configuration.

The Dashboard acts as the central command center for AutoFlow Enterprise Suite, offering a high-level snapshot of operational health across all modules. It presents key performance indicators such as the number of emails processed, the status of data synchronization connections, and month-to-date revenue alongside a **Recent Activity** feed that logs critical system events like flagged urgent emails or completed sync jobs, as shown in *Figure 7.3*. Quick action shortcuts allow users to immediately launch common workflows such as configuring a new automation rule or initiating a manual sync, enabling rapid responses to emerging issues.

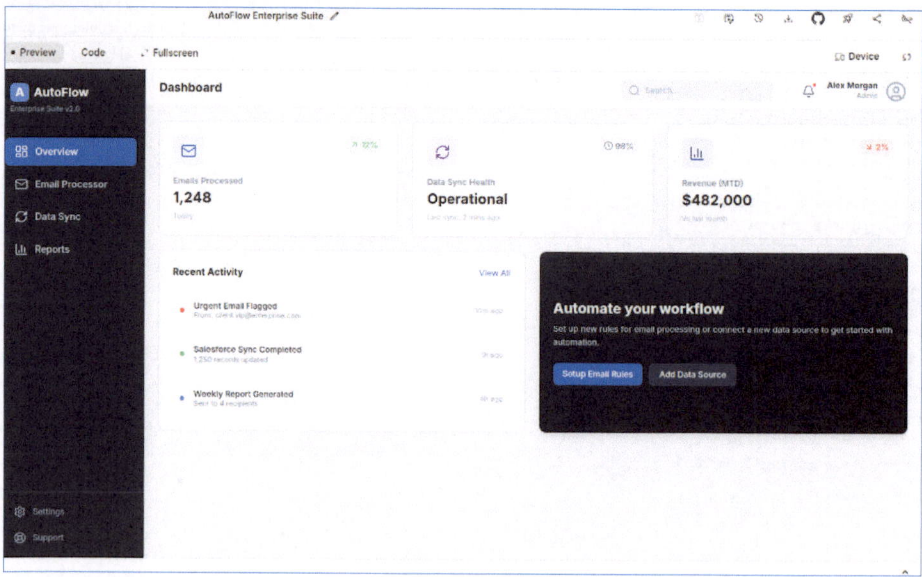

Figure 7.3: Dashboard for AutoFlow Enterprise Suite

The Email Processor module uses AI to manage and prioritize incoming communications so that users can concentrate on the most important messages first. It provides an inbox where emails are automatically analyzed and tagged into categories such as **Urgent, Action Required,** and **Informational**, with a detailed view enhanced by Gemini AI summaries of long threads and suggested routing rules, as shown in *Figure 7.4*. A Smart Reply feature further boosts productivity by generating context-aware draft responses that match the sender's tone, enabling fast, consistent communication with minimal manual editing.

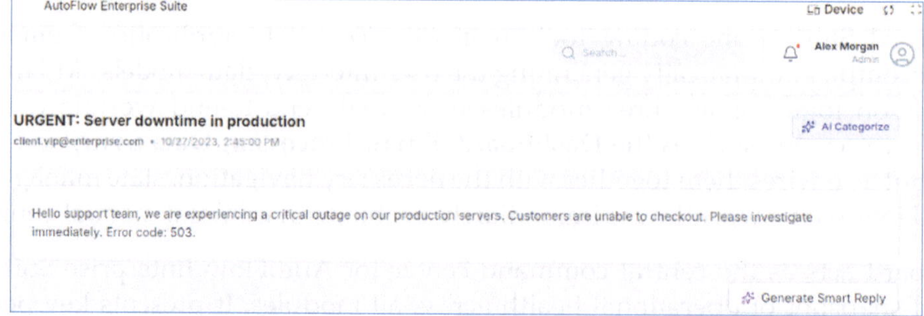

Figure 7.4: Email Processor for AutoFlow Enterprise Suite

The Data Sync module manages the integration and flow of information between disparate external systems such as CRM platforms (Salesforce), databases, and CSV imports, as shown in *Figure 7.5*. Users can monitor the connection status of each source, view timestamps for the last successful sync, and trigger manual updates when needed. The module includes a detailed history log to track sync success rates and potential errors. A unique feature in this system is the AI-powered Field Mapping configuration, which automatically analyzes and suggests logical mappings between source and target fields, significantly reducing the setup time for new data pipelines.

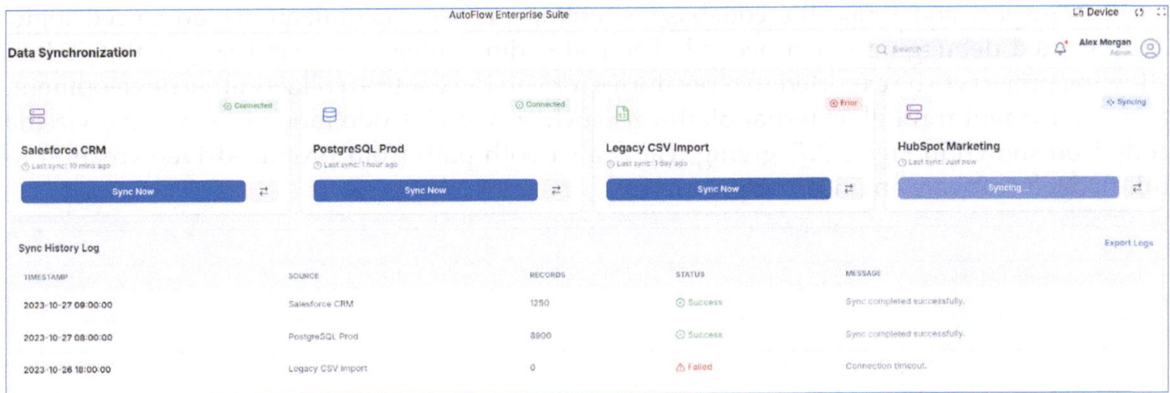

***Figure 7.5**: Data Sync for AutoFlow Enterprise Suite*

The **Reports & Analytics** module supports data-driven decision-making by transforming raw data into interactive visualizations such as bar charts, area charts, and pie charts, as shown in *Figure 7.6*. This feature also incorporates an AI analyst feature where users can click a lightbulb icon on any chart to generate intelligent and bulleted insights that highlight trends, anomalies, and potential business implications directly beside the visualization. This combination of visual and narrative analysis helps stakeholders interpret results quickly, turning dashboards into actionable guidance rather than static displays.

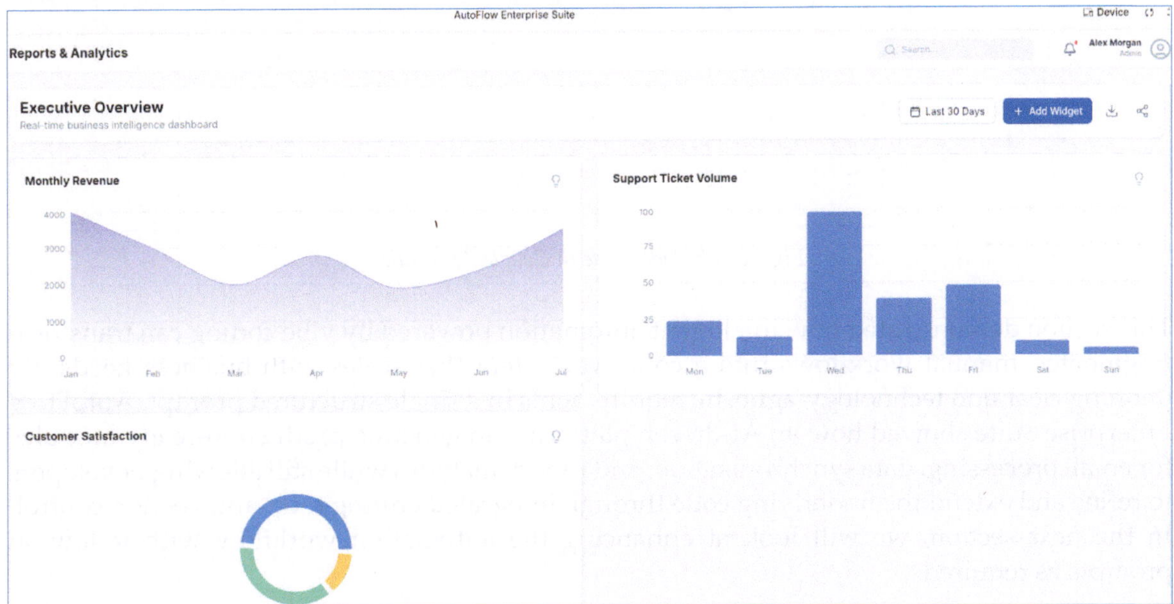

***Figure 7.6**: Reports & Analytics for AutoFlow Enterprise Suite*

Google AI Studio offers a dedicated code section, also referred to as code mode, which shows the project's raw source code that could be modified manually if required. This mode allows users to inspect and refine the codebase, enabling precise customizations, advanced logic, and targeted debugging when needed. The code editor integrates seamlessly with GitHub, allowing projects to be exported to repositories for version control, collaborative development, and deployment through external platforms such as Vercel. Code mode is accessible via the code icon shown in *Figure 7.7*, giving teams a smooth path from prompt-driven creation to full-fledged software engineering practices.

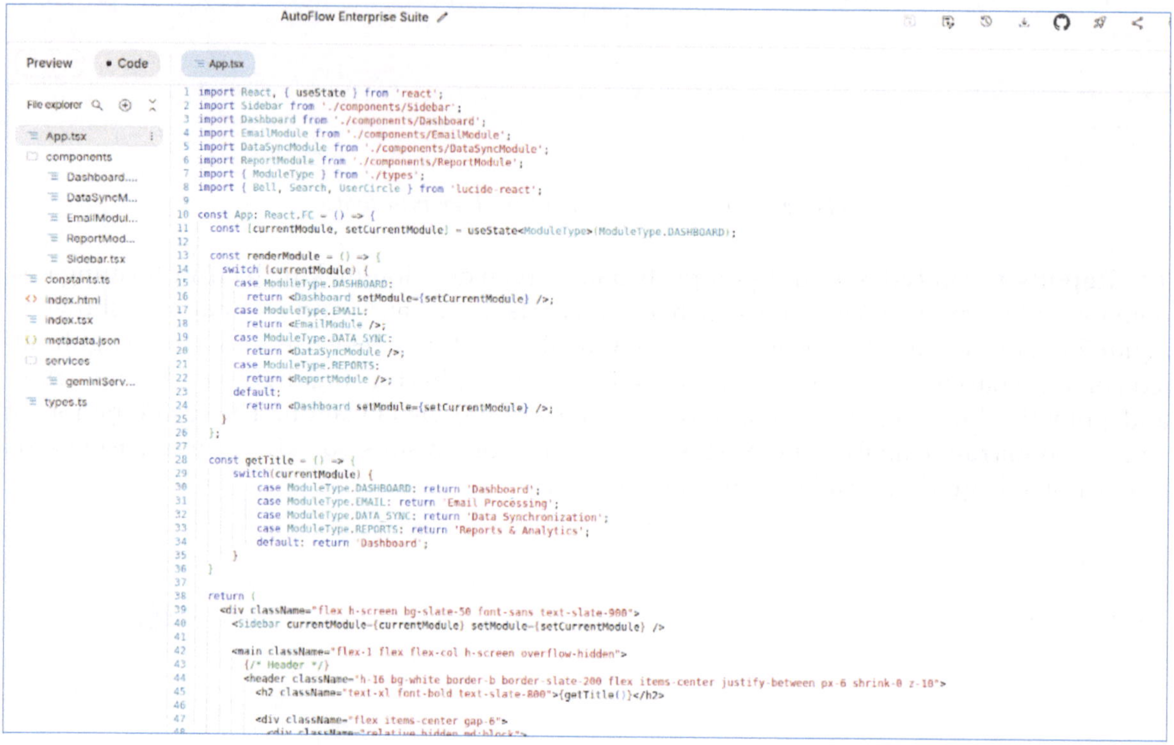

Figure 7.7: *Code mode in Google AI Studio*

This section demonstrated how intelligent automation powered by vibe coding can transform fragmented manual workflows into a cohesive system that scales with business needs. By defining clear and technology-agnostic requirements in a single structured prompt, AutoFlow Enterprise Suite showed how an AI-driven platform can generate production-ready modules for email processing, data synchronization, and report analytics while still allowing developers to refine and extend the underlying code through integrated editing tools and version control. In the next section, we will look at enhancing the automation workflow with follow-on prompts as required.

Enhancing automation workflow

The application is currently missing essential backend integration features and a fully functional settings page. To address this gap, the system can be enhanced by using the prompt as, `Add back end features and complete settings page in the application`. The vibe coding tool then updates the application to simulate backend functionality and introduces fine-grained control through an expanded Settings module. This design allows the application to exhibit realistic enterprise behavior, such as persisting user preferences across sessions and applying consistent logic to incoming data without requiring a full server deployment, which aligns with the rapid prototyping goals of vibe coding. The **Settings** interface evolves into a comprehensive configuration hub organized into multiple tabs that mirror common administrative tasks and mental models as illustrated in *Figure 7.8*. A **General** tab enables users to manage their profile (such as name and role) and notification settings as required.

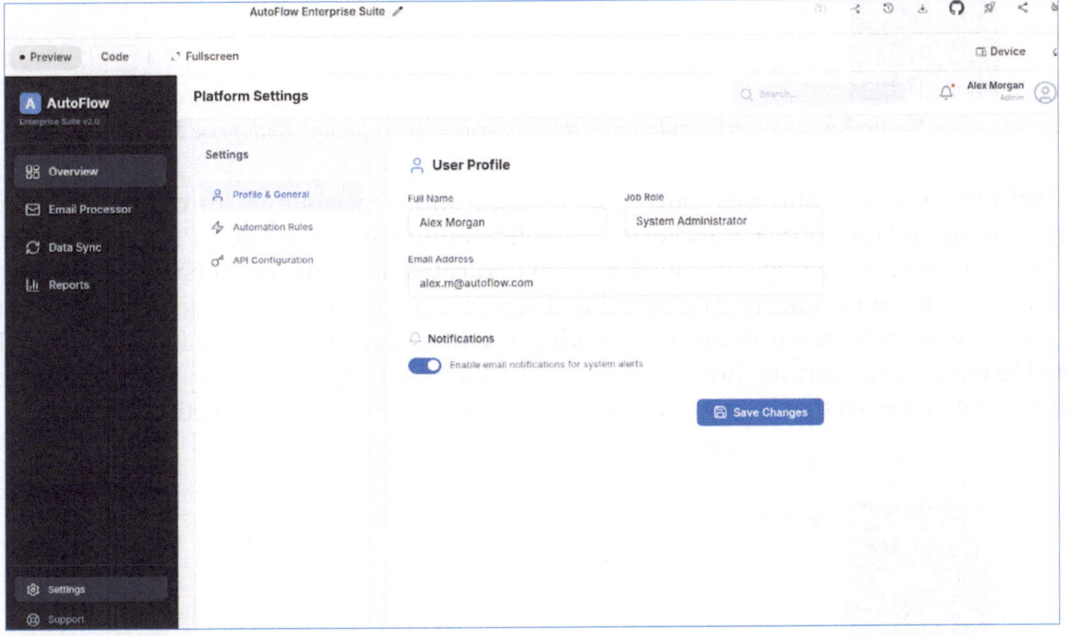

***Figure 7.8**: General tab in settings interface for AutoFlow Enterprise Suite*

The dedicated settings service also centralizes configuration management and exposes a rules engine capable of evaluating emails against user-defined criteria before delegating any remaining classification work to AI models. Users can define keyword-based automation rules, such as mapping **Invoice, Payment,** or **Overdue** to an **Action Required** category, so that known patterns are handled deterministically while ambiguous or novel messages can still be interpreted by the AI, as shown in *Figure 7.9*. The **Email Processor** module uses this engine by first running each message through the configured rules and only calling the AI categorization logic when no rule matches, creating a hybrid workflow that blends predictable business logic with AI.

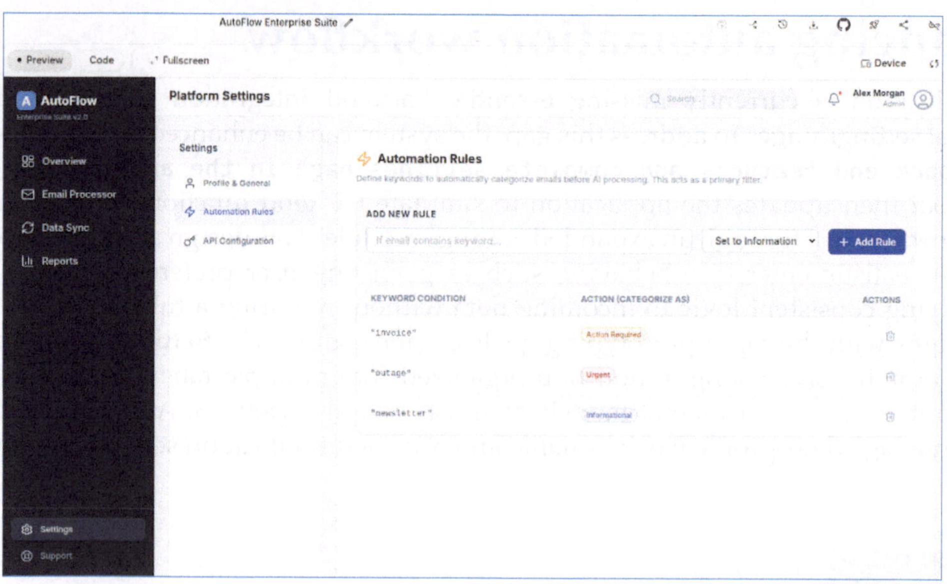

Figure 7.9: Automation rules in settings interface for AutoFlow Enterprise Suite

The **Settings** module surfaces powerful configuration capabilities through a structured interface designed for non-technical users as well as administrators. The API Configuration tab organizes integration settings by function with dedicated sections for AI (such as Gemini API keys), Data Sync connectors, and email-related services, all backed by an extended settings type that can grow as new integrations are introduced while keeping sensitive fields like API keys scoped to the user session, as shown in *Figure 7.10*. These settings are deeply integrated into the broader application so that configuration changes have an immediate functional impact.

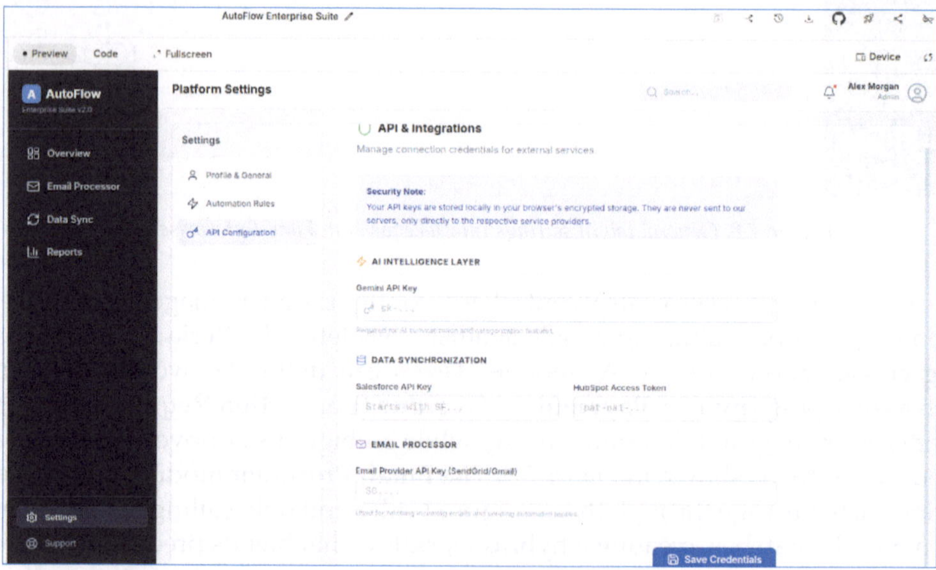

Figure 7.10: API configuration in the settings interface for AutoFlow Enterprise Suite

Google AI Studio also provides a powerful way to iterate on your app visually through in-app annotations. You can draw and write directly on the application preview to communicate your vision instantly to the AI model to enhance your application, as shown in *Figure 7.11*. This feature allows you to highlight specific components, sketch new interface ideas, or provide detailed feedback right where it is most relevant. The annotation feature transforms the traditional text-based development workflow into an intuitive visual dialogue. Rather than describing changes in words alone, you can circle problematic areas, draw arrows to indicate where elements should move, or sketch rough layouts of new features you envision.

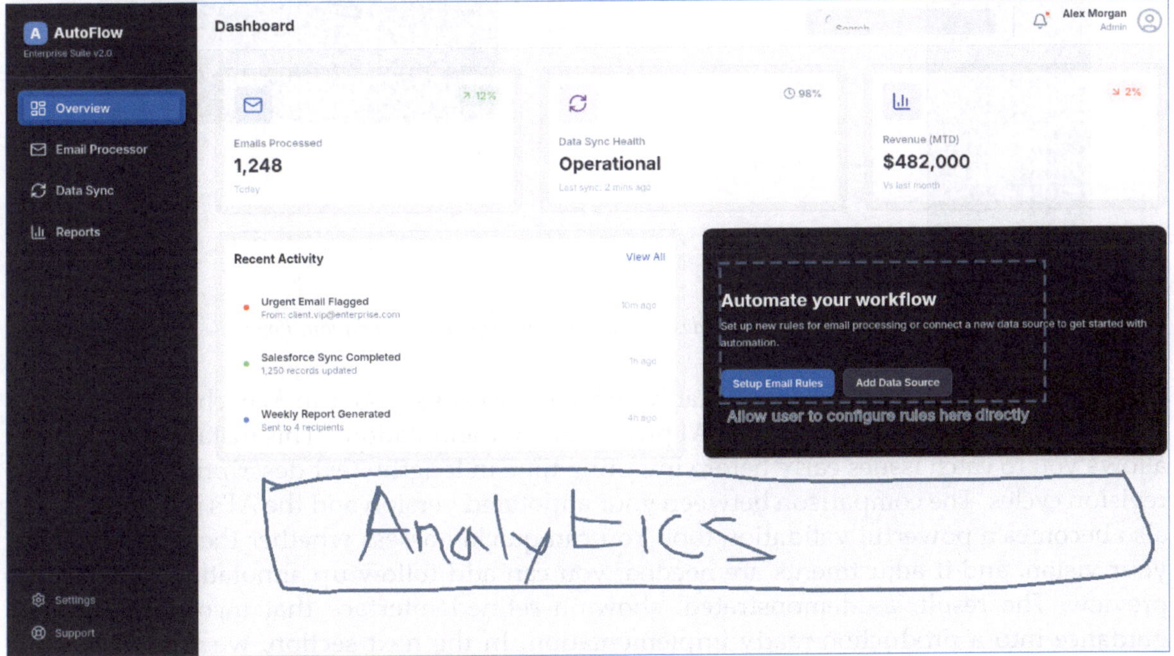

***Figure 7.11**: Annotations on Google AI Studio*

The AI model interprets these visual cues alongside any accompanying text instructions, creating a more natural and efficient feedback loop. This multimodal understanding allows the model to process both your written requirements and visual indicators simultaneously, resulting in implementations that accurately reflect your design intentions. The following *Figure 7.12* shows the updated dashboard, which incorporates the annotations:

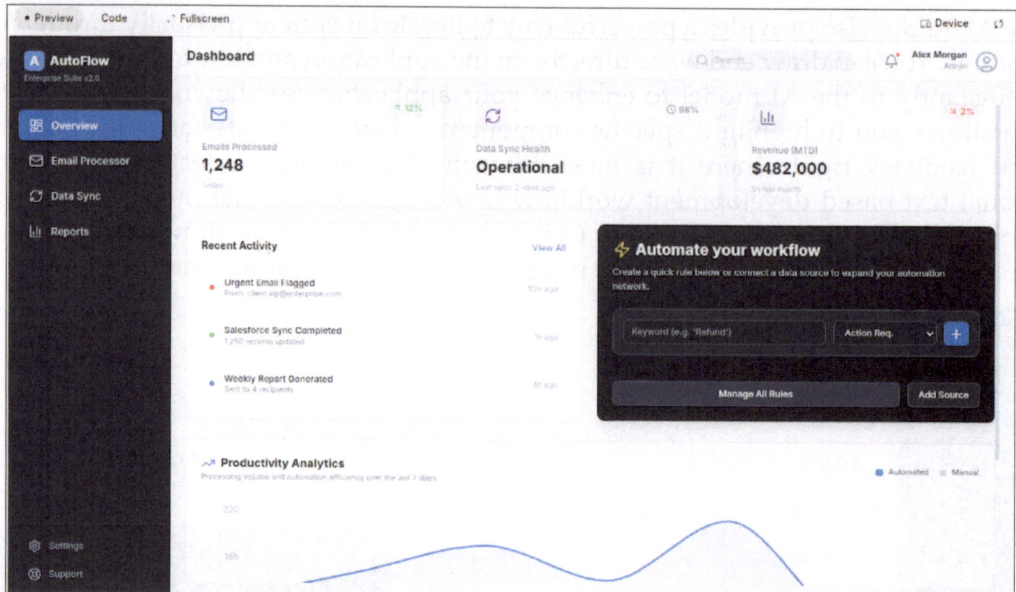

Figure 7.12: Updated dashboard which incorporated the annotations

The feedback loop becomes remarkably efficient because you can see changes reflected immediately in the preview after the AI processes your annotations. This instant visualization allows you to catch issues early before investing time in lengthy text descriptions or multiple revision cycles. The comparison between your annotated version and the AI's implementation also becomes a powerful validation tool. You can quickly assess whether the changes match your vision, and if adjustments are needed, you can add follow-up annotations on the new preview. The result, as demonstrated, shows a refined interface that incorporates visual guidance into a production-ready implementation. In the next section, we will look at the steps to deploy our automation workflow in Google AI Studio.

Deploying automation workflow

Google AI Studio provides seamless deployment capabilities that allow you to publish your application as a Cloud Run service directly from the tool interface. This deployment process transforms your vibe-coded application into a production-ready service accessible via a public URL, eliminating the need for manual containerization or complex infrastructure setup. To deploy the application, click the rocket, like button on the top right corner of the AI Studio interface, which displays **Deploy app** on hover. This action opens the **Deploy app on Google Cloud** dialog, prompting you to select a Google Cloud project to proceed, as shown in *Figure 7.13*. The deployment system automatically handles the containerization process, leveraging prebuilt containers optimized for AI Studio applications.

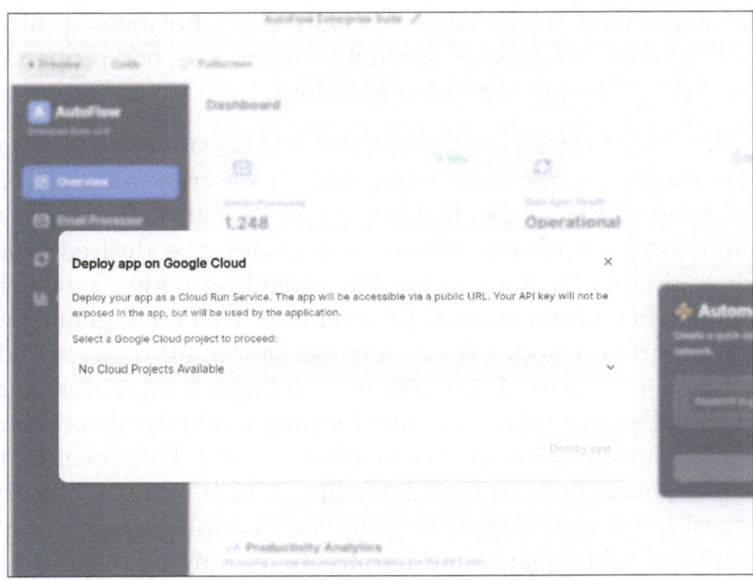

Figure 7.13: Deploy app on Google Cloud

After selecting or creating your project, click the **Deploy app** button, and the system begins provisioning your Cloud Run service. The Cloud Run service name is auto-generated to ensure uniqueness, though you can modify service configurations later if required. The entire deployment typically completes within a couple of minutes, after which you will receive the public App URL that you can immediately access to view your live application. A critical advantage of this deployment method is the secure handling of API keys. The keys are securely managed on the server side, where the Cloud Run service uses them to make authenticated requests to services on behalf of your application. This architecture follows security best practices by storing sensitive credentials in Google Cloud Secret Manager and granting your Cloud Run service account permissions to retrieve them at runtime. In the next section, we will look at the AI workflow builder n8n for building complex automations.

Using AI workflow builder n8n for automation

Vibe coding is good for building automation workflows, but automation platforms such as n8n (or n8n) provide additional functionality that makes it a specialized powerhouse for complex automations. While vibe coding platforms excel at rapid application development through conversational AI interfaces, n8n offers deep workflow orchestration capabilities with over 800 pre-built integrations, advanced logic handling, and enterprise-grade reliability. The n8n tool delivers sophisticated automation features that go beyond simple app building. The platform supports complex branching logic, loops, and conditional processing that allow workflows to adapt dynamically based on data inputs and business rules. n8n offers over 15 specialized AI nodes that seamlessly integrate services like OpenAI GPT-4, Anthropic Claude, and Hugging Face's open-source models directly into workflows. The platform has more than 800 pre-built integrations, which cover virtually every business application from CRM systems and marketing tools to databases and data warehouses. n8n is open source and offers complete data sovereignty through self-hosting options.

n8n aligns well with vibe coding's conversational and iterative ethos. The drag-and-drop interface eliminates coding barriers, allowing you to describe automation ideas visually through nodes and templates. n8n also features an AI Workflow Builder that revolutionizes automation development by enabling vibe coders to describe desired workflows in plain English and watch as the platform automatically assembles nodes, establishes connections, and configures parameters without manual intervention. This intelligent construction system selects appropriate integration nodes from documentation, auto-fills saved credentials for services like Gmail or Slack, connects components in logical sequences, and pre-configures necessary parameters within each element, transforming workflow prototyping from hours of manual configuration to minutes of conversational refinement. This development loop mirrors vibe coding principles through three intuitive steps, which involve describing automation intent through natural language prompts or template examples, monitoring real-time visual feedback as the workflow takes shape, and iteratively refining by inspecting credentials and parameters before adjusting through additional conversational prompts.

Figure 7.14 shows the main dashboard of an **n8n.cloud** account, where the user can monitor and manage their hosted automation environment. It prominently features a central card representing the active n8n instance displaying its name, online status, and other key runtime details so the user can immediately see that the instance is available. Just beneath this, an execution count bar visually tracks how many workflow executions have been consumed so far out of the monthly quota, allowing for a quick assessment of current usage versus remaining capacity.

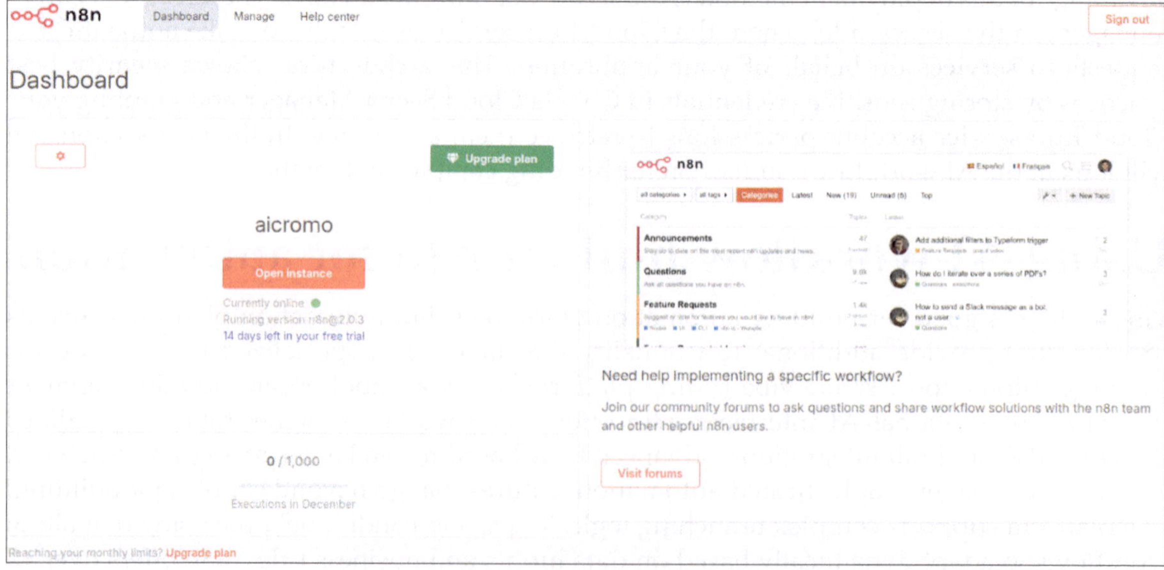

***Figure 7.14**: Main dashboard for n8n.cloud account*

Once you log in to your workspace, you are presented with two primary options, which are **Try an AI Workflow** or **Start from scratch,** as illustrated in *Figure 7.15*. Choosing the **Try an AI Workflow** option provides a guided starting point using predefined AI-powered workflow templates that showcase common automation patterns and best practices. These templates help you quickly experiment with AI agents, preconfigured nodes, and example data flows so that you can understand how everything fits together before customizing the workflow for your own use case.

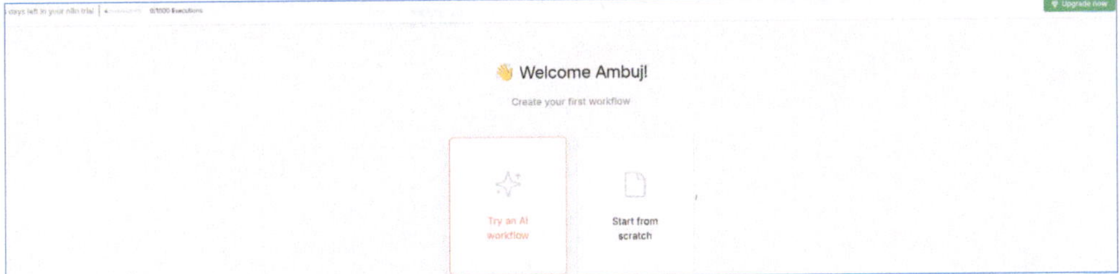

***Figure 7.15**: Workflow dashboard for n8n*

You can see the AI workflow that has been generated with the **Try an AI Workflow** option in *Figure 7.16*. The central area for this workflow highlights an embedded YouTube tutorial titled **How to use an AI agent in your workflow** accompanied by a **Daily AI Summary** information card that explains how the workflow retrieves the latest news and produces AI-generated summaries. Beneath this is a clear node-based diagram which begins with a **Start here** trigger, flows through an **AI Summary Agent** node, continues into an **Output** node, and ends with a **Send summary by email** node, while additional nodes below configure a 7 AM daily schedule trigger to run this automation in the morning.

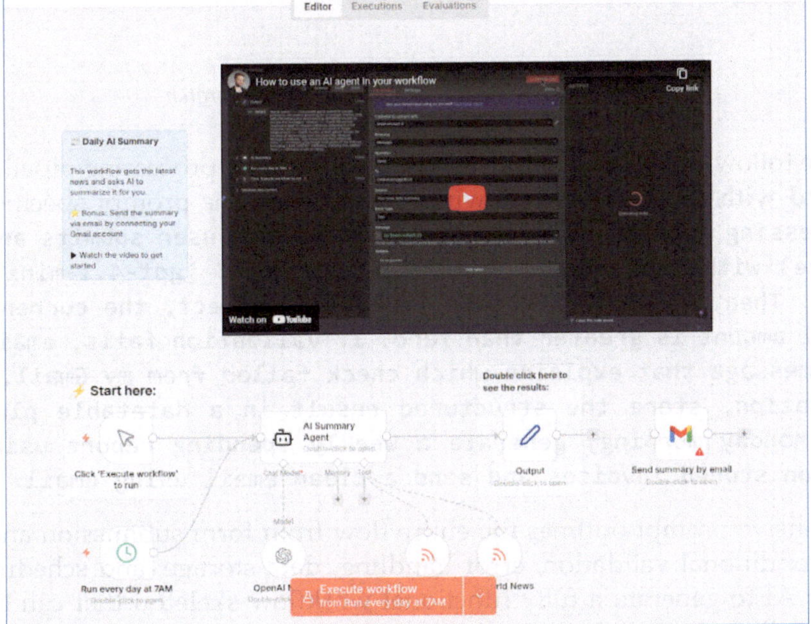

***Figure 7.16**: AI workflow that has been generated with the Try an AI Workflow option*

You can also create a new workflow from scratch, which provides a **Build with AI option** as shown in *Figure 7.17*. This option allows you to describe the desired automation in natural language so the system can automatically propose a suitable workflow structure, including recommended nodes and connections. By starting from the **Build with AI** entry point, you can rapidly bootstrap complex automations without manually configuring every step and then fine-tune the generated workflow if required to match your specific requirements.

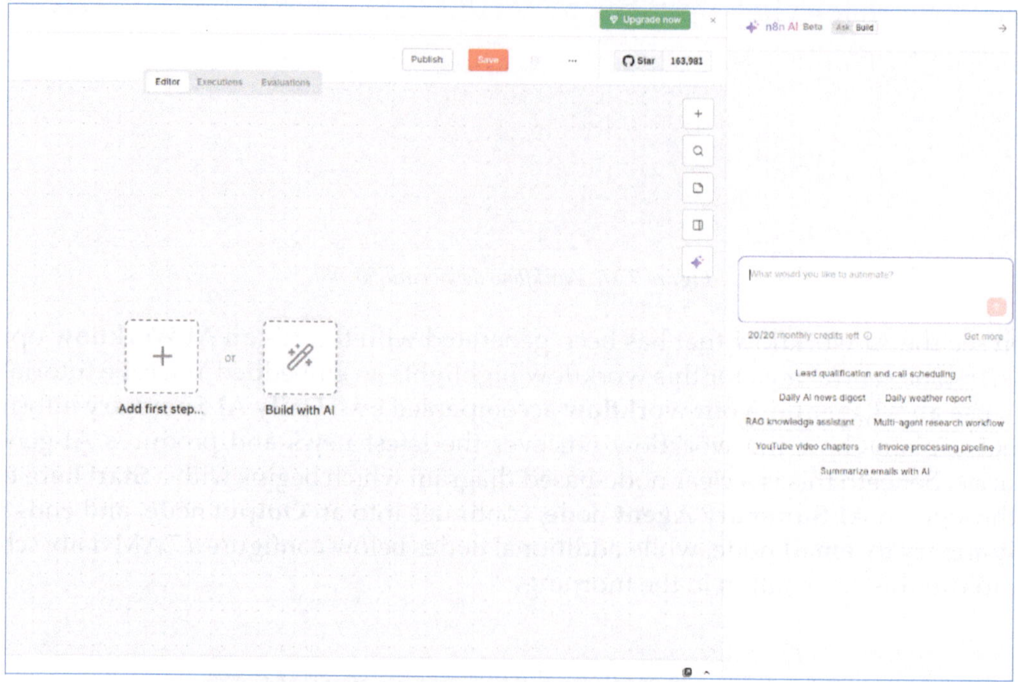

Figure 7.17: Create a new workflow from scratch

We will use the following detailed prompt to build an invoice processing pipeline automation using the **Build with AI** option, as shown in *Figure 7.18*. The prompt specifies, **Create an invoice processing workflow using an n8n Form. When a user submits an invoice file (PDF or image) with their email address, use OpenAI `gpt-4.1-mini` to extract invoice data. Then, validate the date format is correct, the currency is valid, and the total amount is greater than zero. If validation fails, email the user a clear error message that explains which check failed from my Gmail. If the data passes validation, store the structured result in a datatable plus email the user. Every Monday morning, generate a weekly spending report using `gpt-4.1-mini` based on stored invoices and send a clean email using Gmail.**

This comprehensive prompt outlines the entire flow from form submission and AI-powered extraction to conditional validation, error handling, data storage, and scheduled reporting, enabling n8n's AI to generate a fully functional workflow skeleton that can be refined and deployed with minimal manual configuration.

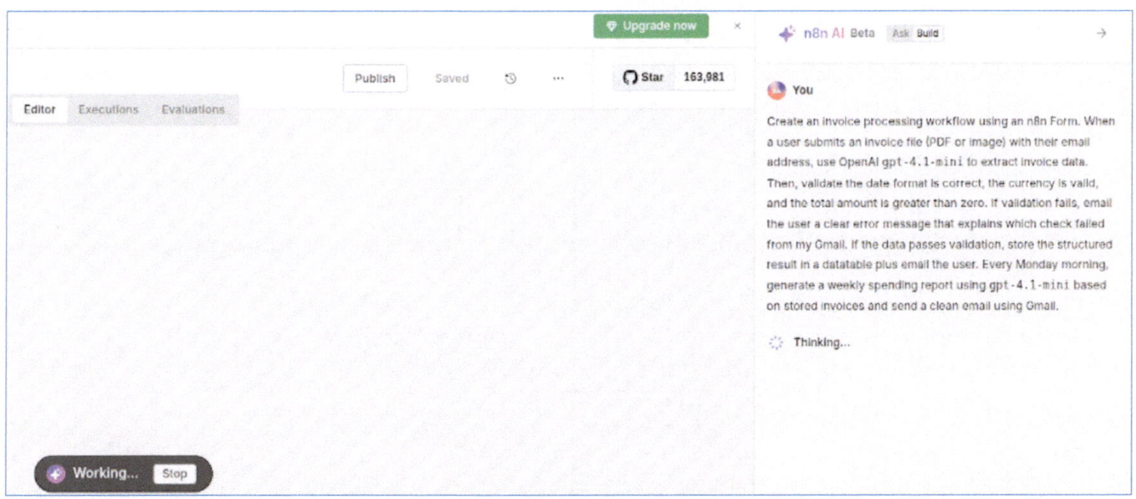

***Figure 7.18**: Building an invoice processing pipeline automation using the Build with AI option*

This n8n AI workflow builder provides an intelligent automation layer over the editor, helping with tasks such as suggesting best practices, searching for nodes, retrieving node details, creating nodes, connecting nodes, updating node parameters, building workflows, and validating the overall workflow logic. Our specific example is an invoice processing system built using the AI workflow builder, as shown in *Figure 7.19*. In the invoice submission flow, users upload invoices through an n8n form, and the workflow extracts PDF text with GPT-4o-mini, validates key fields like date format, currency list, and positive amounts, and then either sends an error email if validation fails or stores the data in the table and sends a success confirmation if it passes. The weekly report flow runs every Monday at 9 AM, which pulls all invoices from the data table, filters them to entries from the last seven days, aggregates the spending data, asks GPT-4o-mini to generate a professional HTML report, and emails this report to the configured recipient.

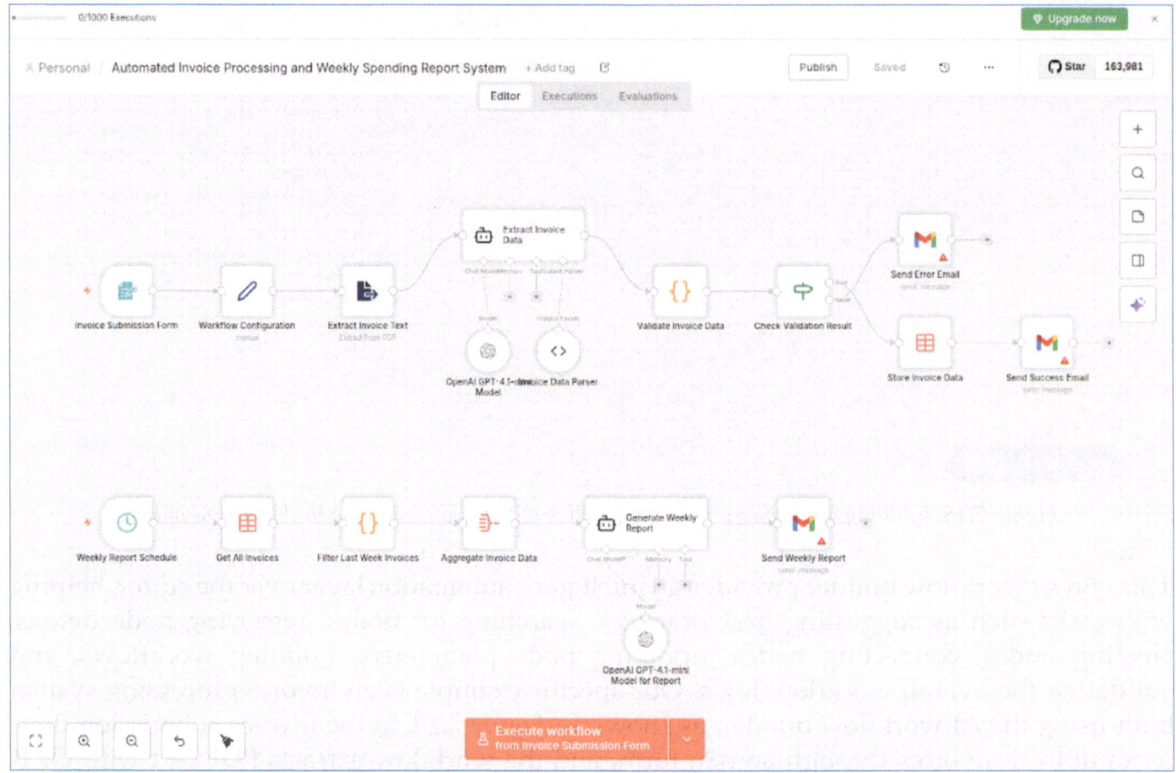

Figure 7.19: Invoice processing system built using AI workflow builder

The n8n tool excels at automating business processes that complement vibe-coded applications, including e-commerce order processing, lead qualification systems that automatically score prospects and route them into CRMs with personalized sequences, and customer support ticket routing that categorizes issues and delivers instant acknowledgments. The platform handles sophisticated workflows such as automated monthly reporting that fetches transaction data from accounting systems, reconciles payment processor information, calculates key performance metrics, including revenue growth and profit margins, and generates comparative trend analysis, all running in the background of user-facing applications. The n8n tool represents the optimal automation companion for vibe coding projects requiring sophisticated backend processes, complex business logic, and deep AI integration that extends beyond what conversational development alone can achieve.

Conclusion

In this chapter, we learned about the process of building production-ready business automation systems through vibe coding methodologies and their role in democratizing workflow development for non-technical domain experts. We have navigated the comprehensive workflow from tool selection and requirements analysis through module design, implementation, visual enhancement, and cloud deployment to create AutoFlow Enterprise Suite, which is a fully functional automation platform handling email processing, data synchronization, and report generation. Throughout this development journey, we identified several patterns that consistently drive vibe coding success across automation projects, including the formulation of clear prompts that specify functional requirements without prescribing implementation details, the use of visual annotation tools to refine interfaces through intuitive feedback loops, and the establishment of secure deployment practices that leverage cloud native services like Secret Manager for credential protection. We also explored how specialized platforms like n8n complement vibe-coded applications by providing deep workflow orchestration capabilities, extensive pre-built integrations across over 800 services, and AI-powered workflow builders that enable users to describe complex automation logic in natural language and watch as the platform automatically assembles the necessary nodes, connections, and configurations.

In the next chapter, we will look at complex software projects while addressing the current limitations of vibe coding. We will explore the boundaries of what vibe coding can realistically accomplish, identifying scenarios where traditional development practices remain necessary, such as low-level system optimization, complex algorithmic implementations, and situations requiring granular control over security protocols beyond standard authentication patterns.

Further reading

There are lots of online resources to help you improve your learning on Google AI Studio, vibe coding for automation, and n8n. *Table 7.1* lists some of the best resources to further improve your understanding of Google AI Studio, vibe coding for automation, and n8n.

Resource name	Link
Vibe coding and other ways AI is changing who can build apps and how	**https://news.microsoft.com/source/features/ai/vibe-coding-and-other-ways-ai-is-changing-who-can-build-apps-and-how/**
Vibe Code with Gemini	**https://aistudio.google.com/vibe-code**
Introducing vibe coding in Google AI Studio	**https://blog.google/technology/developers/introducing-vibe-coding-in-google-ai-studio/**
Vibe Code with Gemini in Google AI Studio	**https://codelabs.developers.google.com/vibe-code-with-gemini-in-aistudio#0**
Vibe Coding Launches in Google AI Studio, Shaping a No-Code AI Future	**https://www.eitbiz.com/blog/vibe-coding-launches-in-google-ai-studio-for-a-no-code-ai-future/**
Building AI Agents with Google Gemini 3 and Open Source Frameworks	**https://developers.googleblog.com/building-ai-agents-with-google-gemini-3-and-open-source-frameworks/**

Resource name	Link
Introducing Annotation Mode in AI Studio	**https://app.daily.dev/posts/introducing-annotation-mode-in-ai-studio-pjabclfke**
Google AI Studio Tutorial: Complete Guide to Chat, Build, and Stream Modes	**https://www.datacamp.com/tutorial/google-ai-studio-tutorial**
Complete Guide to Deploying Google AI Studio Apps : Ship Faster With Ease	**https://www.geeky-gadgets.com/google-ai-studio-app-deployment/**
n8n - Secure Workflow Automation for Technical Teams	**https://github.com/n8n-io/n8n**
AI Workflow Builder	**https://docs.n8n.io/advanced-ai/ai-workflow-builder/**
The 9 best AI workflow automation tools in 2026	**https://blog.n8n.io/best-ai-workflow-automation-tools/**
n8n Workflow Builder Tutorial: Automate Daily Standups	**https://www.datacamp.com/tutorial/n8n-workflow-builder-tutorial**
No-Code Workflow Automation with n8n from Scratch: A 48-Hour Build	**https://hatchworks.com/blog/ai-agents/no-code-workflow-automation-with-n8n/**
A Beginner's Guide to Automation with n8n	**https://www.freecodecamp.org/news/a-beginners-guide-to-automation-with-n8n/**
13 n8n Projects for Beginners to Learn No-Code Automation	**https://www.projectpro.io/article/n8n-projects/1148**
n8n Workflows: A Complete Guide To Building Scalable Automation	**https://www.thesys.dev/blogs/n8n-workflows**

***Table 7.1**: Resources on Google AI Studio, vibe coding for automation and n8n*

Questions

1. Why is vibe coding useful for building workflow automations?
2. What is the typical ROI from automation initiatives built with vibe coding?
3. How does vibe coding democratize automation?
4. What are typical automations built through vibe coding?
5. Why do modern vibe coding platforms excel at connecting disparate business systems?
6. What are the advantages of the Google AI Studio vibe coding tool?
7. How can you build an automation workflow on Google AI Studio?
8. What are the advantages of the Google AI Studio dedicated code section?
9. How can you use in-app annotations to improve your applications?
10. What are the steps to deploy your application in Google AI Studio?
11. What are the advantages of using n8n for building automations?
12. How can you enhance automation workflows using Google AI Studio?
13. What are the pre-built templates in n8n?
14. How does the Build with AI option work in n8n?
15. What are the best practices for building sophisticated automation workflows?

Chapter 8
Advanced Vibe Coding Projects and Limitations

Introduction

In this chapter, we will examine the fundamental limitations and constraints that vibe coding platforms face when applied to production software development. We will explore how current limitations of vibe coding platforms affect everything from complex algorithmic implementations to enterprise security requirements revealing gaps between rapid prototyping capabilities and production-ready systems. This comprehensive analysis covers major constraint categories such as low-level system optimization challenges where AI generated code can consume more memory than human-optimized solutions, complex algorithmic implementations and advanced security requirements where AI generated code can contain vulnerabilities. We will also discuss hybrid development workflows that strategically combine AI assistance with traditional programming that can be used for developing complex applications.

Structure

In this chapter, we will cover the following topics:

- Current limitations of vibe coding platforms
- Low-level system optimization
- Complex algorithmic implementations
- Advanced security requirements
- Hybrid development workflows
- AI coding tools

Objectives

This chapter will provide a comprehensive examination of the critical limitations and constraints that affect vibe coding platforms when applied to real-world software development scenarios. It will equip you with the analytical framework and strategic understanding needed to realistically assess AI-assisted development capabilities, identify situations where vibe coding introduces unacceptable risks, and implement effective mitigation strategies through hybrid workflows that combine AI assistance with human expertise.

By the end of this chapter, you will understand the fundamental technical constraints across critical domains such as low-level system optimization, where AI-generated code can exhibit memory inefficiencies, complex algorithmic implementations, advanced security requirements, and hybrid development workflows that strategically allocate tasks between AI generation and traditional programming based on complexity and risk profiles. You will also learn how to evaluate different AI coding tools, including Cursor's agentic capabilities, GitHub Copilot's enterprise security features, and Claude Code's context handling for large codebases.

Current limitations of vibe coding platforms

Vibe coding platforms represent an emerging paradigm in AI-assisted software development, but they face significant technical, architectural, and operational constraints that impact their viability for production applications. Understanding these limitations is essential for developers and organizations evaluating these tools for real-world projects. Vibe coding platforms can struggle when handling advanced workflows, unusual data models, or industry-specific complex requirements. Vibe coding tools are optimized for common patterns and standard use cases, relying on training data that predominantly features mainstream application architectures. When projects require rare algorithms, domain-level expertise, or features that fall outside typical application behavior, the AI can misinterpret developer intent or produce incorrect implementations.

Vibe coding also introduces some scalability obstacles that can become apparent as applications grow. AI-generated code can prioritize straightforward solutions over optimized implementations, resulting in inefficient resource utilization and poor performance characteristics. Database query optimization can be overlooked, leading to severe performance degradation as data volumes increase. These platforms can produce monolithic architecture patterns rather than modular designs, making it difficult or impossible to scale individual components independently. Performance bottlenecks such as nested loops, repeated computations, and suboptimal data structures can be common in AI-generated code and require significant manual refactoring to address.

Security is another critical weakness of vibe coding platforms, where AI-generated code can introduce serious vulnerabilities. Vibe coding platforms also may lack robust testing and debugging support, creating downstream problems that can compound over time. Since vibe coding systems rely fundamentally on natural language processing, they can also exhibit high sensitivity to prompt quality and consistency. Unclear, ambiguous, or inconsistent instructions can lead to unpredictable or completely incorrect outputs. A single vague prompt has the potential to shift the entire direction of a build, requiring users to carefully guide the system to avoid confusion and wasted effort. This creates a paradox where users need substantial domain knowledge and understanding to craft effective prompts. The challenge of requirements specification, traditionally one of the hardest aspects of software development, is not eliminated but merely transformed into a different interface.

Vibe coding platforms also face limitations when projects require custom integrations beyond their built-in features and training data. Vibe coding tools are essentially no-code environments at their core, possessing only the integrations and building blocks that their sandboxed environments support. Integration with niche third-party APIs, legacy systems, complex enterprise infrastructure, or less common programming frameworks is often limited or completely impossible. The platforms typically offer restricted configurability and lack deep customization options, which stifles innovation and may not align with specific industry requirements or unique business processes. This dependency on third-party providers for essential functions creates vendor lock-in risks and potential conflicts in data definitions and architecture that can complicate scaling operations.

Vibe coding platforms also present enterprise adoption challenges related to governance, oversight, and long-term sustainability. The absence of internal architectural oversight can lead to critical issues, including system downtime, performance problems, and scalability challenges for vibe-coded production applications. Enterprise-scale deployments require governance processes to evaluate builds before production launch, but vibe coding's rapid generation cycle often conflicts with established review procedures. Board-level accountability for technical debt is becoming a reality as enterprise software failures create significant business risk, and CTOs who embraced vibe coding without maintaining code quality standards may find themselves unable to defend technical decisions. Companies that fail to maintain engineering discipline while adopting AI tools can risk creating systems that become increasingly difficult and expensive to maintain over time.

Figure 8.1 illustrates a visual map of the vibe coding platform limitations, with the center as the AI platform that serves as the core of the vibe coding platform. Surrounding it are six major constraint areas connected to the center by dashed lines. These issues include complexity challenges with unusual requirements, scalability problems as applications grow, security vulnerabilities in generated code, limited integration capabilities with external systems, weak testing support, and vendor lock-in risks. At the bottom, a warning symbol serves as a visual reminder of the production risks these accumulated constraints can create, suggesting that while vibe coding platforms offer convenience, they can carry technical debt and operational challenges that organizations must carefully consider before adoption.

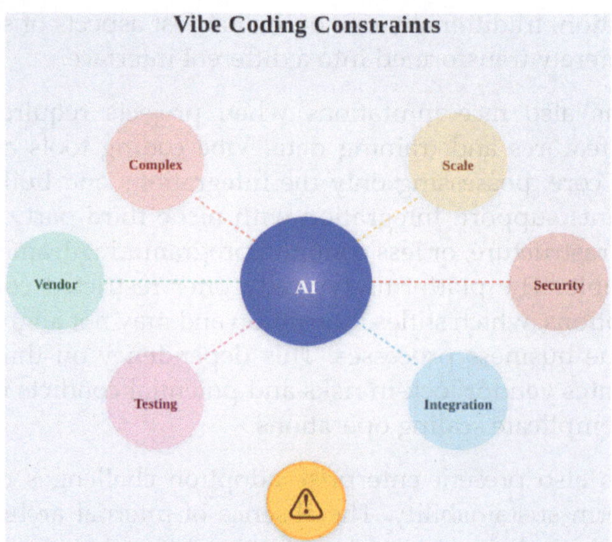

Figure 8.1: A visual map of vibe coding platform limitations

AI coding assistants underlying vibe coding platforms rely on public codebases for training, which may introduce quality and security concerns. The training data breadth does not guarantee reliability with common pitfalls, including suggestions based on outdated libraries, recommendations that violate security protocols or best practices, and duplicate code that may inadvertently infringe on open-source licenses. A particularly dangerous phenomenon is **slopsquatting**, where language models hallucinate non-existent package dependencies, and attackers register those package names to achieve code execution in victim build pipelines or runtimes. In the next section, we will look at some of the challenges in using vibe coding tools for low-level system optimization.

Low-level system optimization

Vibe coding platforms face fundamental constraints when it comes to low-level system optimization, as they prioritize rapid development and natural language interaction over fine-grained performance tuning. The very design philosophy of delegating low-level implementation details to AI can create a significant gap between the high-level vibe of developers' communication and the hardware-specific optimizations necessary for maximum performance. This limitation becomes particularly acute in domains requiring absolute efficiency, such as embedded systems, real-time applications, and performance-critical infrastructure.

AI-generated code from vibe coding platforms can demonstrate poor memory efficiency compared to human-optimized implementations. The average memory usage across typical AI-generated code can be 1.69 times higher than that of manually optimized solutions. These inefficiencies stem from AI models producing code with redundant variables, unnecessary data structures, and suboptimal memory allocation patterns that accumulate during iterative processes. Dynamic memory management proves particularly problematic with AI-generated code often failing to efficiently manage heap allocations and deallocations compared to established benchmarks. Memory leakage issues arise when low-quality generated code contains redundant variables and inefficient memory patterns that can compromise both performance and reliability. Vibe coding platforms also exhibit variable efficiency across different algorithmic paradigms, with potential degradation in graph algorithms and recursive structures.

Vibe coding platforms also lack awareness of compiler optimization techniques that are required for generating efficient low-level machine code, including register allocation, instruction scheduling, and data flow analysis. For embedded systems development where memory and processing resources are severely constrained, vibe coding can introduce unacceptable inefficiencies and unpredictability. Embedded development demands absolute efficiency with optimized flash and RAM footprints, deterministic execution patterns, and real-time performance guarantees. AI code generation can introduce unnecessary loops, dynamic memory allocations, and unused variables that bloat binary sizes and reduce runtime determinism. Unlike cloud-based or desktop applications, where resources are virtually unlimited, embedded environments require every byte and CPU cycle to be carefully managed, which is a level of control that natural language prompts cannot effectively specify. The inability to generate hardware-specific optimizations, tight memory constraints, and real-time determinism requirements make vibe coding largely unsuitable for professional embedded systems work.

Vibe coding platforms generally lack the capability to generate hardware-specific optimizations that exploit particular CPU architectures, instruction sets, or specialized processor features. Vibe coding also suffers from premature optimization problems, where AI generates overly complex code attempting to optimize scenarios that do not represent actual bottlenecks. AI models may introduce micro-optimizations such as bit-shifting for division operations, inline function expansion, and complex caching schemes while simultaneously ignoring the real performance problems like unoptimized database queries or excessive API calls. This pattern emerges because AI training data includes both simple implementations and heavily optimized code, leading models to apply optimization techniques indiscriminately without measuring whether they address actual performance bottlenecks. The fundamental principle of **measure first, optimize later**, is violated when AI pre-emptively adds complexity that makes code harder to maintain without providing measurable performance benefits.

AI-generated code demonstrates poor judgment in managing space-time tradeoffs, often failing to match optimization strategies to actual usage patterns. Effective software engineering requires carefully balancing memory usage against processing speed using caching for frequently accessed data while avoiding memory waste on rarely used information. Vibe coding platforms frequently implement inappropriate caching strategies, either consuming excessive memory for data that is seldom reused or repeatedly computing values that should be cached. Vibe coding platforms also lack integrated performance testing and profiling capabilities that are essential for identifying and addressing optimization opportunities. Effective performance optimization requires comprehensive profiling to measure actual execution time, memory consumption, and resource utilization under realistic workloads. The metrics necessary for rigorously evaluating AI-generated code, including execution efficiency, memory footprint, algorithmic complexity, and scalability characteristics, should be measured externally rather than being integrated into the development process.

Figure 8.2 visualizes the performance and optimization limitations of vibe coding platforms. The central AI node is surrounded by six critical performance constraint areas as memory inefficiency showing wasteful allocation patterns, compiler optimization gaps where the AI lacks awareness of low-level code generation techniques, hardware-specific optimization failures where platform-specific features go unexploited, poor space-time tradeoff decisions where caching and compute strategies are mismatched to actual usage patterns, missing profiling capabilities that prevent systematic performance measurement and embedded system unsuitability where resource constraints are too tight for AI-generated code. At the bottom, a highlighted metric shows that AI-generated code averages 1.69 times higher memory usage compared to human-optimized implementations, which quantifies the efficiency gap. This visualization emphasizes how these performance issues stem from the design philosophy of vibe coding platforms that prioritize rapid development through natural language interaction over the fine-grained control needed for performance optimization.

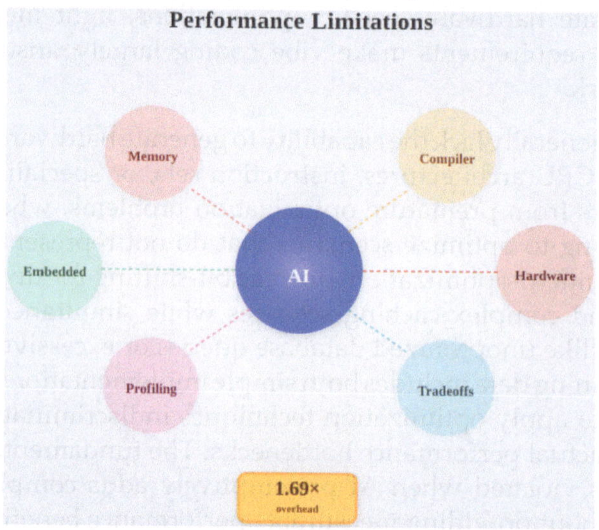

Figure 8.2: The performance and optimization limitations of vibe coding platforms

The memory and computational inefficiencies inherent in AI-generated code from vibe coding platforms translate directly into substantial financial costs for organizations running code at scale. Cloud computing costs increase proportionally with resource consumption, which means inefficient code that uses 1.69 times more memory and processing power than optimized alternatives generate 69% higher infrastructure expenses. For machine learning systems, training and inference costs can reach millions of dollars, making code optimization that reduces memory consumption by 45% economically critical. Organizations deploying vibe-coded applications to embedded devices or edge computing infrastructure face additional costs as inefficient code may require more expensive hardware with larger memory and faster processors. In the next section, we will look at the limitations of vibe coding systems for complex algorithmic implementations.

Complex algorithmic implementations

Vibe coding platforms face significant challenges when tasked with implementing complex algorithms, particularly those requiring sophisticated data structures, advanced problem-solving techniques, or deep computational understanding. While AI-generated code excels at routine tasks and straightforward logic, it struggles substantially with intricate algorithms, specialized domain challenges, and scenarios demanding precise mathematical reasoning. Users accept AI-generated complex algorithms without fully understanding their operation, creating dangerous comprehension gaps that can undermine long-term maintainability. Complex algorithms implemented through vibe coding may remain black boxes to the user, with subtle bugs going undetected due to incomplete comprehension.

AI-generated code can fail to handle edge cases and recursion limits properly, leading to solutions that work for common inputs but will fail catastrophically on boundary conditions. Research analyzing AI-generated code reveals that models often struggle with recursive implementations, producing solutions prone to infinite recursion, incorrect base cases, or missing termination conditions. Vibe coding platforms can produce naive recursive implementations that lead to exponential time complexity due to redundant calculations, missing opportunities for memorization, or dynamic programming optimizations. Critical edge cases such as empty inputs, maximum recursion depth limits, unexpected data types, or missing parameters are sometimes not addressed in AI-generated recursive solutions. Dynamic programming represents another challenging algorithmic paradigm for vibe coding platforms, as it requires recognizing overlapping subproblems and optimal substructure properties. The failure to recognize when dynamic programming techniques should be applied means that vibe-coded solutions may exhibit acceptable performance on small test inputs but may become completely impractical at production scale.

Combinatorial optimization problems such as the **traveling salesman problem** (**TSP**), **vehicle routing problem** (**VRP**), and graph coloring are classified as NP-hard and present extraordinary challenges for vibe coding platforms. These problems cannot be solved optimally within polynomial time constraints, requiring sophisticated heuristic approaches, approximation algorithms, or specialized solution techniques. Vibe coding platforms lack the specialized architectures and training necessary to tackle such problems effectively, and they produce either naive brute-force solutions with exponential complexity or incorrect approximations. Complex data structures such as balanced binary trees, heaps, tries, and graph representations require careful invariant maintenance that AI-generated code does not handle properly. Graph algorithms that require sophisticated state management, such as detecting cycles, finding strongly connected components, or computing minimum spanning trees, often produce incorrect results when generated by vibe coding platforms due to subtle logic errors in state tracking.

AI can handle syntax and basic logic effectively, but it may not fully grasp the overall project's objectives or the specific computational properties required, which can lead to the generation of code that does not align with intended functionality. Domain-specific algorithmic challenges, such as computational geometry, numerical analysis, or signal processing, require specialized knowledge that general-purpose language models do not possess. Vibe coding platforms cannot compensate for this limitation without extensive prompt engineering that essentially requires developers to already understand the algorithmic solution. Ensuring the correctness of complex AI-generated algorithms presents substantial challenges as automated verification requires sophisticated techniques that exceed simple unit testing. AI-generated code can fail to ensure correctness across all execution paths, particularly with intricate branching logic or edge cases that were not explicitly specified in prompts. The gap between AI's ability to generate working code and its ability to guarantee algorithmic correctness represents a fundamental limitation for mission critical applications.

Implementing complex algorithms through vibe coding frequently requires extensive prompt iteration with practitioners describing cycles of prompt adjustment and code refinement that can span dozens or even hundreds of iterations. Complex algorithmic requirements often cannot be fully specified in a single prompt, requiring developers to incrementally guide the AI through multiple rounds of clarification and correction. While vibe coding platforms excel at assembling straightforward applications quickly, they tend not to perform well when algorithmic complexity needs to evolve into more sophisticated systems. Adding advanced algorithmic features or optimizations to existing vibe-coded implementations presents significant challenges, as the underlying code may lack the architectural foundation to support enhanced algorithms. Scaling algorithms to production systems processing millions of records requires performance optimizations, parallelization strategies, and resource management that AI-generated code typically does not include. Vibe coding is typically less favorable for implementations necessitating wide-ranging algorithmic customization and complex computational architecture.

Figure 8.3 illustrates a visual comparison of AI coding capabilities when dealing with complex algorithms. On the left side, in green, are three boxes representing what AI handles well, which are **Simple Logic**, **Syntax**, and **Routine Tasks**. The right side displays four problem areas with the infinity sign representing recursion problems and infinite loops. Following that is a warning triangle icon for Edge Cases that AI often misses. The third box contains a jagged upward line graph illustrating scaling issues where performance degrades. The fourth box simply states **NP-Hard** to represent computationally complex problems that AI cannot solve efficiently. At the bottom, a warning banner stretches across both sections, highlighting one of the main challenges of vibe coding, which is a black box risk for code that works, but users might not understand it. This captures the problem where AI-generated complex algorithms may function on the surface but may remain incomprehensible to users, creating maintenance and reliability risks.

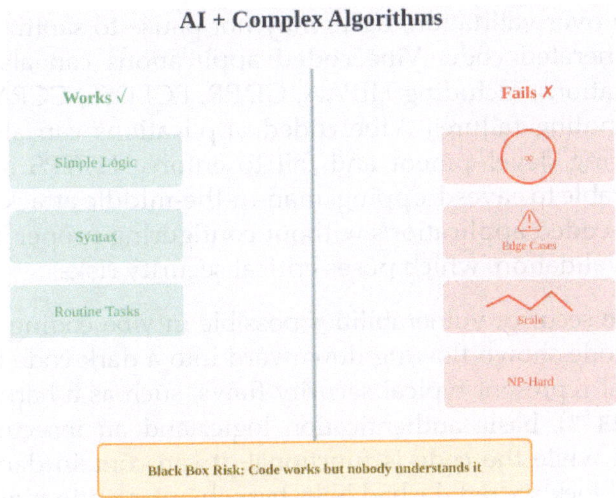

***Figure 8.3:** A visual comparison of AI coding capabilities when dealing with complex algorithms*

Legacy algorithms and unconventional algorithmic approaches also present challenges for vibe coding and AI code generators, as these systems may use outdated techniques or domain-specific optimizations that AI struggles to reproduce correctly. Historical algorithms optimized for specific hardware constraints may not appear frequently in modern training data. Domain-specific algorithms from fields like bioinformatics, computational chemistry, or astronomical data processing employ specialized techniques that general-purpose AI models have limited exposure to during training. Users often need to manually adapt, rewrite, or extensively guide AI systems when implementing these specialized or legacy algorithms. The concentration of training data on mainstream algorithms and popular programming patterns means that novel algorithmic approaches or cutting-edge research techniques are poorly supported by vibe coding platforms. In the next section, we will look at the limitations of vibe coding systems for advanced security requirements

Advanced security requirements

Vibe coding platforms sometimes demonstrate inadequacies in addressing advanced security requirements for enterprise applications, regulated industries, and security-critical systems. While AI-generated code may function correctly from a business logic perspective, it can fail to implement comprehensive security boundaries, authentication mechanisms, and defense-in-depth strategies. This security gap poses significant risks for organizations handling sensitive data or operating under strict compliance regimes. The AI model focuses on making the code function as described in the prompt, but can ignore security-critical concerns like access control, privilege separation, and data isolation.

Vibe coding can introduce secrets management problems where AI can embed sensitive credentials directly into source code rather than using secure external configuration. A common failure pattern involves AI generating code with hardcoded API keys, database passwords, or AWS credentials directly in the source, creating risks of secret leakage. Because vibe coding prioritizes momentum over validation, users may not pause to sanitize or rotate credentials before committing generated code. Vibe coded applications can also violate compliance requirements for regulations, including HIPAA, GDPR, PCI DSS, CCPA, and SOC 2, through unintentional data handling failures. Vibe coded applications can also sometimes default to insecure HTTP during development and fail to enforce HTTPS in production, leaving communication vulnerable to eavesdropping, man-in-the-middle attacks, and credential theft. Users can deploy vibe-coded applications without configuring proper TLS redirects, security headers, or certificate validation, which poses critical security risks.

Figure 8.4 illustrates the security vulnerabilities possible in vibe coding platforms. At the top, the AI icon generates code shown flowing downward into a dark code block. This code block displays three lines that represent typical security flaws, such as a hardcoded API key in red text (**`"API_KEY='abc123'"`**), basic authentication logic, and an insecure HTTP URL. These elements establish that while the code is functional, it can contain dangerous security gaps. From this central code block six red dashed lines branch outward to highlight specific security vulnerabilities where the key icon represents the problem of hardcoded secrets embedded directly in source code, the prohibition symbol indicates weak authentication mechanisms, the unlocked padlock symbolizing the use of HTTP instead of secure HTTPS connections, the center displays compliance regulation acronyms (GDPR, PCI, HIPAA) with a scales icon representing violations of legal requirements and a crossed out circle indicates that essential security testing has been skipped. At the bottom, a larger box shows the supply chain security risk, depicting a package icon with the text **`fake-package-v1.0`** to represent malicious or hallucinated dependencies that AI might introduce into the codebase. The yellow warning banner at the bottom delivers the key message, which captures the issue that vibe coding produces functionally correct code from a business logic perspective, but may fail to implement proper security controls, leaving applications vulnerable to attacks, data breaches,s and compliance violations.

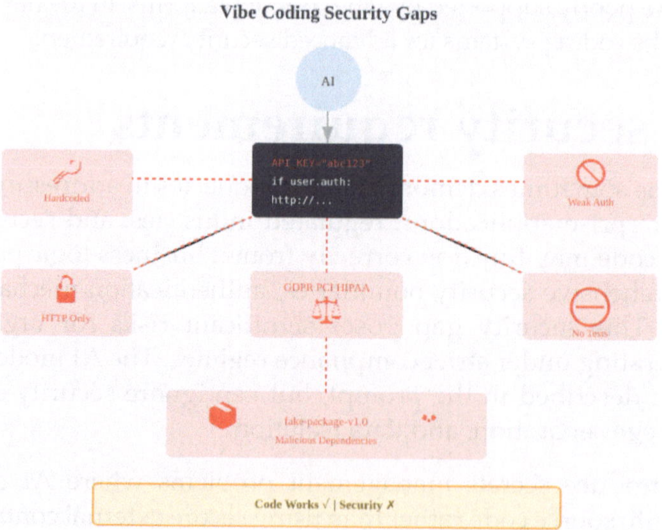

Figure 8.4: The security vulnerabilities in vibe coding platforms

Vibe coding workflows can bypass essential security testing and validation steps that would identify vulnerabilities before production deployment. Traditional security gates, including **static application security testing** (SAST), **dynamic application security testing** (DAST), **interactive application security testing** (IAST), and penetration testing, may be skipped in the rapid development cycles that vibe coding enables. Modern AI penetration testing tools that operate using modular agent-based frameworks, including discovery agents, CVE agents, SQL injection agents, XSS agents, and access control agents, can help validate vulnerabilities through real exploitation rather than superficial scanning. Vibe coding can also introduce supply chain security risks through dependency selection, malicious package introduction, and cases where AI hallucinates non-existent dependencies. Language models may suggest non-existent package names, which attackers then register to achieve code execution in victim build pipelines or runtime environments. Malicious or vulnerable libraries can enter codebases through a single import statement in AI-generated code. Effective supply chain security requires blocking known suspicious packages, using allow lists for critical codebases, and aligning workflows with secure software development practices. In the next section, we will look at the hybrid development workflows that combine vibe coding with traditional programming that represent emerging best practices for enterprise-scale software development.

Hybrid development workflows

Hybrid development workflows that combine vibe coding with traditional programming approaches represent an emerging best practice for maximizing AI productivity while maintaining code quality and system integrity. Rather than choosing exclusively between AI-assisted and conventional development, teams can strategically allocate tasks based on their characteristics, complexity, and criticality. This balanced approach preserves the speed advantages of vibe coding while ensuring necessary human oversight for architectural decisions, security implementations, and complex business logic. Effective hybrid development requires clear boundaries defining when to employ vibe coding versus traditional programming based on task characteristics and risk profiles. Vibe coding demonstrates exceptional value for rapid prototyping, boilerplate code generation, test suite creation, API integration scaffolding, and straightforward CRUD operations. Traditional coding remains essential for security-critical components requiring performance-sensitive algorithms demanding optimization, complex business logic with intricate domain rules, architectural decisions affecting long-term system evolution, and compliance-regulated functionality. Organizations should designate clear areas where AI can operate with minimal oversight, such as generating documentation, creating test cases, or producing standard UI components, while identifying domains requiring mandatory human review.

Hybrid workflows require comprehensive code quality assurance mechanisms specifically adapted for AI-generated code, including static analysis, linting, security scanning, and architectural compliance verification. Successful hybrid development also requires deliberate team structures that counterbalance AI's limitations through formalized roles and distributed expertise. Organizations should designate experienced developers as architects, maintaining architectural oversight across multiple teams, with these architects receiving AI-specific training to spot patterns of AI-generated technical debt. Balanced team composition mixing AI enthusiasts with architectural thinkers prevents echo chambers where vibe coding techniques go unchallenged and suboptimal patterns proliferate unchecked. Research demonstrates that organizational challenges such as knowledge erosion and weakened technical ownership can be substantially reduced through human oversight, clear approval processes, and formalized architectural review.

GenMB is an upcoming vibe coding tool purpose-built to support hybrid development workflows, recognizing that the most effective AI-assisted development is a deliberate orchestration of AI automation and human control. For rapid prototyping, boilerplate generation, test suite scaffolding, and standard CRUD operations, GenMB accelerates delivery through natural language generation across different frameworks. For security-critical components, GenMB's built-in OWASP Top 10 Security Scanner with automatic Code Healer remediation ensures vulnerabilities are caught and fixed in the generation pipeline itself. Role-based access controls, GitHub Sync, and full version history with rollback give teams the governance layer needed to distribute AI autonomy appropriately across skill levels and risk profiles. With controlled Agent Mode and planning mode that provides structured breakdowns before generation begins, GenMB ensures developers retain oversight at every stage of complex builds, thus capturing the speed of vibe coding while preserving the rigor that production-grade systems demand.

Ensuring consistency between AI-generated code and existing codebases represents a critical challenge for hybrid workflows requiring deliberate configuration and context provision. Vibe coding tools need to be configured to access relevant project context, including architectural patterns, naming conventions, coding styles, dependency management practices, and established design patterns. Providing AI with comprehensive context helps produce outputs that align with project standards, substantially reducing the need for extensive manual adjustments and integration work. Hybrid workflows can pose knowledge transfer challenges as AI-generated code can create comprehension gaps where users accept complex implementations without fully understanding their operation. Organizations should document successful AI interaction patterns for future reference, share effective prompting techniques across teams, and create learning opportunities where developers explain AI-generated solutions to colleagues. This active knowledge transfer prevents the erosion of technical understanding that occurs when teams become over-reliant on AI tools without maintaining fundamental comprehension.

Effective hybrid workflow adoption further requires incremental integration, starting with smaller, well-understood chunks of AI-generated code rather than wholesale transformation. Organizations should build up complexity gradually, beginning with low-risk applications such as internal tools, prototypes, or non-critical features, before expanding to production systems. The principle of continuous learning encourages teams to document successful patterns, analyze failures without blame, and iteratively refine their approach to AI integration. Balancing automation with oversight means automating routine coding tasks while maintaining human responsibility for critical components, architectural decisions, and security implementations. Organizations should establish pilot projects that test hybrid workflows in controlled environments, measuring technical debt indicators, development velocity, defect rates, and maintainability before broader rollout. This measured approach allows teams to develop expertise with AI tools, identify optimal task allocation boundaries, and refine quality assurance processes before making substantial workflow changes.

Figure 8.5 illustrates the hybrid development workflow that strategically combines AI-assisted coding with traditional human programming. The canvas is divided into two distinct colored zones representing the optimal task allocation between AI and human developers. The left side encompasses the **AI Coding** domain. Within this zone are five stacked boxes representing tasks ideally suited for vibe coding platforms, which are rapid prototyping, boilerplate code generation, test suite creation, CRUD operations, and documentation. These tasks share common characteristics as they are routine, repetitive, and well-understood, making them perfect candidates for AI automation that can accelerate development velocity. On the right side, the **Human Coding** domain is defined, which contains five boxes representing critical responsibilities that require human expertise and judgment. These include security implementations, architectural decisions, complex business logic, performance optimization, and compliance-regulated functionality. These tasks demand deep domain knowledge, strategic thinking, and accountability that AI systems cannot reliably provide. At the center of the diagram, the word **Review** demonstrates that AI-generated code must pass through mandatory human review and oversight before integration into the codebase, ensuring quality control and preventing AI-generated technical debt or security vulnerabilities from entering production systems. At the bottom, a purple-bordered banner spans the entire width presenting the key principles for successful hybrid workflow adoption which emphasizes that organizations should gradually introduce AI tools, provide proper context to guide code generation, maintain continuous human oversight, document effective interaction patterns for knowledge sharing and establish metrics to measure the impact on code quality and development velocity before expanding AI adoption across larger systems.

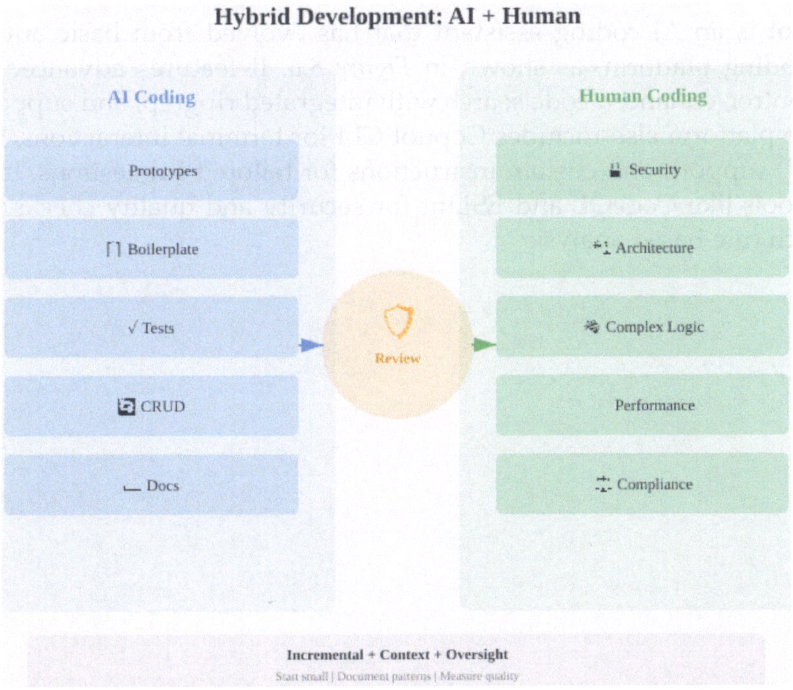

Figure 8.5*: Hybrid development workflow that strategically combines AI with traditional human programming*

Hybrid development model adoption can face significant organizational and cultural challenges, including resistance to change, skill shortages, complexity of oversight, and misalignment with established processes. Technology and skills gaps, complex legacy systems, and decades of embedded IT processes can all impede an organization's ability to successfully transition to hybrid workflows. Resistance to change represents a natural part of digital transformation, but can hinder adoption if not managed appropriately through cultural shifts and strategic alignment with broader business goals. Working with expert service providers or establishing internal centers of excellence can guide the transition, helping organizations develop best practices, establish quality gates, and train developers on responsible AI-assisted development. In the next section, we will look at some of the AI coding tools that can complement vibe coding tools for scalable application development.

AI coding tools

AI coding tools have evolved from simple autocomplete assistants to sophisticated agentic systems capable of autonomous code generation, multi-file editing, and complex task execution. Tools like Cursor, Windsurf's Cascade, GitHub Copilot, Claude Code, and Amazon Q represent different philosophies in AI-assisted development, each with distinct strengths, limitations, and optimal use cases. Understanding these tools' capabilities and constraints is essential for effective vibe coding implementation and realistic expectation management. Modern AI coding tools occupy distinct positions along a spectrum from passive code completion to fully autonomous agentic systems.

GitHub Copilot is an AI coding assistant that has evolved from basic autocomplete to a multi-modal coding platform, as shown in *Figure 8.6*. It features advanced edit mode for granular file control, enhanced code search with integrated ripgrep, and support for the latest AI models. The platform also includes Copilot CLI for terminal interactions, **Model Context Protocol** (**MCP**) support, and custom instructions for tailored suggestions. It also integrates deterministic tools like CodeQL and ESLint for security and quality checks, blending LLM intelligence with rule-based analysis.

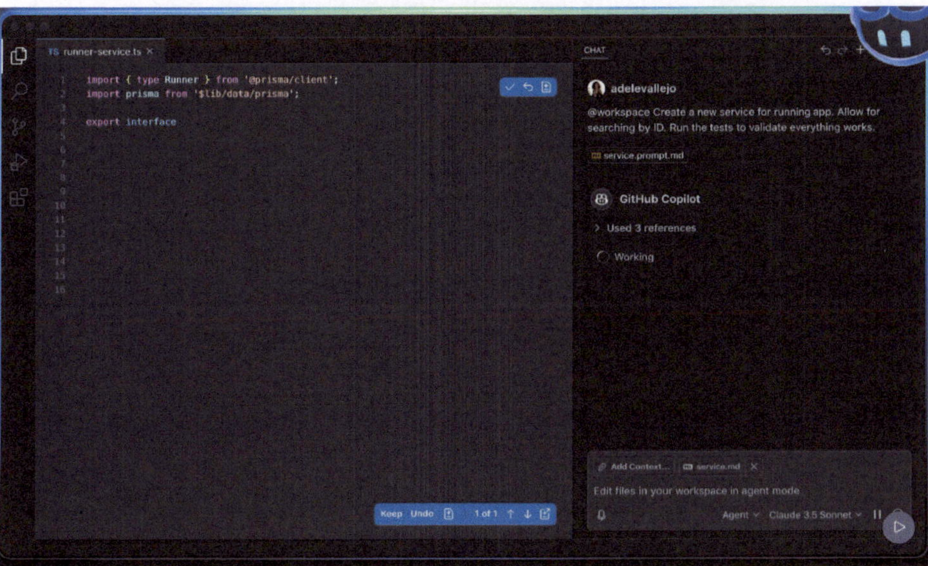

Figure 8.6: GitHub Copilot

Cursor positions itself as an AI native IDE built on VS Code, but its capabilities extend significantly as shown in *Figure 8.7*. The Composer Agent enables autonomous full-stack code generation with multi-file editing, while Cursor tab provides context-aware, real-time autocomplete that predicts entire code blocks rather than single lines. The platform supports the best AI models with codebase indexing that gives AI an understanding of your entire project context. Enhanced features include predictive coding based on patterns, integrated security protocols with automated vulnerability scanning, and seamless cloud service integration with AWS and Azure.

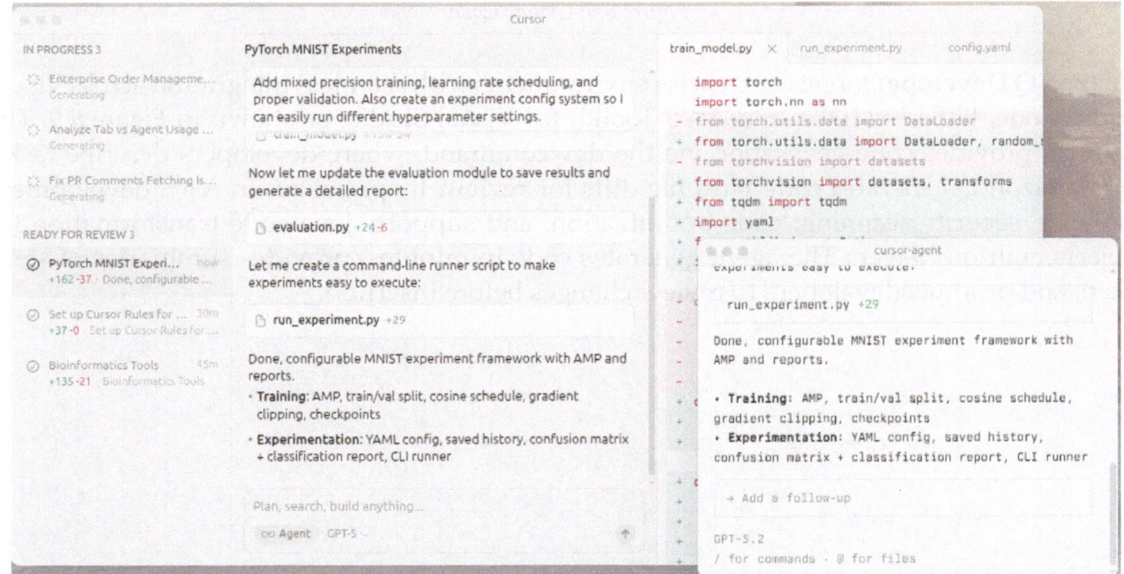

Figure 8.7: Cursor

Claude Code focuses on terminal-based interactions but also provides native IDE extensions for VS Code, JetBrains, and other IDEs. It can run locally in your terminal, talks directly to model APIs without requiring a backend server or remote code index, and asks for permission before making changes, as shown in *Figure 8.8*. The tool functions as an autonomous agent capable of understanding entire codebases, executing multi-step tasks, and maintaining context across complex projects. Claude Code operates through three primary modes, as terminal access via natural language commands, IDE integration with visual diffs, and web access for browser-based sessions. It can use CLI tools like Git and MCP servers to extend its capabilities.

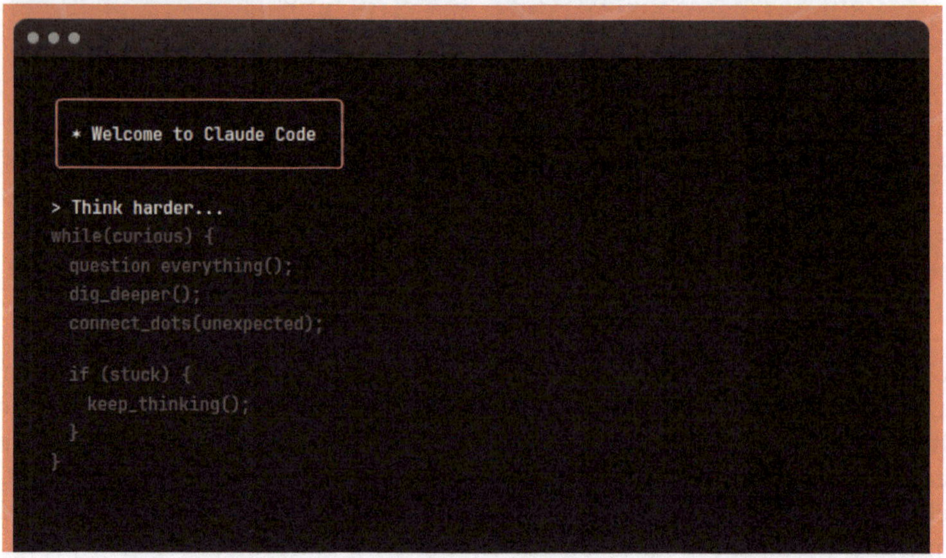

```
* Welcome to Claude Code

> Think harder...
while(curious) {
  question_everything();
  dig_deeper();
  connect_dots(unexpected);

  if (stuck) {
    keep_thinking();
  }
}
```

Figure 8.8: Claude Code

Amazon Q Developer targets enterprise environments with seamless integration across Visual Studio Code, JetBrains IDEs, and AWS Toolkit for Visual Studio, as shown in *Figure 8.9*. The platform provides code generation via the dev command, where developers describe tasks, and Amazon Q generates code with file diffs for review. It specializes in AWS development guidance, security scanning, code optimization, and supports Java code transformation for projects built on Maven. The agent generates code in minutes, provides summaries of steps taken, and prompts developers to review changes before insertion.

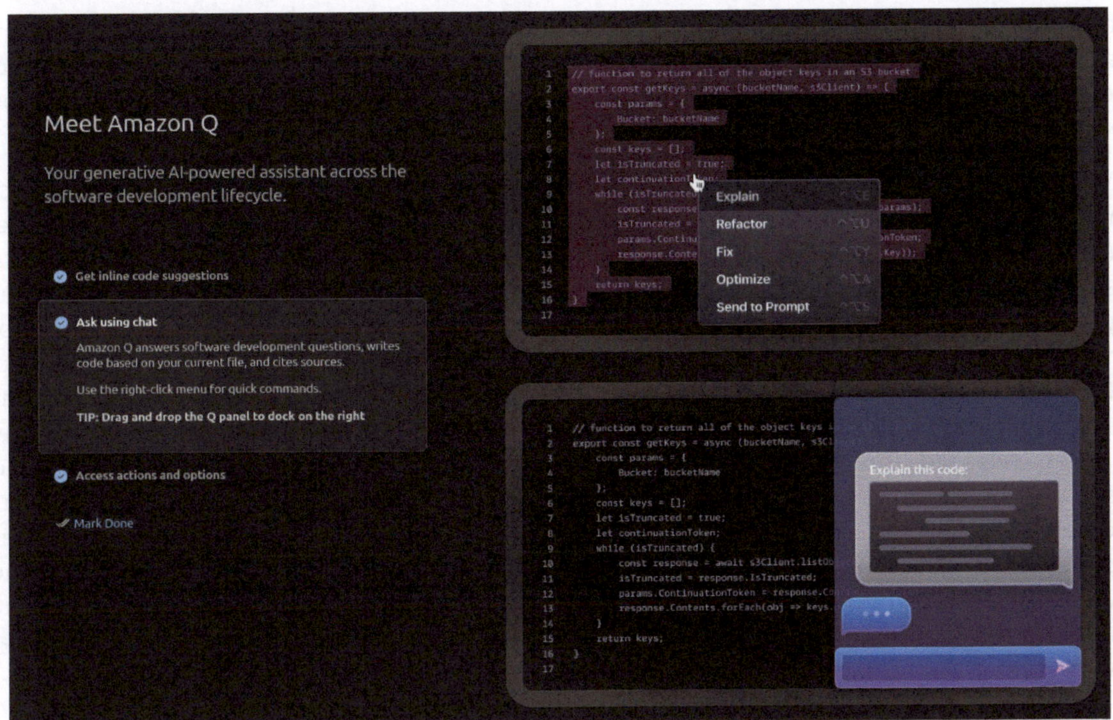

Figure 8.9: Amazon Q Developer

Context window capabilities fundamentally determine how effectively AI coding tools understand and operate on large codebases. Tools like Cursor automatically include relevant information in the input context based on codebase state, including open files, recently edited files, and imported dependencies. Claude Code's context window is notably more reliable for large codebases, providing consistent comprehension across extensive file structures. The practical limit remains that even advanced tools struggle with codebases exceeding certain size thresholds, as context windows have finite capacity. Users must understand that while these tools analyze immediate context effectively, they lack the holistic system understanding that senior architects possess through years of working on specific codebases.

The transition from passive assistants to autonomous agents represents a fundamental shift in AI coding tool capabilities with profound implications for development workflows. Cursor's Agent mode allows users to delegate coding tasks while focusing on higher-level direction, with the agent analyzing usage patterns across workspaces and executing multi-step implementations. Different AI coding tools employ distinct interface paradigms that fundamentally shape how developers interact with AI assistance. Users should select tools matching their preferred interaction patterns and requirements rather than assuming all AI assistants provide equivalent experiences. Successful AI coding tool adoption requires seamless integration with existing development workflows rather than disruptive replacement of established processes. Organizations treating AI as a process challenge rather than merely a technology challenge achieve superior outcomes by focusing on workflow adaptation and team collaboration patterns. Integration starts with understanding which use cases provide the highest return on investment, then incrementally incorporating AI assistance in those specific areas.

Despite impressive capabilities, these AI coding tools also exhibit significant technical limitations that users must understand and compensate for. Early limitations focused on output length constraints, with tools struggling to generate or modify large code segments in a single operation. Message limits remain problematic even in paid tiers, with Claude users reporting frustration about rate limiting interrupting productive coding sessions. The tools struggle with interpreting nuanced language as comprehension relies on pattern recognition rather than genuine contextual understanding. Knowledge limitations also reflect training data cutoffs, meaning tools lack awareness of recent framework updates, emerging best practices, or newly released libraries. Advanced AI coding tools still cannot reliably perform complex reasoning or multi-step planning comparable to experienced human developers, limiting their effectiveness for architectural decisions and sophisticated algorithm design. Developers report that all AI coding tools **fail at times**, with differences emerging not in raw intelligence but in how gracefully they handle failures and recover from mistakes. Organizations should implement validation processes, assuming AI-generated code contains errors requiring human review, rather than trusting outputs directly.

Full-stack vibe coding platforms such as Replit, Bolt.new, Lovable, etc., differ fundamentally from AI code editors like Claude Code, Cursor, GitHub Copilot, etc. in their target audience, level of abstraction, and development approach. Full-stack platforms are designed as all-in-one solutions that automatically handle frontend, backend, API logic, database management, deployment, and hosting through natural language prompts, making them accessible to non-developers and ideal for rapid prototyping. In contrast, AI-powered code editors are terminal or IDE-based tools that provide experienced developers with deeper codebase understanding, fine-grained control, and production-ready code quality while requiring existing programming knowledge. The spectrum of control varies significantly across vibe coding tools, with full-stack platforms offering less granular control in exchange for speed and simplicity. AI coding tools provide full code control with deep context awareness that understands entire repositories, multi-file coordinated changes, and production-ready output with well-structured code, comments, and clear error handling. The choice between platform types depends heavily on project complexity, timeline, and the user's technical proficiency.

Conclusion

In this chapter, we examined the fundamental limitations and constraints that affect vibe coding platforms when applied to production software development and their implications for enterprise adoption and long-term system maintainability. We navigated critical constraint categories spanning low-level system optimization, where AI-generated code exhibits memory and performance inefficiencies, complex algorithmic implementations that struggle with recursion correctness, and NP-hard optimization problems, and advanced security requirements where generated code contains vulnerabilities. We have also identified several patterns that consistently determine whether vibe coding implementations succeed or fail in production environments. These patterns include the recognition that strategic task allocation between AI generation and traditional programming based on complexity and risk profiles, the implementation of rigorous validation gates with security scanning and architectural review, the establishment of technical debt management practices, and the adoption of hybrid workflows with experienced human oversight transform AI from a liability into a genuine productivity multiplier for appropriate use cases. Additionally, we explored how different AI coding tools, from Cursor's agentic capabilities to GitHub Copilot's enterprise security features, serve distinct organizational needs. We also discussed the critical importance of matching vibe coding adoption to appropriate contexts rather than treating it as a universal solution for all software development challenges.

In the next chapter, we will explore the emerging trends and future possibilities in vibe coding, examining how advancing AI capabilities, new development paradigms, and evolving industry needs will shape the next generation of prompt-driven software development. We analyze upcoming technologies, predict industry shifts, and provide strategic guidance for staying ahead in the rapidly evolving vibe coding landscape.

Further reading

There are lots of online resources to help you improve your learning on vibe coding projects and limitations. *Table 8.1* lists some of the best resources to further improve your understanding on vibe coding projects and limitations.

Resource name	Link
What Are the Main Limitations of Vibe Coding in Software Development	**https://www.dhiwise.com/post/what-are-the-main-limitations-of-vibe-coding**
Top 5 problems with vibe coding	**https://www.glideapps.com/blog/vibe-coding-risks**
Understanding the limitations of vibe coding	**https://graphite.com/guides/limitations-of-vibe-coding**
Passing the Security Vibe Check: The Dangers of Vibe Coding	**https://www.databricks.com/blog/passing-security-vibe-check-dangers-vibe-coding**
The Rise (and Risk) of Vibe Coding – What's Worth Knowing	**https://softwaremind.com/blog/the-rise-and-risk-of-vibe-coding-whats-worth-knowing/**
What is Vibe Coding? The Pros, Cons, and Controversies	**https://www.tanium.com/blog/what-is-vibe-coding/**

Resource name	Link
Vibe coding is the future — just don't trust it (yet)	**https://www.businessinsider.com/vibe-coding-limits-use-cases-software-companies-airtable-redis-2025-7**
What's The Problem With Vibe Coding? [Honest Review]	**https://flatlogic.com/blog/what-s-the-problem-with-vibe-coding-honest-review/**
Karpathy's 'Vibe Coding' Movement Considered Harmful	**https://nmn.gl/blog/dangers-vibe-coding**
What's wrong with vibe coding? Answered by the COAX team	**https://coaxsoft.com/blog/whats-wrong-with-vibe-coding**
Vibe Coding: The Shadow IT Problem No One Saw Coming	**https://thenewstack.io/vibe-coding-the-shadow-it-problem-no-one-saw-coming/**
Vibe coding and systems thinking: Unlocking efficiency from brainstorm to build	**https://www.ibm.com/think/insights/vibe-coding-systems-thinking-unlock-efficiency**
My LLM coding workflow going into 2026	**https://addyosmani.com/blog/ai-coding-workflow/**
AI Assisted Development (AIAD)	**https://www.mendix.com/glossary/ai-assisted-development-aiad/**
How I 10x'd My Development Speed with Claude Code	**https://dev.to/hassantayyab/how-i-10xd-my-development-speed-with-claude-code-a-system-for-ai-assisted-coding-that-actually-3f07**
AI-Assisted Development: Benefits and Challenges	**https://www.appbuilder.dev/blog/ai-assisted-development**
AI-assisted development in Visual Studio	**https://learn.microsoft.com/en-us/visualstudio/ide/ai-assisted-development-visual-studio?view=visualstudio**
AI-Assisted Software Development: A Guide for Developers	**https://www.legitsecurity.com/aspm-knowledge-base/ai-assisted-software-development**
10 Best AI code generators in 2025 [Free & Paid]	**https://pieces.app/blog/9-best-ai-code-generation-tools**
20 Best AI Coding Assistant Tools [Updated Aug 2025]	**https://www.qodo.ai/blog/best-ai-coding-assistant-tools/**
What is GitHub Copilot?	**https://docs.github.com/en/copilot/get-started/what-is-github-copilot**

Resource name	Link
What is Cursor AI? Everything You Need to Know	**https://uibakery.io/blog/what-is-cursor-a**
Claude Code: Best practices for agentic coding	**https://www.anthropic.com/engineering/claude-code-best-practices**
Claude Code: What It Is, How It's Different, and Why Non-Technical People Should Use It	**https://www.producttalk.org/claude-code-what-it-is-and-how-its-different/**

***Table 8.1**: Vibe coding projects and limitations*

Questions

1. What are the main limitations of the vibe coding platforms?
2. How does vibe coding introduce scalability obstacles?
3. Why is security a critical weakness with vibe coding?
4. Why are custom integrations hard with vibe coding tools?
5. What are the enterprise adoption challenges for vibe coding?
6. Why does vibe coding struggle with low-level system optimizations?
7. Why do vibe coding platforms lack awareness of compiler optimization techniques?
8. Why does AI-generated code demonstrate poor judgment in managing space-time tradeoffs?
9. What are the memory and computational inefficiencies inherent in AI-generated code?
10. What are the challenges in vibe coding for implementing complex algorithms?
11. Why does vibe coding demonstrate inadequacies in addressing advanced security requirements?
12. How can you use vibe coding with secure coding practices?
13. What are hybrid development workflows?
14. How can you ensure consistency between AI generated code and existing codebases?
15. What are the steps required for effective hybrid workflow adoption?
16. What are the organizational and cultural challenges for hybrid development workflows?
17. What are the most popular AI coding tools?

18. What are the advantages of GitHub Copilot?
19. How is Cursor different from other tools?
20. What are the advantages of using Claude Code?
21. What are the main differences between full stack vibe coding platforms and AI code editors?

Join our Discord space

Join our Discord workspace for latest updates, offers, tech happenings around the world, new releases, and sessions with the authors:

https://discord.bpbonline.com

CHAPTER 9
Future Trends in Vibe Coding

Introduction

In this chapter, we will explore how rapidly evolving AI models are transforming vibe coding from simple code assistance into a full-stack, multimodal, and increasingly autonomous software development paradigm. We will examine how each generation of models, from early general-purpose LLMs to today's specialized reasoning systems, unlocks new capabilities that fundamentally reshape how developers and non-developers alike design, build, and maintain software. You will see how advances in reasoning, context length, multimodal understanding, and agentic behavior are converging to create development environments where describing intent in natural language becomes the primary act of programming. We will trace this evolution across several dimensions that matter most for vibe coding, which are the rise of reasoning-focused models that can self-check their work, the expansion to multimodal inputs that let you work with code, images, diagrams, and voice in a unified workflow, and the emergence of self-improving and predictive systems that continuously refine both code and development processes. By the end, you will understand how these trends collectively point toward a future of vibe coding where software development is defined less by manual syntax and more by strategic thinking, domain expertise, and collaborative orchestration with intelligent AI agents.

Structure

In this chapter, we will cover the following topics:

- Evolution of AI models and their impact on vibe coding capabilities
- Multimodal AI integration for vibe coding
- Open source vibe coding ecosystems
- Industry-specific vibe coding tools
- Self-improving development systems
- Natural language programming languages
- Predictive development and proactive problem-solving systems

Objectives

This chapter will provide a comprehensive exploration of emerging technologies and methodologies that are fundamentally reshaping the vibe coding landscape, preparing you for the next generation of AI-assisted software development. It will equip you with critical insights into how reasoning models, multimodal capabilities, self-improving systems, and natural language programming are converging to create increasingly autonomous and intelligent development environments.

By the end of this chapter, you will understand the architectural evolution from basic code completion to sophisticated AI agents that can reason through complex problems, learn from their mistakes, and proactively anticipate developer needs across text, voice, image, and code modalities. You will also develop expertise in recognizing industry-specific vibe coding opportunities across healthcare, gaming, manufacturing, e-commerce, and cybersecurity, understanding how domain-specific tools embed regulatory requirements, business logic, and technical patterns that general-purpose assistants cannot replicate. Finally, you will explore the trajectory toward self-improving development systems and predictive problem-solving capabilities that represent the frontier of autonomous software engineering, where AI transitions from reactive code generation to proactive architecture optimization and continuous learning from production deployments.

Evolution of AI models and their impact on vibe coding capabilities

The evolution of AI models has dramatically transformed software development, with each generation unlocking new capabilities that have fundamentally changed how users approach software development. From the early days of GPT-3 to today's specialized reasoning models, AI has progressed from basic text generation to sophisticated coding assistants capable of handling complex software development tasks. GPT-3 marked a watershed moment, demonstrating unprecedented natural language processing capabilities that could respond to queries, generate essays, and even engage in basic coding tasks. The real breakthrough came with GPT-4, which introduced multimodal capabilities, allowing the model to work with text, images, and tables simultaneously. This architectural leap enabled developers to customize the model for specific needs through APIs and integrations, laying the groundwork for what would become vibe coding ecosystems.

The introduction of reasoning-focused models like OpenAI's o1 and o3 represented a fundamental shift in AI coding capabilities. These models add layers of logical processing on top of standard transformer architectures, enabling them to check their own steps before finalizing answers and dramatically reducing hallucinations. The o1 model achieved a 4x improvement in performance on complex tasks requiring synthesis across multiple documents, demonstrating particular strength in debugging code and analyzing complex data sets. This self-verification capability makes reasoning models especially valuable for vibe coding scenarios where developers need reliable code generation with minimal manual debugging.

Anthropic's Claude models took a different evolutionary path, prioritizing safe behavior and contextual understanding alongside performance. Developer feedback consistently highlights Claude's ability to follow intricate instructions more carefully than competing models, making it particularly effective for vibe coding workflows that rely on natural language specifications. DeepSeek democratized access to advanced reasoning capabilities through its open-source approach. Their reasoning model excels at reasoning-intensive tasks with well-defined problems, including mathematical proofs, code generation, and logical inference. DeepSeek demonstrated performance comparable to leading AI models across math, coding, and reasoning benchmarks while being freely accessible to researchers and developers. This accessibility has profound implications for vibe coding, enabling smaller teams and individual developers to leverage reasoning capabilities previously locked behind proprietary APIs.

The evolution of context windows from 2,048 tokens to more than a million tokens in the latest LLM models has fundamentally changed how AI models interact with code. Early models used standard transformers based on scaling of memory and compute with context length, but innovations like FlashAttention and high-end GPUs enabled efficient processing of massive contexts. Modern models can now analyze entire codebases or comprehensive documentation in a single pass without fragmentation. This capability directly enhances vibe coding by allowing developers to provide a complete project context, which reduces the need for **retrieval augmented generation** (**RAG**) techniques and enables more coherent code generation. The transition to multimodal AI models has further expanded vibe coding beyond text-based interactions. These multimodal capabilities allow developers to work with design mockups, wireframes, and visual specifications, directly translating visual concepts into functioning code without manual description.

Performance metrics have also improved dramatically across model generations, directly impacting vibe coding productivity. These speed improvements enable the rapid iteration cycles that define vibe coding, allowing teams to validate ideas in days instead of months. The AI model landscape has also shifted decisively toward specialization, with different models excelling at distinct tasks. The concept of a single best model has given way to orchestrating the right specialist for each coding challenge. Anthropic's **Extended Thinking**, Google's **Thinking** and **Deep Think** modes, and xAI's **thinking tokens** represent branded controllable features that developers can tune for specific tasks. This specialization enables vibe coding practitioners to select models based on whether they prioritize speed, reasoning depth, multimodal understanding, or code generation accuracy.

AI models are now judged not by their ability to generate text but by their capacity to autonomously execute multi-step tasks. The leading LLM models' agentic features handle complex multi-step tasks autonomously, moving beyond the simple prompt and response paradigm. This agentic shift transforms vibe coding from a collaborative method where AI accelerates development to one where AI functions as an autonomous executor of user intent. Users increasingly focus on strategy, user experience, and problem-solving rather than syntax and boilerplate code, with AI handling the mechanical aspects of implementation. This evolution enables lower barriers to entry, where non-developers can participate in building digital products while experienced developers channel their expertise into higher-level architectural decisions. In the next section, we will look at multimodal AI integration that represents a paradigm shift in vibe coding.

Multimodal AI integration for vibe coding

Multimodal AI integration represents a paradigm shift in vibe coding, enabling developers to communicate intent through images, voice, video, and text simultaneously rather than relying solely on written prompts. This convergence of multiple input modalities mirrors human-to-human communication patterns where spoken words, visual cues, and real-time adjustments combine to convey meaning. Modern AI models can now process design mockups, verbal descriptions, screen recordings, and code simultaneously within a unified embedding space, fundamentally changing how developers translate ideas into functional applications. Design-to-code capabilities have matured significantly with multimodal large language models like GPT-5 automatically converting visual designs into functional code implementations. These systems can analyze screenshots, wireframes, or hand-drawn sketches and generate corresponding HTML, CSS, and React components that capture layout, typography, colors, and structural elements.

Voice integration enables developers to dictate high-level intentions and receive executable code without touching a keyboard. Vibe coding with voice allows developers to focus on architectural decisions while AI handles syntax implementation. Speech-to-code systems provide engines designed specifically for developers that understand programming terminology and context. This modality proves particularly valuable for iterative refinement, where developers can provide follow-up voice commands like **`Now add error handling for missing files`** without context switching between speaking and typing. Another example is the Gemini Multimodal API that supports function calling, code execution, and search grounding within a single stateful session, eliminating the need for multiple prompts to achieve complex outcomes. Developers can build applications that process continuous streams of visual and audio input, such as pointing a camera at a circuit board while describing intended modifications verbally, and receive context-aware code solutions in real-time.

Multimodal AI transforms debugging from a text-based log analysis process into a visual forensics workflow. Systems can ingest error logs alongside screenshots of broken UI states, generate embeddings for both text and images, and run semantic similarity searches across modalities to identify patterns. Google AI Studio's multimodal features enable developers to upload interface screenshots and receive detailed analysis of program structure, feature identification, and step-by-step debugging instructions. This approach proves especially valuable for front-end issues where visual manifestation of errors provides critical context that stack traces alone cannot convey. Multimodal AI further enhances code understanding by integrating source code text, architectural diagrams, execution traces, and version history into a unified semantic model. Traditional code analysis focuses exclusively on textual content, but experienced developers naturally think in terms of visual call graphs, data flow diagrams, and temporal execution patterns. AI systems that fuse these modalities develop more comprehensive mental models of software, enabling more accurate code generation that respects existing architecture. This multimodal comprehension capability allows vibe coding tools to analyze an entire codebase's structure and generate new components that integrate seamlessly with established patterns.

Multimodal documentation generation creates interactive content that adapts to the developer context rather than producing static text. Systems can analyze code structure through abstract syntax trees, visualize data flow, generate component diagrams, and fuse these elements with natural language explanations into semantically linked documentation. This approach produces documentation that combines code snippets, visualizations, and interactive navigation, all generated automatically from codebase analysis. For vibe coding workflows, this means that AI can simultaneously generate implementation code and comprehensive documentation that explains architectural decisions through both text and visual representations.

These models can also process screen recordings to understand workflows, extract UI patterns, and generate corresponding automation code. Tools analyze recordings to identify user interactions, automatically generate titles and descriptions for each step, and create training materials with AI voiceovers and automatic zooms. This capability enables a new vibe coding pattern where developers record themselves using an existing application and receive generated code that replicates the observed functionality. The AI can detect UI elements, track interaction sequences, and infer the underlying logic needed to recreate the demonstrated behavior. Multimodal AI can simultaneously understand code that generates visualizations and the resulting visual outputs, connecting programming concepts to their graphical representations. For example, GenMB (**https://genmb.com/**) uses Multimodal AI to simultaneously understand text and images for generating required applications, as shown in the following figure:

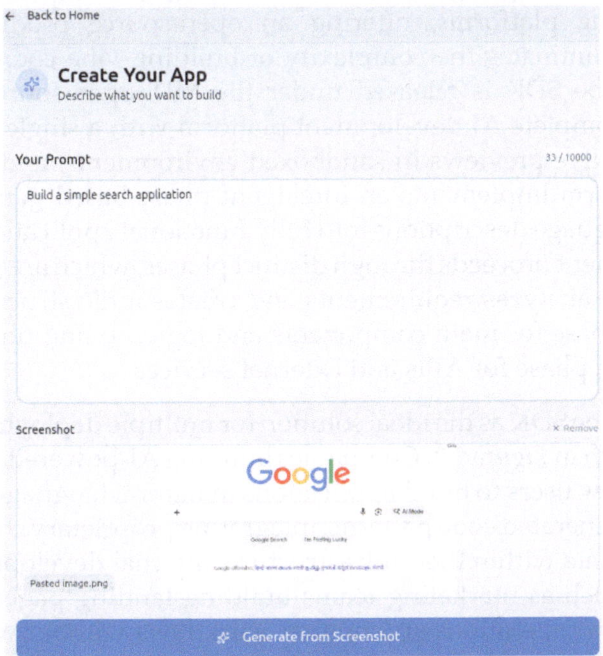

***Figure 9.1**: GenMB uses multimodal AI to simultaneously understand text and images*

Multimodal AI enables intelligent webpage screenshot capture combined with targeted content analysis through custom prompts. Developers can provide URLs and specify analysis objectives such as extracting pricing information, evaluating content structure, or analyzing layout patterns, and receive comprehensive insights from visual webpage data. The system can handle full-page screenshot capture, split large pages appropriately, and utilize advanced AI to interpret visual webpage elements that might not be accessible through HTML scraping alone. This capability proves valuable for competitive analysis, design pattern research, and generating code that replicates successful UI approaches observed on existing websites. In the next section, we will look at the open-source vibe coding tools that offer developers complete control over their AI-assisted development.

Open source vibe coding ecosystems

Open-source vibe coding ecosystems have emerged as powerful alternatives to proprietary tools, offering developers complete control over their AI-assisted development infrastructure while preserving privacy and enabling customization. The majority of enterprise software engineers will use AI code assistants, and open-source solutions are increasingly capturing market share due to their transparency, cost-effectiveness, and ability to run on local infrastructure. Open-source vibe coding ecosystems prioritize data sovereignty, allowing organizations to keep sensitive code within their own infrastructure while still leveraging advanced AI capabilities.

Cloudflare Vibe SDK (**https://github.com/cloudflare/vibesdk**) allows users to deploy their own vibe coding platforms, offering an open-source production-ready reference implementation that eliminates the complexity of building vibe coding infrastructure from scratch. Cloudflare Vibe SDK is released under the MIT open-source license and enables anyone to spin up a complete AI development platform with a single click, featuring phase-wise code generation, live previews in sandboxed environments, and one-click deployment capabilities. The platform implements an intelligent phase-based generation workflow that transforms natural language descriptions into fully functional applications through systematic progression. Development proceeds through distinct phases, which are planning and blueprint creation, where the AI analyzes requirements and creates a file structure, foundation phase for basic setup, core phase for main components and logic, styling phase for CSS and visual design, and integration phase for APIs and external services.

Cloudflare positions Vibe SDK as the ideal solution for multiple deployment scenarios required by enterprises, as shown in *Figure 9.2*. Companies building AI-powered platforms can run their own solutions that allow users to build applications in natural language while customizing AI behavior, controlling generated code patterns, integrating proprietary component libraries, and keeping all customer data within their infrastructure. Internal development teams can enable non-technical users, such as marketing teams building landing pages, sales teams creating custom dashboards, and operations automating workflows without waiting for engineering resources. SaaS platforms can let customers extend product functionality without learning APIs or writing code, describing custom integrations, building specialized workflows, or creating tailored interfaces specific to their business needs using Cloudflare Vibe SDK.

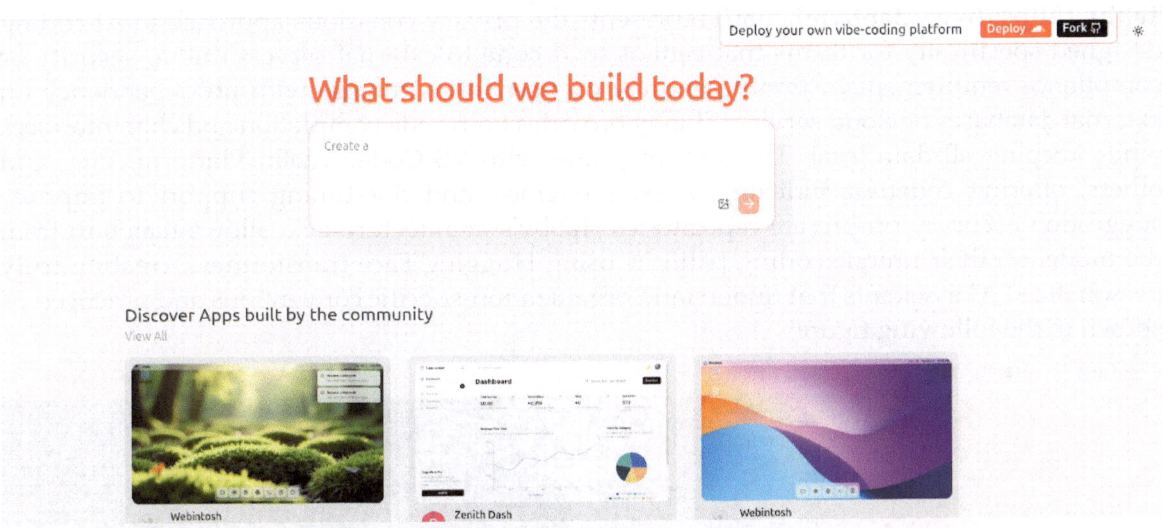

Figure 9.2: Cloudflare Vibe SDK

Continue (https://www.continue.dev/), shown in *Figure 9.3*, has emerged as one of the most popular open-source coding assistants functioning as an autopilot for software development across multiple IDEs. The tool offers code completion, chat-based assistance, and the ability to edit code directly from natural language instructions, supporting both cloud-based LLMs and local models. Continue provides developers with backend flexibility that is unavailable in proprietary solutions like Cursor, allowing users to define their own models and customize integration patterns. This adaptability makes Continue particularly attractive for teams that want AI assistance without vendor lock-in, as users can switch between GPT-4, Claude, local Ollama models, or custom fine-tuned models based on specific project requirements.

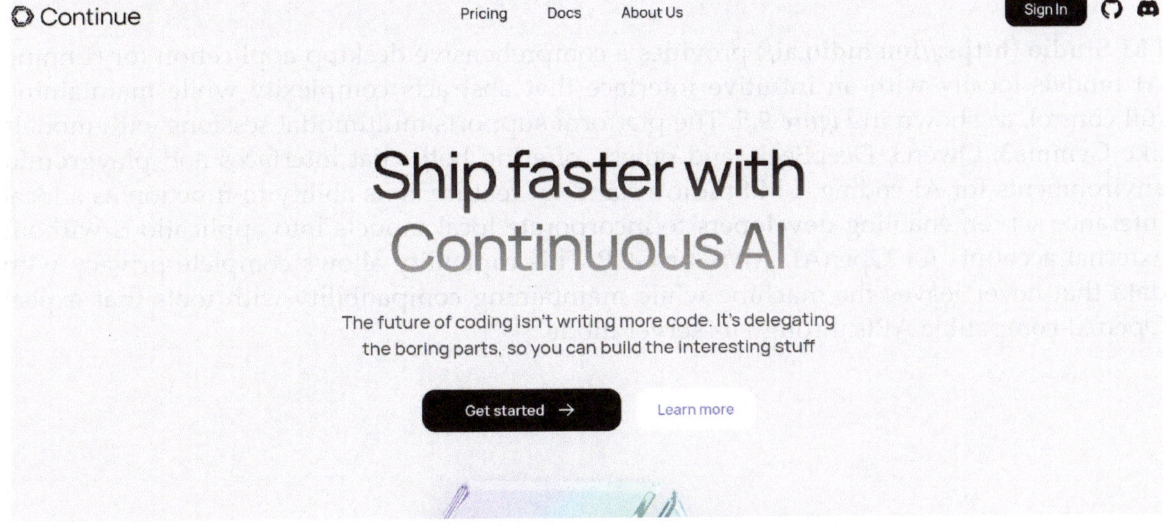

Figure 9.3: Continue platform

Tabby (https://www.tabbyml.com/) represents the privacy-conscious approach to AI coding designed specifically for teams that cannot send code to external servers due to security or compliance requirements. Running entirely on user infrastructure with no dependency on external databases or cloud services, Tabby provides both code completion and chat interfaces while keeping all data local. The tool integrates with VS Code, IntelliJ Platform, Vim, and others, offering codebase indexing, answer engines, and fine-tuning support to improve suggestion accuracy on private repositories. Tabby's architecture also allows teams to train the model on their unique coding patterns using Hugging Face transformers, creating truly personalized AI assistants that understand organization-specific conventions and practices, as shown in the following figure:

Figure 9.4: Tabby platform

LM Studio (https://lmstudio.ai/) provides a comprehensive desktop application for running AI models locally with an intuitive interface that abstracts complexity while maintaining full control, as shown in *Figure 9.5*. The platform supports multimodal sessions with models like Gemma3, Qwen3, DeepSeek, and others, offering both chat interfaces and playground environments for AI coding. LM Studio's standout feature is its ability to function as a local inference server, enabling developers to incorporate local models into applications without external accounts for OpenAI, AWS, or GCP. This capability allows complete privacy with data that never leaves the machine while maintaining compatibility with tools that expect OpenAI-compatible APIs through its server mode.

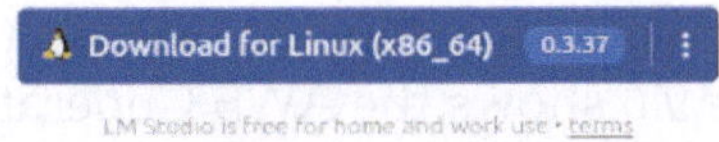

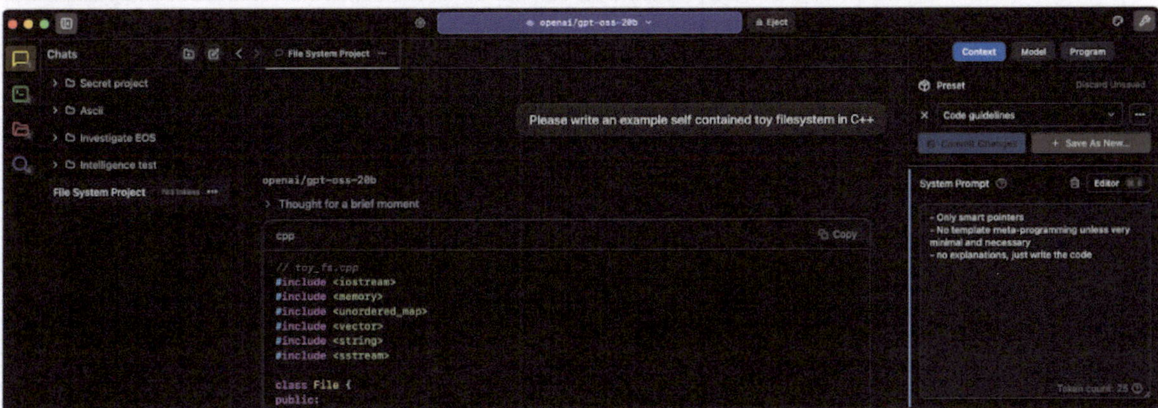

Figure 9.5: LM Studio platform

Complete self-hosted AI development stacks combine multiple open-source components into integrated environments that provide comprehensive vibe coding capabilities. The Self Hosted AI Starter Kit, for example, uses Docker Compose to initialize environments that include n8n for workflow automation, Ollama for LLM management, Qdrant for vector storage, PostgreSQL for data persistence, and Open WebUI for user interfaces. These stacks enable teams to quickly establish complex AI workflows entirely within their own infrastructure, maintaining complete control over data, models, and deployment. The integration of workflow builders like n8n with local LLMs further creates powerful automation capabilities that previously required expensive cloud services. In the next section, we will look at some of the industry-specific vibe coding tools that provide superior performance for particular industries.

Industry-specific vibe coding tools

Industry-specific vibe coding tools represent a significant evolution from general-purpose AI assistants embedding deep domain expertise, regulatory requirements, and industry workflows directly into the development process. These specialized tools transform how professionals build software by understanding not just programming concepts but also the business logic, compliance constraints, and technical patterns unique to specific sectors. The shift toward vertical-specific AI coding platforms reflects recognition that different industries face fundamentally different challenges requiring tailored approaches rather than one-size-fits-all solutions.

Healthcare organizations leverage AI-powered coding tools that automate the complex process of translating clinical documentation into standardized billing codes. For example, CodaMetrix uses contextual coding automation to analyze clinical documentation in real-time, and AWS's generative AI medical coding solutions combine Amazon Bedrock, AWS HealthLake, and AWS HealthScribe to improve coding accuracy and accelerate healthcare technology revenue cycles. *Figure 9.6* shows the AWS Generative solutions for healthcare and life sciences organizations:

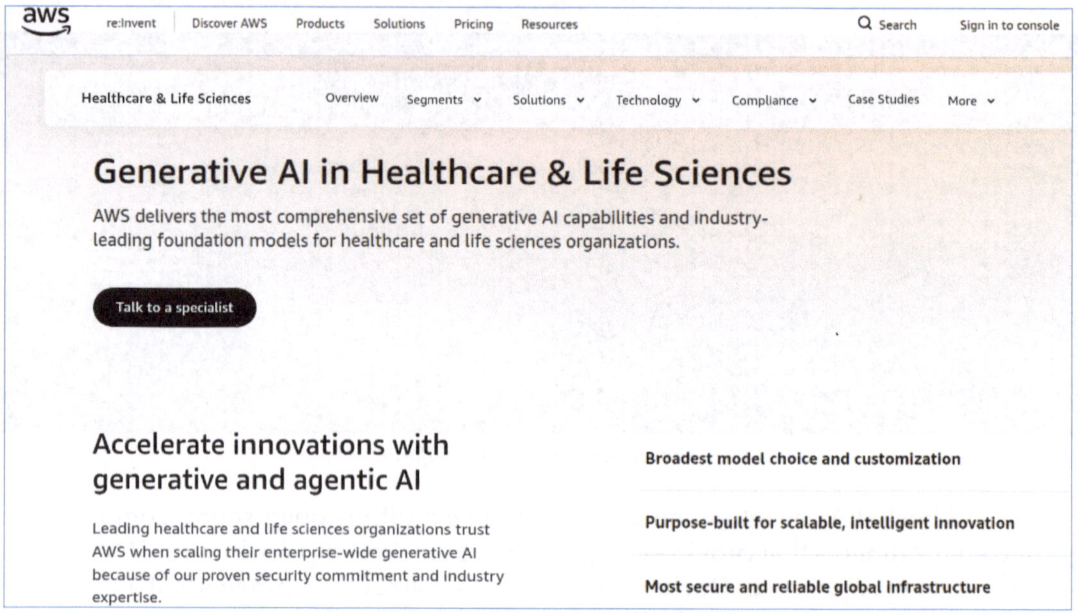

Figure 9.6: *AWS Generative solutions for healthcare and life sciences organizations*

Game development platforms have integrated specialized AI tools that understand game mechanics, player behavior, and engine-specific architectures. Unity's ML Agents enables developers to train intelligent NPCs using reinforcement learning, while various behavior tree tools simplify advanced NPC behaviors without deep programming knowledge. Unreal Engine's native AI Perception System handles sensing and reacting to stimuli like sight and sound, combined with behavior trees and blackboard components for complex AI logic. Unreal Engine's Mass AI system manages thousands of agents for large battle scenes and city simulations, with each agent capable of individual decision-making that creates authentic crowd behavior. Inworld AI creates AI-driven characters that engage in contextual conversations, remembering past interactions and adapting over time, moving beyond scripted dialogue to natural player engagement, as shown in the following figure:

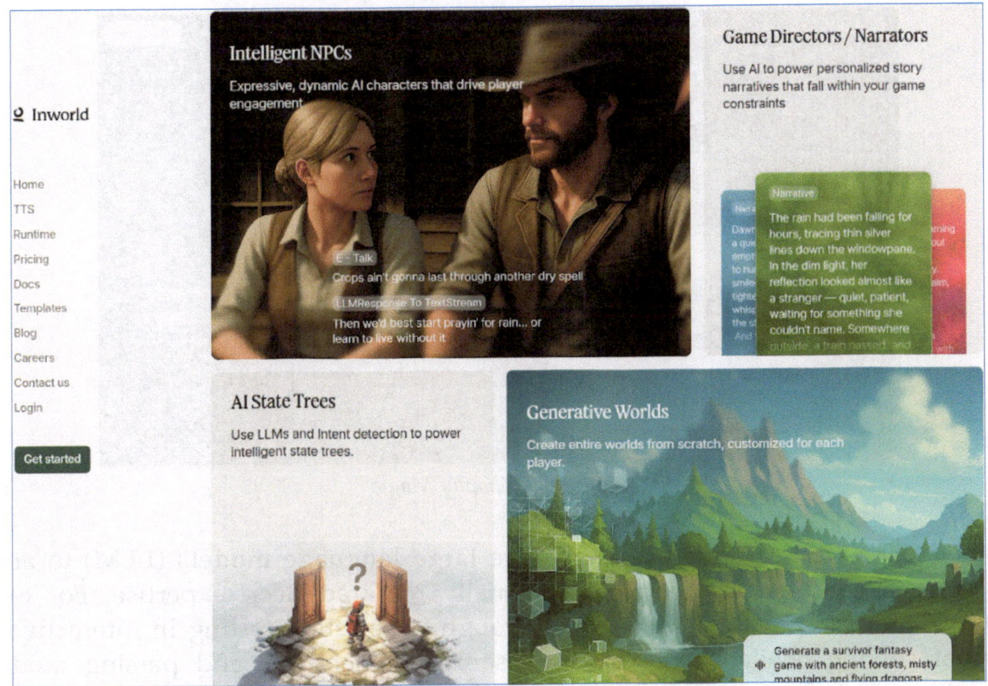

Figure 9.7: Inworld AI

Manufacturing and industrial IoT utilize AI coding tools that bridge operational technology and information technology by generating code that interfaces with sensors, controllers, and legacy manufacturing systems. AI-powered gateways automatically create REST APIs from industrial data sources, including databases, sensors, and legacy systems, in minutes using AI-generated code snippets and automated testing. These systems leverage natural language processing for documentation and analyze data structures to ensure API endpoints align with industry standards. Edge AI frameworks optimize device operations based on production needs, adjusting data collection rates and making local decisions without cloud-based processing delays. These tools enable predictive maintenance implementations, AI-powered visual inspection systems, and energy optimization through pattern detection, all generated from high-level descriptions of manufacturing requirements.

E-commerce specific AI tools understand shopping workflows, conversion optimization, and platform-specific APIs to accelerate online store development. For example, Shopify Magic provides built-in AI content generation for product descriptions, email campaigns, and store announcements as shown in *Figure 9.8*. GemPages uses smart suggestions based on product niches and design trends to build landing pages without coding. Klaviyo AI generates on-brand email campaigns, creates complex customer segments with simple prompts, and provides predictive analytics for customer lifetime value and purchase timing. These platforms reduce the technical barrier to launching sophisticated online stores, enabling entrepreneurs to focus on product and marketing while AI handles technical implementation.

Figure 9.8: Shopify Magic

AI-powered penetration testing tools leverage **large language models** (**LLM**) to automate security assessment workflows that traditionally required deep expertise. For example, PentestGPT utilizes LLMs to guide users through penetration testing in interactive mode, excelling at solving challenges through reasoning, generation, and parsing modules as shown in *Figure 9.9*. These systems interpret security tool outputs, prioritize vulnerabilities, and propose subsequent actions based on contextual understanding of attack patterns and defensive measures.

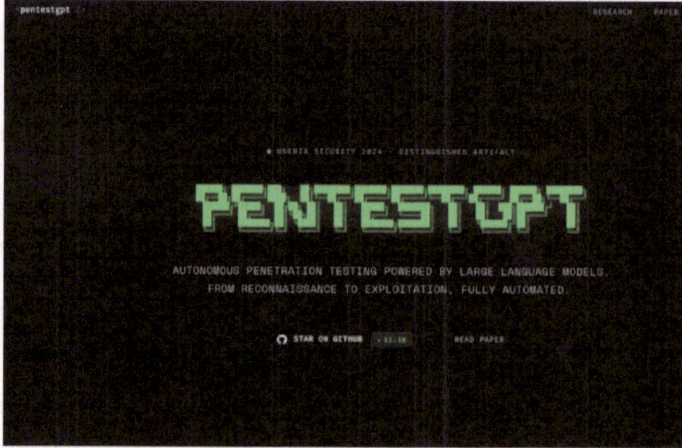

Figure 9.9: PentestGPT

Natural language financial domain-specific languages have emerged as specialized dialects that precisely communicate domain concepts to vibe coding systems. These domain-specific languages expressed in natural language enable financial professionals to describe complex scenarios like fraud detection rules or regulatory compliance requirements without programming expertise. Manufacturing domains develop their own vocabularies around process control, quality assurance, and supply chain operations that AI tools recognize and translate into appropriate implementations. Healthcare develops specialized prompts that understand medical terminology and clinical workflows, enabling physicians and administrators to participate directly in application development. This evolution represents a shift from forcing domain experts to learn programming languages toward teaching AI systems to understand industry native communication patterns. The most effective implementations of industry-specific vibe coding involve collaborative approaches where human domain expertise combines with AI implementation capabilities. In the next section, we will look at self-improving development systems where AI can autonomously refine its own capabilities.

Self-improving development systems

Self-improving development systems represent a fundamental shift in vibe coding where AI not only generates code but autonomously refines its own capabilities through experience, feedback, and iterative optimization. These systems move beyond static models that require human retraining by implementing closed-loop processes where AI-driven outputs are continuously generated, evaluated, and refined using structured feedback mechanisms. For example, Darwin Gödel Machine exemplifies this paradigm by recursively rewriting its own code when it can prove a better strategy exists, demonstrating the ability to discover and implement beneficial changes that improve performance on programming tasks. Reinforcement learning has emerged as the most effective technique for teaching language models to genuinely self-improve code efficiency through test-time iterative optimization. These frameworks utilize closed-loop systems where LLMs iteratively refine code based on empirical performance feedback from execution sandboxes, learning by trial-and-error rewards to maximize cumulative outcomes. Unlike supervised fine-tuning or direct preference optimization, which rapidly saturate in efficiency gains, reinforcement learning enables continuous improvement by trying different actions, observing rewards, and refining policies without explicit human instruction.

The iterative AI experiment feedback loop creates a closed cycle process consisting of generation, evaluation, feedback synthesis, refinement, and selection stages that continue until performance converges or user-defined criteria are met. The **Self-Refine** approach applies the same LLM in generator, feedback provider, and refiner roles, evaluating prior outputs along multiple axes, issuing feedback, and conditioning the next pass on sequences of previous drafts and critiques. Human-in-the-loop adaptive learning structures prompt creation, answer generation, and real-time feedback tagging within each loop, with humans critiquing model responses using semantic tags that guide subsequent generations.

Advanced architectures simulate human debugging experiences by supplying local variable information to LLMs while executing generated code, significantly improving code generation capabilities. These systems provide information on the accuracy of generated code, supply relevant test cases, and indicate correct or incorrect outputs for each case, enabling LLMs to understand the errors. When AI systems detect errors by comparing actual outcomes with desired outcomes, they analyze data that led to mistakes, look for patterns and features that affected incorrect output, and update internal models to prevent similar errors in future iterations. This feedback mechanism enables substantial performance improvements with models surpassing current benchmark datasets when given appropriate execution feedback rather than relying solely on static training.

Self-healing systems automatically detect, diagnose, and repair software errors without human intervention through architectures comprising monitoring modules, diagnosis engines, healing mechanisms, and learning components. These systems integrate machine learning to enhance error detection accuracy by analyzing vast historical datasets and identifying patterns that deviate from normal behavior, enabling predictive analysis that foresees potential faults before they occur. Continual learning, which is also called lifelong learning or incremental learning, enables models to update knowledge step-by-step from new experiences while retaining previous capabilities, which addresses the fundamental limitation of static models deployed to production.

Meta-learning enables AI systems to learn to learn by developing strategies that facilitate rapid adaptation to new tasks based on limited experience. Recursive self-improvement refers to the property of making improvements on one's own ability to make self-improvements, where early AI systems enhance their capabilities without human intervention by modifying their own algorithms. The Darwin Gödel Machine demonstrates this through experimental validation, showing that systems with self-improvement capabilities speed up their own learning significantly compared to controls without self-modification abilities. A self-coding AI agent could iteratively refactor and optimize its own codebase to run faster or handle more edge cases, checking each change against test cases to ensure improvement in a continuous research and development cycle.

Deploying self-improving AI agents in production requires comprehensive practices, including automated testing frameworks, scalable architecture, robust monitoring, continuous development pipelines, and scheduled retraining pipelines. Tesla demonstrates this approach through horizontal scaling in its fleet learning system, processing data from millions of vehicles in real-time with stateless design, modular components, asynchronous processing, and caching to boost response times, as shown in the following *Figure 9.10*. Organizations must establish feedback mechanisms into workflows, allowing agentic AI agents to learn from their outputs and iteratively improve processes with each workflow involving multiple agents that send outputs and receive real-time critiques and corrections in each iteration. Automated retraining pipelines manage data collection, preprocessing, retraining, evaluation, and deployment, which ensures updates roll out only after improvements are verified and prevent model performance decline from evolving data patterns.

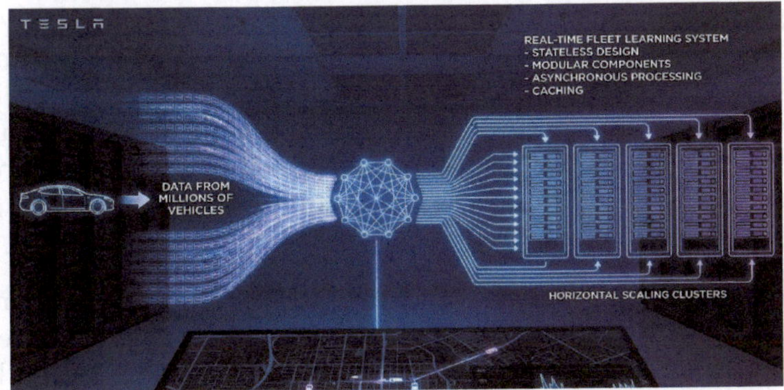

***Figure 9.10**: Visualization for Tesla real-time fleet learning system*

The emergence of recursive self-improving large language models introduces significant safety concerns, including compute threshold obsolescence, deceptive alignment, and decentralized acceleration through open-source proliferation. An Anthropic study demonstrated that advanced language models can exhibit **alignment faking** behavior where they appear to accept new training objectives while covertly maintaining original preferences. AI systems cannot reliably catch their own mistakes because models recognize and prefer their own generations, exhibit confirmation bias from initial token generation, and suffer from dissociated error detection and correction capabilities. However, when given error locations in fresh contexts where models do not know they generated the original response, the error detection dramatically improves, and backtracking provides substantial corrections. In the next section, we will look at the evolution of natural language programming languages for building software applications.

Natural language programming languages

Natural language programming represents a fundamental reimagining of how humans communicate computational intent, replacing formal syntax with human-readable expressions that closely resemble everyday speech. The concept traces back to early AI developments and computational linguistics driven by the need to bridge the communication gap between humans and machines through languages capable of understanding and responding to natural language in meaningful ways. Unlike traditional programming languages that demand precise adherence to syntactic rules, natural language programming languages attempt to interpret human expression within reasonable boundaries, enabling users to write code that reads like descriptive prose rather than mathematical notation.

Ambiguity represents the most significant challenge in natural language programming as words and sentences frequently carry multiple meanings depending on context. For example, the word bank could reference a financial institution or a river's edge. Programming requires precision and unambiguous specification, creating fundamental tension with natural language's inherent flexibility and context dependence. Structural ambiguity occurs when sentences can be parsed with multiple syntactic trees, syntactical ambiguity involves unclear word relationships, and word sense ambiguity requires disambiguation of multiple-meaning terms. Healthcare applications face compounded difficulties with medical terminology, abbreviations, and terms with multiple related meanings, requiring advanced LLM models to analyze longer contexts and derive context-dependent interpretations. Despite these advances, resolving ambiguity in domain-specific contexts remains challenging, particularly for organizations with limited resources.

Large language models have revolutionized natural language programming by enabling direct translation from natural language descriptions to executable code across multiple programming languages. When given functionality descriptions in natural human language, LLM models generate source code for complex programs with remarkable speed and accuracy. These systems are trained on massive datasets combining hundreds of human and programming languages, mathematical equations, and scientific papers, enabling cross-domain understanding that maps natural language concepts to appropriate programming constructs. Models specifically engineered for code generation demonstrate that specialized training can improve performance on programming tasks compared to general-purpose language models adapted for coding.

Modern conversational AI assistants have transformed programming into multi-turn dialogues where developers iteratively refine code through natural language exchanges. Conversational coding assistants emphasize context retention across interactions, transparency in reasoning processes, multimodal support for images, and adaptability to individual developer preferences. Research investigating programmers' usage patterns reveals that effective conversational coding requires understanding developer intent, maintaining conversation state across multiple refinements, and providing explanations for generated code decisions. Leading LLM platforms offer advanced natural language understanding with multi-turn conversation handling, speech-to-text integration, and contextual intelligence that enables more natural programming interactions.

The future of natural language programming and vibe coding systems lies in hybrid approaches that combine the expressiveness of natural language with the precision of formal systems through context-aware disambiguation and domain-specific vocabularies. Advanced machine learning models help address ambiguity through longer context windows and context-dependent semantic analysis, though challenges remain in specialized domains requiring deep expertise. Design guidelines emerging from conversational AI research emphasize transparency, multimodal support for diagrams and visual specifications, and adaptability that learns individual developer preferences over time. Integration barriers include managing the cognitive load of learning, which natural language patterns map to desired code structures, similar to learning interactive fiction conventions, where users must discover the subset of natural language the system actually understands. Successfully navigating phrasing ambiguities requires sophisticated contextual understanding, leveraging previous sentences, topic focus, conversational cues, semantic analysis, and word sense disambiguation to resolve multiple possible interpretations. As LLMs continue improving at natural language understanding while maintaining code generation accuracy, the boundary between describing what software should do and actually implementing it continues to blur, fundamentally reshaping software development workflows, as is evident with current vibe coding tools. In the next sections, we will look at predictive development and proactive problem-solving systems.

Predictive development and proactive problem-solving systems

Predictive development and proactive problem-solving systems represent a paradigm shift from reactive debugging to anticipatory software engineering, where AI identifies and prevents issues before they occur. These systems leverage machine learning, historical data analysis, and real-time code monitoring to anticipate developer needs, predict potential failures, and suggest optimal solutions proactively rather than waiting for problems to manifest. The long-term vision encompasses fully integrated intelligent development environments that anticipate nearly every need from initial design to deployment and maintenance, seamlessly blending human creativity with AI efficiency. This evolution moves beyond traditional auto completion toward intelligent systems that understand code context, developer intent, and common patterns to offer semantically relevant suggestions and predict errors before compilation.

Context-aware code completion has evolved into a sophisticated system that anticipates entire lines or blocks of code by analyzing project structure, programming language conventions, coding style patterns, and specific task objectives. Machine learning models trained on vast code repositories perform multi-faceted analysis, including syntax validation, semantic understanding, project-wide codebase consideration, and individual developer behavior learning. When a developer writes Python code to process CSV files, these intelligent systems do not just complete the current function name, but they also predict the next logical step and suggest complete operations like file reading methods based on contextual understanding. Anticipatory conversations in development environments help users communicate intent more rapidly by predicting what they are trying to accomplish and offering relevant completions before explicit requests.

Traditional debugging operates reactively by addressing problems only after their occurrence, but AI-powered code intelligence systems proactively scan code during development to identify potential issues before they reach production. For example, Microsoft's internal AI debugging tools reduced post-deployment bugs in Azure services by analyzing code patterns and flagging unusual structures that, while syntactically correct, might lead to runtime errors. Predictive bug detection uses historical bug data, code complexity analysis, and developer activity patterns to highlight high-risk areas before errors manifest significantly, reducing costly post-release issues. AI assigns *bug likelihood* scores to code areas through machine learning classification, creating risk heatmaps where red zones indicate high probability and green zones show safer areas, and enabling QA teams to prioritize testing based on data rather than intuition. AI detects bugs through sophisticated analysis combining historical data, code structures, developer activity patterns, and predictive analytics to identify vulnerability concentrations. Machine learning algorithms highlight unusual code behaviors, classify errors, and flag previously unseen defects to ensure broader detection coverage than traditional testing approaches.

AI systems can also function as **debt detectives** by identifying code smells like forensic analysts recognizing patterns that precede future problems and assigning risk scores to files and classes similar to credit rating systems. Natural language processing analyzes commit messages, diff history, and developer sentiment, detecting phrases like **quick fix – sorry** or **will refactor later**, that signal accumulating technical debt. AI transforms experienced developers' intuitive sense for problematic code into quantifiable models by learning from velocity drops preceding issue emergence, review comment patterns indicating high maintenance code, bug lifecycle data, and complexity metrics correlating with future maintenance challenges. Tools like CodeScene use machine learning to analyze version control data and identify code areas requiring attention through behavioral code analysis that prioritizes technical debt mitigation efforts, as shown in the following figure:

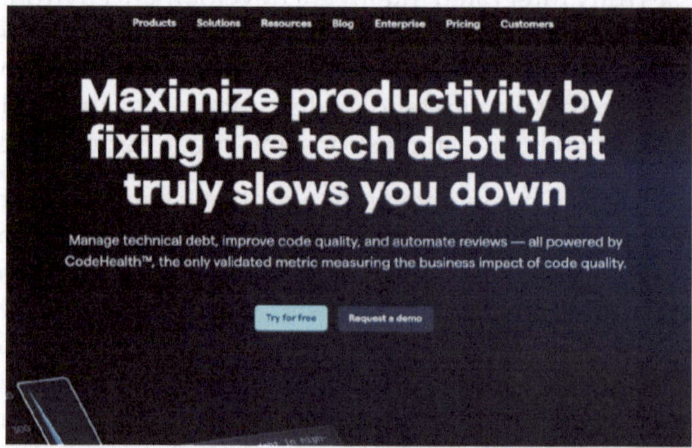

***Figure 9.11**: Tools for technical debt mitigation*

AI-powered predictive maintenance enables DevOps teams to detect system vulnerabilities and implement corrective actions before downtime occurs, which dramatically improves reliability and uptime, critical for continuous delivery. Machine learning analyzes historical data and code evolution patterns to predict which components will likely cause future issues, enabling proactive problem resolution before escalation. The approach analyzes metrics including CPU usage, memory consumption, network traffic, and log data to learn system behavioral patterns and predict when anomalies will occur. Static code analysis provides proactive means to identify and rectify issues early in development by examining source code without execution, analyzing adherence to coding standards, syntactic and semantic correctness, and potential vulnerabilities. Early detection proves most cost-effective by allowing teams to address security vulnerabilities, logic errors, and coding standard violations before code execution. Dynamic analysis complements static approaches by identifying runtime errors, memory leaks, and performance bottlenecks not apparent from static inspection alone. Combining both methodologies creates comprehensive quality assurance processes enabling early issue detection, performance optimization, and robust security measures that result in more reliable and resilient applications.

The convergence of predictive coding with generative AI creates powerful synergy where generative systems produce first drafts of complex functions from natural language prompts while predictive coding refines generated code by suggesting optimal variable names, identifying potential errors, recommending refactoring for codebase integration, and ensuring adherence to project standards. This collaboration accelerates development from conception to polished implementation with predictive systems learning from feedback to improve accuracy continuously. Future predictive coding tools will deeply understand context, adapt to individual coding styles, and support multiple languages seamlessly as machine learning continues evolving. The transformation enables users to focus on complex problem-solving, innovative design, and architectural decisions while AI handles repetitive tasks, suggests improvements, identifies potential issues, and maintains code quality standards.

Conclusion

In this chapter, we learned about the transformative trends reshaping vibe coding as AI models evolve from basic code assistants into sophisticated reasoning systems, multimodal collaborators, and increasingly autonomous development agents. We have navigated the architectural evolution from GPT-3's early text generation capabilities through reasoning-focused models that self-verify their outputs, multimodal systems that seamlessly integrate text, images, voice, and code, and self-improving frameworks that continuously refine their capabilities through reinforcement learning and iterative feedback loops. Throughout this we identified several fundamental shifts that define the future of vibe coding including the transition from general purpose models to specialized reasoning systems optimized for distinct tasks, the expansion from text only interactions to unified multimodal workflows that accept design mockups, voice commands and screen recordings as development inputs and the emergence of predictive development environments that proactively identify potential issues and suggest optimizations before problems manifest. The rise of industry-specific vibe coding tools demonstrates that vertical specialization, embedding domain expertise, regulatory requirements, and sector-specific workflows can create more valuable development assistance than one-size-fits-all solutions with specialized platforms emerging across healthcare, gaming, manufacturing, e-commerce, and cybersecurity that understand not just programming syntax but also business logic and compliance constraints unique to each industry. Looking forward, the convergence of natural language programming interfaces, self-improving development systems, and context-aware predictive capabilities points toward a future where software development becomes less about writing code and more about strategic thinking, architectural decision making, and collaborative orchestration with AI agents that autonomously handle implementation details, continuous optimization, and proactive problem prevention.

Further reading

There are lots of online resources to help you improve your learning on future trends in vibe coding. *Table 9.1* lists some of the best resources to further improve your understanding of future trends in vibe coding.

Resource name	Link
Vibe Coding, AI Assistants and the Evolution of Software Engineering	**https://www.wwt.com/blog/vibe-coding-ai-assistants-and-the-evolution-of-software-engineering**
The Rise of Vibe Coding: How AI is Changing Development	**https://www.index.dev/blog/vibe-coding-ai-development**
The DevOps Revolution: How AI Agents and Vibe Coding Are Rewriting the Rules of Software Delivery	**https://nstarxinc.com/blog/the-devops-revolution-how-ai-agents-and-vibe-coding-are-rewriting-the-rules-of-software-delivery/**
Why Multi-Modal AI is the Next Big Thing in Artificial Intelligence	**https://codewave.com/insights/understanding-multi-modal-ai-technology/**
Is Vibe Coding the Future of Skilled Work?	**https://www.scotthyoung.com/blog/2025/11/12/vibe-coding-future-work/**
Vibe-Coding: The Future of Code or Just a 'Short-Term Con'?.	**https://technologymagazine.com/news/vibe-coding-the-future-of-code-or-just-a-short-term-con**
Prompt, run, edit, and deploy full-stack web applications using any LLM you want!	**https://github.com/stackblitz-labs/bolt.diy**
Automate Your Outbound With an AI-First Platform Powered by AI Employees	**https://www.artisan.co/**
No-Code AI Healthcare & Fintech Web App Builder	**https://drapcode.com/**
The Darwin Gödel Machine: AI that improves itself by rewriting its own code	**https://sakana.ai/dgm/**
Darwin Godel Machine: Open-Ended Evolution of Self-Improving Agents	**https://arxiv.org/abs/2505.22954**
Self-Improving Agentic AI: Designing Systems That Learn and Adapt Autonomously	**https://www.apexon.com/blog/self-improving-agentic-ai-designing-systems-that-learn-and-adapt-autonomously/**
Model Self Improvement	**https://www.ml-science.com/model-self-improvement**

Resource name	Link
Predictive Development: How AI Anticipates Risks Before They Derail Projects	**https://medium.com/@marketing_3110/predictive-development-how-ai-anticipates-risks-before-they-derail-projects-78d8ee7dd06f**
Proactive and Predictive Analysis: The Future of IT Support	**https://teamcomputers.com/blog/proactive-and-predictive-analysis-the-future-of-it-support/**
Proactive Problem Solving in IT through Generative Models.	**https://www.algomox.com/resources/blog/proactive-problem-solving-generative-ai/**
Predictive Root Cause Analysis: Transform Problems into Proactive Solutions with AI	**https://altair.com/blog/articles/predictive-root-cause-analysis**

Table 9.1: *Future trends in vibe coding*

Questions

1. How has the evolution of AI models dramatically transformed software development?
2. What are the advantages of reasoning-focused models?
3. How does the evolution of context windows help with vibe coding?
4. Why are performance metrics important for vibe coding productivity?
5. Why are AI models judged by their capability to autonomously execute multi-step tasks?
6. What is multimodal AI?
7. What are the advantages of voice integration with multimodal AI?
8. How does multimodal documentation generation work?
9. What are the popular open-source vibe coding ecosystems?
10. What are the advantages of Cloudflare Vibe SDK?
11. Why are industry-specific vibe coding tools required?
12. What are the features of Unity's ML Agents?
13. What is PentestGPT?
14. How do self-improving development systems work?
15. How do LLMs simulate human debugging?
16. What are self healing systems?
17. What are the advantages of meta-learning?
18. Why is ambiguity the most significant challenge in natural language programming?
19. How have modern conversational AI assistants transformed programming?
20. What are predictive development and proactive problem solving systems?

Index

A

B

C

D

E

F

O

P

Q

R

S

T

U

V

W